RETHINKING MEDIA COVERAGE

In the post-9/11 era, media technologies have become increasingly intertwined with vertical power as airwaves, airports, air space, and orbit have been commandeered to support national security and defense. In this book, Lisa Parks develops the concept of vertical mediation to explore how audiovisual cultures enact and infer power relations far beyond the screen. Focusing on TV news, airport checkpoints, satellite imagery, and drone media, Parks demonstrates how "coverage" makes vertical space intelligible to global publics in new ways and powerfully reveals what is at stake in controlling it.

Lisa Parks is Professor of Comparative Studies at Massachusetts Institute of Technology and Director of the Global Media Technologies and Cultures Lab. She is the author of *Cultures in Orbit: Satellites and the Televisual* and co-editor of *Life in the Age of Drone Warfare*.

RETHINKING MEDIA COVERAGE

Vertical Mediation and the War on Terror

Lisa Parks

Routledge
Taylor & Francis Group

NEW YORK AND LONDON

First published 2018
by Routledge
711 Third Avenue, New York, NY 10017

and by Routledge
2 Park Square, Milton Park, Abingdon, Oxon OX14 4RN

Routledge is an imprint of the Taylor & Francis Group, an informa business

Library of Congress Cataloging-in-Publication Data
Names: Parks, Lisa, author.
Title: Rethinking media coverage : vertical mediation and the war on terror /
Lisa Parks.
Description: New York ; London : Routledge, Taylor & Francis Group, 2018. |
Includes index.
Identifiers: LCCN 2018002561| ISBN 9780415999816 (hardback) |
ISBN 9780415999823 (pbk.) | ISBN 9780203879641 (ebk.)
Subjects: LCSH: Television broadcasting of news. | Artificial satellites in
telecommunication. | Television broadcasting of news—Technological
innovations. | Telecommunication—Social aspects. | Mass media and war.
Classification: LCC PN4784.T4 P375 2018 | DDC 070.1/95—dc23
LC record available at https://lccn.loc.gov/2018002561

ISBN: 978-0-415-99981-6 (hbk)
ISBN: 978-0-415-99982-3 (pbk)
ISBN: 978-0-203-87964-1 (ebk)

Typeset in Bembo and Stone Sans
by Florence Production Ltd, Stoodleigh, Devon, UK

CONTENTS

ACKNOWLEDGMENTS

This book started in pieces that scattered in different directions. Over the years, I have attempted to pull them together in efforts to try and make sense of a changing mediated world. Many people have assisted me in this process. First and foremost, I am grateful to many colleagues and students at UC Santa Barbara, who challenged and supported me as I worked on this book, including Paul Amar, Peter Bloom, Anna Brusutti, Julie Carlson, Alenda Chang, Mona Damluji, Susan Derwin, Anna Everett, Cynthia Felando, Lisa Hajjar, Dick Hebdige, Jennifer Holt, Bishnu Ghosh, Avery Gordon, Giles Gunn, Carl Gutierrez-Jones, David Marshall, Mireille Miller-Young, Chris Newfield, Marko Peljhan, Constance Penley, Patrice Petro, Rita Raley, Russel Samolsky, Bhaskar Sarkar, Laila Sakr, Greg Siegel, Winddance Twine, Cristina Venegas, Janet Walker, Elisabeth Weber, and Chuck Wolfe. I also thank former graduate students in Film and Media Studies for their research assistance and support, especially Alex Champlin, Hannah Goodwin, Daniel Grinberg, Lisa Han, Jennifer Hessler, Abigail Hinsman, Lan Xuan Le, Rahul Mukherjee, Lindsay Palmer, Jade Petermon, and Nicole Starosielski. I send special thanks to Nicole Strobel, who was a tremendous help during the project's home stretch. Staff members Kathy Murray, Joe Palladino, and Dana Welch created a wonderful department to work in at UCSB, and I miss them all.

I presented portions of this book during lectures at various institutions and received crucial feedback. I am grateful to colleagues and students who attended my talks, asked questions, or offered suggestions, enabling me to evolve my ideas. I thank the following institutions for supporting these lectures: American University of Beirut, Bahcesehir University, Birbeck, University of London, Brown University, Carleton University, Duke University, Goldsmith's College of London, Miami University of Ohio, Northwestern University-Qatar,

Oklahoma State University, San Francisco Museum of Modern Art, UC Davis, UC Irvine, UC Santa Barbara, University of Alberta, University of Glasgow, University of Ljubljana, University of Oslo, University of Queensland, University of Sao Paulo, University of Toronto, and University of Wisconsin-Milwaukee.

In 2014, I had the privilege of working as a Visiting Professor at the Annenberg School of Communication at the University of Pennsylvania. This was a generative time for me, and I continue to be inspired by the dynamic intellectual environment of that department. Faculty and graduate students shared encouragement and ideas, and I especially benefitted from the questions and input of Michael Delli Carpini, Marwan Kraidy, Carolyn Marvin, Monroe Price, Joe Turow, and Barbie Zelizer.

At Routledge, Erica Wetter has been a wonderful editor. I am extremely grateful for her patience and ongoing support of this project. Thanks also to her associate, Mia Moran, who helped move the book through production. Copy editor, Betsy Lane, was very helpful during an early iteration of the project, and I greatly benefitted from consultations with professional editor, Cathy Hannabach, as I was completing the final draft as well. Quentin Scott and Josh Curtis helped tremendously in the final phases of the book's production as well.

After moving to MIT in 2016, I brought this project to the finish line. I am grateful to my new colleagues and the staff in the Comparative Media Studies/ Writing Department for creating a stimulating place to work. Graduate students Vicky Zeamer and Sonia Banaszczyk provided helpful research assistance as well.

Over the years, I have remained connected with friends, colleagues, and mentors who have inspired and supported this project in many different ways. I am grateful to Mark Andrejevic, Megan Boler, Simone Browne, Lisa Cartwright, Wendy Chun, Julie D'Acci, Kelly Gates, John Fiske, Anne Friedberg, Michele Hilmes, Julia Himberg, Vicky Johnson, Vicki Mayer, Anna McCarthy, Nicholas Mirzoeff, Lisa Nakamura, Trevor Paglen, John Durham Peters, Jim Schwoch, Jonathan Sterne, Heather Hendershot, and Fred Turner.

During the final weeks of writing, I was fortunate to reconnect with my dear friends in Missoula, Montana, philosopher, Michel Valentine, and political theorist, William "Chip" Stearns, both of whom have offered support over the years. I also sought advice from treasured mentors and collaborators, Caren Kaplan, Constance Penley, and Janet Walker. Each of them helped me to see the relationship between the big picture and little details. I have been so fortunate to work with and learn from each of these intelligent, powerful, and inspiring women.

My dear friends Moya Luckett, Jenny Thomas, and Shari Goldin have been in my life for over two decades now. Their enduring friendship is a pleasure and honor. I also thank my dear Santa Barbara pals, Jennifer Holt and Cristina Venegas, for their wit, bravery, and love. Without them, I would be lost. My parents, Marilyn and Sam Lemaich and Ron and Debbie Parks, and my Aunt Maureen Mann, have provided guidance, love, and much, much more. Most of all, I thank my husband, John Harley, the most brilliant, compassionate, and loving person I could imagine being by my side.

Earlier versions of this work appeared as Lisa Parks, "Points of Departure: the Culture of US Airport Screening," *Journal of Visual Culture* 6, no. 22 (2007): 183–200; Lisa Parks, "Vertical Mediation and the Wars in Afghanistan and Iraq," in *Mediated Geographies/Geographies of Media*, Susan Mains, Julie Cupples, et al., Eds. (Dordrecht: Springer, 2015), 159–175; and Lisa Parks, "Vertical Mediation and the US Drone War in the Horn of Africa," in *Life in the Age of Drone Warfare*, Lisa Parks and Caren Kaplan, Eds. (Durham: Duke University Press, 2017), 134–158.

INTRODUCTION

FIGURE 0.1 A fireball erupts from the south tower of the World Trade Center as the second of two hijacked airplanes crashes into the building on the morning of September 11, 2001. Photo by Dan Doane Jr./SIPA Press.

Source: https://upload.wikimedia.org/wikipedia/commons/5/51/South_Tower_gets_hit_on_911.JPG
—public domain, via Wikimedia Commons

The 9/11 attacks were a vertical event. To orchestrate the attacks, members of Al Qaeda commandeered the electromagnetic spectrum, air, and orbit. They used the spectrum to communicate before and during the attacks, hijacked commercial US airplanes in flight, and used satellites to guide them to their targets. The attackers also anticipated that an armada of cameras would record the event and instantly transmit footage of the aftermath around the world. Air traffic controllers used global positioning satellites and screen interfaces to monitor American Airlines flight 11 and United Airlines flight 175 as the planes drifted off-course and rammed into the twin towers of the World Trade Center, and then witnessed American Airline flight 77 plummet into the Pentagon and United Airlines 93 crash to the ground in Shanksville, Pennsylvania. In New York, cameras on the ground tilted up to capture the mid-air collisions and television networks transmitted scenes of air filled with thick clouds of smoke and debris live via satellite to news outlets worldwide. In the days after 9/11, remote sensing satellites captured images of the attack sites as if revealing giant open wounds on the earth's surface. As these scenes were aired, they vividly ruptured US vertical hegemony, and created a crisis for the US that for the next two decades would be managed and contained in multiple ways. These events played out through the vertical field: the US sought to reassert its global dominance by controlling orbit, air, and airwaves using satellites, aircraft, and broadcasting, and by doing so, to regulate conditions on the ground.

One way that President George W. Bush tried to manage the crisis was to declare a "war on terror" in the days after the attacks. The "war on terror," Bush explained, "begins with al Qaeda, but it does not end there. It will not end until every terrorist group of global reach has been found, stopped and defeated." Then, emphasizing how this war on terror differed from other recent US military interventions, Bush announced, "Americans should not expect one battle, but a lengthy campaign, unlike any other we have ever seen. It may include dramatic strikes, visible on TV, and covert operations, secret even in success. We will starve terrorists of funding, turn them one against another, drive them from place to place, until there is no refuge or no rest."[1] The war on terror, in other words, would be a war of boundless battlefronts and endless timeframes—a "perpetual," "forever," and "everywhere" war, as critics have described it, a war that would match the scale and proportion of its initiating event, its vertical surprise.[2] If an event like 9/11 could be successfully orchestrated inside the US, so the logic went, then US national security was in at risk in any place at any time.

This book explores how media technologies and cultures have worked to reassert US vertical hegemony after 9/11. By *vertical hegemony*, I am referring to the ongoing struggle for dominance or control over the *vertical field*, which here includes combinations of terrestrial, aerial, spectral, and/or orbital domains. While air space, spectrum, and orbit each have distinct legal definitions and histories, I approach them in this book as constituting the vertical field—an extensive realm of movement, occupation, appropriation, and demonstration.

Vertical hegemony involves efforts to maneuver through, activate technologies within, occupy, or control the vast stretch of space between the earth's surface and the outer limits of orbit as well as the kinds of activities that can occur there. The struggle for vertical hegemony is undergirded by the assumption that controlling orbit, air, and spectrum is tantamount to controlling life on earth. By controlling these vertical domains, a state can monitor sovereign territories from above, transmit signals across national borders, and strike targets on the earth's surface. While satellites, aircraft, and broadcasting operate through these extraterritorial domains, their operations are always linked to ground stations, runways, and receivers on earth. Vertical hegemony cannot simply be achieved "out there" in open skies. To register or take effect, it must be communicated through and materialized as part of culture on earth. This book conceptualizes these processes of communication and materialization as *vertical mediation*.

Given the remoteness and vastness of vertical domains, media technologies and discourses are vital to establishing their materiality and intelligibility. Orbit, air, and spectrum usually only become significant to publics when objects or people move through them or when historic events happen in them. During such occasions, the area surrounding the earth's surface—its *circumterrestrial space*— becomes as a site of world history. Media enable the airwaves, sky, and orbit to matter as they transform these realms into intelligible discourses and forms that can be sensed and made sense of and that produce affects. Rather than think of the vertical field as a domain that is simply there to be mapped, I imagine it as a dynamic field of power and mediation. By mediation I am referring not only to content or representation; mediation is a performative enactment in time—a materialization of particular conditions.[3] In this way, mediation involves demonstrating, putting forward, or bringing to life as much as it involves representing or depicting something that has already occurred. If this is the case, then *vertical mediations* are audiovisual discourses that enact, materialize, or infer power relations as conditions or qualities of the vertical field. They demonstrate what is happening in and through orbit, air, and spectrum and how those happenings impact life on earth. They assert what the vertical field is and who controls it. And they expose how the US uses the vertical field to monitor and intervene in others' lifeworlds and how those on the ground in turn respond.

When developing the concept of vertical mediation throughout this book, my analyses extend from conventional forms of media such as television shows, films, photographs, and maps produced by what James Der Derian calls the military-industrial-media-entertainment-network[4] to more militaristic forms such as airport body scans, geospatial images, airplane leaflets, drone imagery, and photographs of bombed landscapes, all of which communicate vertical dynamics of the war on terror. The concept of vertical mediation, then, signals both the integral relation of orbit, air, and spectrum to the production of contemporary global media cultures and the need to consider different kinds of (non-celluloid/ electronic/digital) domains and materials as *environmental, elemental, and geological media*.[5] Orbit, air, spectrum, and ground each have the potential to function as sites of mediation. As technologies and objects move through these domains they leave traces with varying degrees of presence and legibility. As satellites and drones move through orbit and air, they have the potential to sense and transform the geophysical territories and oceans below. Their vertical maneuvers can alter soils and seas and dynamically reshape the bodies and objects that inhabit them. Only by recognizing a broad array of potential mediations is it possible to grasp the vicissitudes of the vertical, the complex materialities of media, and the changes in strategic power since 9/11.

One of my intentions in focusing on media culture and the war on terror is to foreground the constructedness of vertical forms of power and work to challenge their stronghold on political imaginaries and everyday social relations. There is nothing inevitable or natural about top-down domination, subjugation, oppression, exploitation, observation, or violence. And yet the modern nation-state, the world order, and socio-economic systems are structured in ways that continue to reproduce and even intensify such relations along multiple axes of social difference. This remains the case, despite the fact that feminists, critical race theorists, postcolonial critics, and others have for decades exposed the inequalities, injustices and discriminatory practices enabled by such power relations. The critical analysis of vertical power probes some of the deepest structural problems of our times. Vertical concepts of hierarchization and stratification continue to govern the ways people imagine and exercise power, even as technophiles celebrate a horizontal and rhizomatic Internet and its supposedly radical and revolutionary potentials to transform top-down political, economic, and cultural relations. If anything, the potential for anyone, including "terrorists," to horizontally access the Internet seems to have become a rationale for intensifying and extending vertical forms of strategic power. The more horizontal freedom, the more vertical control.

Rethinking Media Coverage

In order for vertical mediations to be intelligible, acts of communication are required. This book explores various vertical mediations by adopting a new approach to the concept of media coverage. Rather than think of *coverage* as a catchall term for electronic or digital news reporting, I situate the concept within the historical conjuncture of the war on terror, a period in which US media cultures exhibited increasing attention to vertical fields and operations. Historically, the word coverage is derived from the verb "to cover," which comes from the old French verb *couvrir* (circa 1150). It meant "to put or lay something over with the effect of hiding from view, protecting or enclosing; to overlay, overspread (with)." Military use of the verb began in 1687 as it was used to refer to the act of "presenting a gun or pistol at (something) so as to have it directly in the line of fire; to aim directly at." By the early twentieth century the verb was used to describe the practice of "reporting for a newspaper, broadcast or the like; to attend, investigate." And by 1919 to cover described the act of "photographing the whole of an area from the air."[6] That the etymology of coverage is articulated with practices of reporting, mapping, and monitoring positions it as a useful term for thinking about the relationship between vertical spaces, media cultures, and the war on terror. In this book, coverage refers to media content that draws attention to vertical space or power relations, whether through display or inference, while participating in practices of reporting, mapping, and/or monitoring.

The war on terror occurred in relation to major transformations in the media industries. On September 11, 2001 there was no Facebook, YouTube, Google Earth, Twitter, Samsung Galaxy, or iPhone. During the past decade a proliferating array of media platforms, applications, and formats has surfaced, and emergent media have been used to produce coverage of the US war on terror. Citizen-viewers could consume news media accounts of the war on terror in the newspaper, on television, or the Internet as the war on terror played out amid (and some might argue helped to fuel) increasing competition among news-papers, television networks, web portals, and mobile telephone carriers. Cable TV networks embedded reporters in the wars of Afghanistan and Iraq in an effort to deliver footage straight from the battlefront. Websites enabled users to read, download, upload, and/or share news reports and videos and fly though the simulated landscapes of the war theater. And mobile phone companies allowed subscribers to receive war-related news alerts on their mobile devices. Roger Stahl refers to the period between the 9/11 attacks and the 2003 war in Iraq as the "militainment bubble," suggesting that, "audience attention, rallying effects, culture industry profit, and Pentagon interests aligned to produce a certain kind of consumable war."[7] As war has taken on increasingly interactive and immersive dimensions, Stahl argues, "discourses of militainment have burrowed deeper into the capillaries of the subject, working internally to intensify a prescribed posture toward state violence and thereby widen the 'coalition of the willing.' "[8]

Building on the research on militainment, this book explores how different forms of coverage, including television news broadcasts, geospatial images, leaflets, airport security scans, Google Earth interfaces, YouTube videos, and digital photographs, rendered vertical forms of power intelligible to publics and in the process worked to reassert US vertical hegemony after 9/11. The war on terror has been a multiple platform and intermediale war—a war tailor-made for the media savvy citizen-consumer who could afford a cable or satellite TV sub-scription, knew how to surf the Internet, and use applications on a mobile phone as well. Though citizens relied on newspapers and radio during World War II and television during the Vietnam and Persian Gulf Wars, the war on terror provided viewers/users with opportunities to consume a vast assemblage of media forms. Remarking on the extensive array of war on terror media, the editors of *Observant States* note that "One could conduct a detailed visual exegesis of, say, television news; military-themed video games; embedded photo-journalism; Internet sites such as YouTube; the so-called 'martyr' videos; cartographic representations, from Geographical Information Systems (GIS) to the Olympian satellite visions of Google; popular cinema; 'high' art; closed-circuit television (CCTV); bio-surveillance techniques such as retinal scanning; all the way through to relatively mundane and domestic technologies such as Microsoft PowerPoint or mobile camera-phones."[9] Citizens had access to such a plethora of media coverage of the wars in Afghanistan and Iraq that Nicholas Mirzoeff characterized the moment as one of information overload, suggesting, "So many images were being created that there was never time to pause and discuss any one in particular."[10]

As coverage is transmitted and displayed to viewers/users through various media platforms and devices, it is important to recognize that these technologies too are the products of militarized technoscience. The GPS chips in mobile phones, the satellite images in Google Earth, and the Internet networks that connect users to websites were all designed with strategic military agendas in mind. Some scholars have argued that such media technologies inevitably extend militarization into the everyday lives of consumer-citizens. In her analysis of the emergence of Geographic Information Science (GIS) and Global Positioning Satellite (GPS) technologies, Caren Kaplan suggests, "Regardless of whether or not we serve in the military or have the means to afford the latest electronics, residents of the United States are mobilized into militarized ways of being" by virtue of their participation in a society that is increasingly structured by GIS and GPS.[11] Rey Chow echoes this sentiment when she observes:

> As a condition that is no longer separable from civilian life, war is thoroughly absorbed into the fabric of our daily communications—our information channels, our entertainment media, our machinery for speech and expression. We participate in war's virtualization of the world as we use—without thinking—television monitors, remote controls, mobile phones, digital cameras, PalmPilots, and other electronic devices that fill the spaces of everyday life.[12]

For Caplan and Chow, there is no hard line between media machines used by military units and civilian experiences. The consumption of media technologies designed for military contexts results in a generalized militarization of everyday life.

While militarization often assumes subtle ideological and material forms, it is equally important to note the myriad ways in which consumer-citizens in the US and beyond register, respond to, contest, struggle over, reject, or rework such militarization. Media and communication scholarship on anti-war movements, the Arab Spring revolutions, and the Occupy Wall Street protests, for instance, has emphasized the vital role of media in social movements against forces of militarization, totalitarianism, and corporate corruption.[13] Furthermore, as citizen-consumers occupy positions in an expanding and diversified field of media technologies, they are arguably more aware than ever of the precarious truth status of the information they consume, the highly constructed and regimented geographic locations they move through and inhabit, and the systems through which they are monitored, profiled, and surveilled. Rather than use the concept of coverage to advance notions of an uninformed media-consuming public overrun by processes of militarization, I approach the concept as a contentious field defined by changing media industries and overlapping practices of reporting, mapping, and monitoring in the context of the war on terror.

These practices of coverage—reporting, mapping, and monitoring—each are aligned with particular epistemologies. Typically thought of as reporting, coverage refers to the practice of documenting and producing interpretive accounts of world events for media consumers. To cover is to put historical experience into media discourse. Yet, it is important to nuance this meaning because as newsmakers produce coverage they also necessarily "provide cover"—that is, protect their sources and insulate or shield citizens from particular kinds of truths, realities, or views. They provide only partial accounts. There is, in other words, always negation or exclusion involved in the production of coverage and often what is negated or excluded is as significant or interesting as what is covered. This is likely why there has emerged in recent years an entire intellectual movement dedicated to the investigation of US histories of secrecy, black projects, cover ups, and covert operations and to the leaking of classified documents.[14] Coverage is not ubiquitous or total; it is always partial and involves the production and exclusion of information.

In the context of this book, coverage is also linked to mapping. Though the history of cartography dates back centuries, since the late nineteenth century citizen-viewers have used audiovisual media—photography, films, radio, and later television—to formulate cognitive maps of and position themselves in relation to the world historical events.[15] Media have become important tools of global mobility, orientation, and navigation, and, as have facilitated the production of the world as picture as well as worldviews.[16] Satellite and aerial images—often referred to as geospatial imagery—literalize this media mapping by fusing the overhead projections of traditional cartography together with digitized photorealist perspectives from above. This kind of coverage privileges panoptic logics as it presents the world from an imagined and omniscient position in the sky, which Denis Cosgrove calls the Apollonian view.[17] During the past two decades there has been an increasing integration of satellite and aerial imagery within media culture. Such images have been used to "cover" myriad events, ranging from the 9/11 attacks to the US wars in Afghanistan and Iraq, from disasters such as Hurricane Katrina in 2005 to the 2011 tsunami in Japan. Geospatial images also form the backbone of heavily trafficked digital platforms such as Google Maps and Google Earth. More and more we are watching life on earth as if seated in the atmosphere supervising, overlooking, and monitoring human and non-human movements and events on earth. Imaging systems from orbit to the ground structure the ways we perceive and respond to world events as well as the power to see and know.

As geospatial images are integrated within media events they become part of hierarchies of discourse, struggles over knowledge and interpretation, and practices of media literacy.[18] On the one hand, US political officials and TV news anchors have used these images to map and reinforce a changing world order governed by "us and them" logics and to construct new zones of security and conflict, risk and danger. On the other hand, others have used satellite images to expose the CIA's secret drone program in Pakistan, to assess collateral damage in Afghanistan and Iraq, and to map the flight paths of the US torture and rendition program, and other sites of state secrets.[19] As a practice of mapping, then, coverage can be used by viewers/users to position themselves and to navigate the world's politically charged and contested terrains.

Finally, as a practice of monitoring, coverage involves the use of media for surveillance, profiling, and targeting. Since 9/11, public and private spaces in the US and beyond have been monitored or "covered" arguably more than ever as part of coordinated efforts by federal, state, and local law enforcers to pre-empt future terrorist attacks.[20] The intensification of surveillance has been sanctioned by the USA Patriot Act of 2001 and the 2011 Patriot Sunsets Extension Act, which have given federal and state law enforcement agencies unprecedented authority to search individuals' property and profile their behavior, track their movements, and detain them for interrogation. Daily transactions and movements have come to define what Armand Mattelart calls "A new mode of governing society by tracking . . . in which everyone who circulates is liable to be under surveillance."[21] The tracking of movement extends from the micro movements of facial expressions to daily navigations on the Internet, from a trip to the grocery store to travel abroad in an airplane. As David Lyon suggests, "The 'age of terror' is turning its surveillance gaze on ordinary citizens in unprecedented and unconscionable ways."[22] As movement itself generates cause for suspicion and as media are mobilized to document, archive and analyze it, new classes of disenfranchisement have emerged—"the profiled" and "the targeted," as discussed in Chapters 2 and 4.[23] Within these conditions, coverage's monitoring mode enables surveillance and tracking in macro and micro scales and from orbit to the ground.

What is distinctive about this book's definition of coverage is its foregrounding of the potential of media to oscillate between modes of communication such as reporting, mapping, and monitoring. In the context of the war on terror, these modes have overlapped and alternated with one another. Actors ranging from state officials to anti-war activists, from television anchors to satellite operators have produced coverage to map terrorist activity, report on US air strikes, and monitor US military interventions. In addition to recognizing convergent and multi-modal media, this book explores how coverage is organized along a vertical axis of power. Rather than define coverage only as a news story presented on paper or screen; the concept is used to activate understandings of vertical mediation practices—extensive and sometimes imperceptible operations involving aero-orbital platforms that take shape between orbit and ground.

Vertical Mediation

One of the main arguments of this book is that media coverage of the war on terror made vertical space intelligible to global publics in new ways and power-fully revealed what is at stake in being able to control the vertical field. While media and communication scholars have analyzed how news media, prime time dramas, and digital media have been mobilized to support the war on terror, few have concentrated specifically on media and vertical space.[24] By vertical space I am referring to a continuous field of orbital, aerial, spectral, and terrestrial domains, a field that extends from the beneath the earth's surface to the outer limits of orbit. Aero-orbital space includes only the extra-territorial domains of orbit, air, and spectrum. These extra-territorial domains are trafficked by satellites, aircraft, and signals, and used by military, commercial, and civilian organizations. Although orbit, air, and spectrum have each been defined legally in international treaties, these domains have historically also been sites of contestation where sovereignty is qualified, does not apply, or has been applied unevenly.[25] Since 9/11 the US has used aero-orbital space aggressively, violating international law and others' sovereignty, to restore its global power and achieve vertical hegemony.

As media coverage has drawn attention to the vertical field it also signals *vertical mediations*—the use of aero-orbital technologies (satellites, aircraft, transmitters) and spaces (orbit, air, spectrum) to support such activities as the international distribution of audiovisual signals, the patrolling of movements on and beneath the earth's surface, and the physical destruction and reconstruction of lifeworlds from above. Though vertical mediations involve technological objects situated beyond the earth, they are intricately interwoven with terrestrial systems of biopower. US forces have mobilized these technologized practices to (re)shape material conditions for individual and social bodies, produce and circulate views of life on earth, and assert new global hegemonies.

The political significance of vertical space became known to publics long before the war on terror, for instance, with the rise of telecommunications, airlines, and the space age during the late nineteenth and early twentieth centuries. I argue, however, that the 9/11 attacks and their aftermath made vertical space intelligible and meaningful in new ways by demonstrating that the commandeering and coordinated use of the vertical field could have disastrous consequences upon civilians in US territory during a time of peace. Some have compared 9/11 to the attack on Pearl Harbor during World War II, since both events were surreptitious attacks on US territory by foreign forces in which approximately 3000 people died.[26] Unlike 9/11, Pearl Harbor was a military attack on a military target. I show throughout this book that 9/11 was in fact more similar to the Soviet Union's launching of Sputnik on October 4, 1957, which shocked the US and dramatically showcased Soviet aero-orbital domination.[27] That event created a long-term crisis of control for the US, which became known as the Cold War.[28] In the context of that crisis the US strengthened and accelerated vertical maneuvers ranging from nuclear weapons testing to satellite launchings, from aerial espionage to signal intelligence. Both Sputnik and the 9/11 attacks delivered powerful psychic jolts to US leaders and triggered substantive changes in areas of national security, military-industrial development, and telecommunication. Like the 9/11 attacks, Sputnik's launch was a vertical event. While the Soviets shot Sputnik up through the atmosphere auguring the Cold War, the 9/11 terrorists hijacked US commercial airplanes and slammed them fatefully into targets on earth, igniting the war on terror. Both were paradigm-changing events—one catalyzed decades of skyrocketing defense funding and nuclear weapons programs that could wipe out the entire planet and the other led to a state of perpetual war that involved intensified global surveillance and targeted killings.

Strategic forms of vertical power that have evolved during the latter half of the twentieth century have become more pronounced and valued in the context of the war on terror. Mediated US air strikes—so-called "surgical strikes"— that surfaced in coverage of the 1991 Persian Gulf War[29] and US "full spectrum dominance" tested during the war in the former Yugoslavia from 1991–1999, have continued during the war on terror.[30] Describing the US strategy of "full spectrum dominance," Paul Virilio suggests the US war in Kosovo marked a "deep transformation . . . in the nature of conflict between nations," demonstrating that the "ground offensive" has been replaced by the "aero-orbital offensive."[31] This was a "war of the airwaves," Virilio claims—a clash "carried on in the electromagnetic ether over the Balkans."[32] By attempting to control Serbia's spectral, aerial and orbital domains—its "circumterrestrial space"—Virilio contends, the US sought to create a "Hertzian ecosystem"[33] which it could use to jam, destroy and/or commandeer the enemy's telecommunication infrastructure and control the space around it. Total war, according to Virilio, was now directed "against the *atmospheric ecosystem* of the target country."[34] A defining moment of this offensive, Virilio explains, was the suspension of national Serbian radio and television feeds to a Eutelsat satellite on May 26, 1999, followed by the flights of a Hercules EC 130E, a "plane bristling with directional aerials and carrying a radio and television station in its cargo hold," which broadcast messages in Serbo-Croatian pre-recorded by the psychological operations department at Fort Bragg.[35] Similar missions against the "atmospheric ecosystem" have been carried out in Afghanistan, Iraq, and elsewhere as part of the war on terror as I discuss in this book.

Reinforcing the idea that strategic power can take vertical form, Eyal Weizman analyzes a similar dynamic at work in Israel-Palestine. Since the 1990s, many Israeli Defense Force projects, he explains, have been "built up in the air" such that they occupy the space above the Palestinian territories. These spatial relations produce a "politics of verticality" that enables Israel to maintain a position of dominance. As Weizman puts it, "Occupation of the skies gives Israel a presence across the whole spectrum of the electromagnetic field, and enables total observation. The airspace became primarily a place to 'see' from, offering the Israeli Air Force an observational vantage point for policing airwaves alive with electromagnetic signals—from the visible to the radio and radar frequencies of the electromagnetic spectrum."[36] A close ally of Israel, the US military has adopted similar techniques in the war on terror, using aircraft, satellites, telecommunication, and intelligence systems to patrol territories and target sites in Afghanistan, Iraq, and beyond.[37] Stephen Graham reformulates Weizman's concept as the "(geo)politics of verticality," reinforcing the point that vertical power always takes shape in relation to specific conditions on the ground. For instance, US military strategies of "full spectrum dominance" and "shock and awe" during the 2003 war in Iraq were designed in relation to the urban terrain of Baghdad.[38] Vertical power not only involved the capacity to see, know, and strike targets from the air, but also to transform the city's material layout.

While Virilio and Weizman explore the significance of the aero-orbital offensive and the politics of verticality, Peter Sloterdijk traces the logics of the "war on terror" back to instances of chemical warfare during World War I, when, as he suggests, "the air lost its innocence."[39] For the first time in history, the enemy's environment—literally the air he breathed—became the target. Sloterdijk finds the birth of "atmo-terrorism" and environmentalism within these earlier military campaigns, which powerfully demonstrated that breatheable air was no longer a given, marking a modern era of "air conditioning."[40] He uses the scenario of chemical warfare to call for a "process of atmosphere explication," suggesting the need for criticism to make the "air conditions explicit."[41] Combining the physicality (and necessity) of air with more metaphoric notions of cultural immersion, Sloterdijk understands the war on terror as part of a longer trajectory of air conditioning and climate control. Concerns about chemical attacks on civilians were used to rationalize US weaponization of the air—using bombing—during the Persian Gulf War and the current war in Syria. Terror is generated through the manipulation of air—whether filling it with a noxious gas, controlling the messages transmitted through it, or constructing it as a domain of limitless war and bombardment. What is ultimately important here is the insistence that the air cannot be thought about as a given.[42] Its politics must be explicated.

Such explication often occurs in relation to aerial or satellite views, which are used to contain complex events and produce particular ways of understanding them. To grasp what is at stake in the control of the vertical field, it is vital to again consider work by feminist postcolonial scholar Rey Chow, who has critiqued the historical militarization of the aerial view and its relation to the practice of targeting. In *The Age of the World Target*, Rey Chow discusses the iconic images of atomic mushroom clouds hovering over Hiroshima and Nagasaki as she interrogates "what politics of vision—of viewing the world—accompanied the strategic decision to drop the bombs."[43] Chow links this aerial view of nuclear destruction to an episteme in which the "world has come to be grasped and conceived as a target—to be destroyed as soon as it can be made visible."[44] This image, she writes, "is not only a picture . . . it has become in itself a sign of terror, a kind of gigantic demonstration with us, the spectators, as the potential target."[45] Chow's analysis not only shows how a media form—an iconic photograph—enacts vertical power and terror. She also reveals that the aerial view has been become tantamount to acts of targeting and destroying, and thus terror. How to sustain an oblique or diffractive perspective in relation to such optics remains a key issue.[46]

This book explores the specific role of media culture in making the air explicit, constructing the world as a target, and waging aero-orbital offensives. In the process, this book treats vertical spaces and operations as part of world history—as sites of domination and contestation, control and uncertainty, spectacle and the unknown. In an effort to think about vertical space, media, and the war on terror I rethink an existing concept whose meanings are often taken granted—*coverage*—and create a new concept that builds upon the work of scholars I have discussed—*vertical mediation*. I offer a critique of verticality that emphasizes the role of media in communicating how aero-orbital domains and technologies are defined, who controls them, and why they matter. Verticality is not something that simply occurs "out there." It is continuous with terrestrial legacies of state power—the securing of territories and administering populations, the extractive pursuits of imperialism, and the outsourcings of neoliberal governance. In the current historical conjuncture US vertical strategies have been reconfigured in the guise of an exceptional *democratic imperialism* asserted transparently and extensively without questioning. Inderpal Grewal describes this as an "advanced neoliberalism" characterized by conditions of endless war and increasing surveillance that produce "exceptional citizens" who reinforce the security state and protect the country from racialized others.[47] Though the US touts democratic liberalism as a guiding principle, post-9/11 US vertical strategies make patently clear that this state's current objective is to use aero-orbital platforms to sort, stratify, subject, occupy, and dominate particular territories and populations from above. To allow such vertical strategies to go unnoticed and uncontested is to accept a model of power that naturalizes the state's militarized and patriarchal hierarchy as a way of life and to enable its horizontal replication and extension as well as its trickling into myriad spheres of life. To name and critique verticality, I want to suggest, is a feminist post-structuralist project: it is to respond to and challenge some of the most sedimented features of strategic power and to explicate their imagining and materialization as hierarchization and stratification. A feminist critique of verticality not only calls attention to power's vertical operations and materializations, but, in the process, weaves in an analysis of the politics of difference and conditions of embodiment on earth. This is precisely what I offer in this book.

The concept of vertical mediation combines post-structuralist and feminist critiques of verticality with recent theories of mediation and new materialism.[48] Throughout this book, I explore how acts of mediation have the potential to both operationalize strategic vertical power plays and make them intelligible. This articulation—the capacity to materialize and communicate—enables media to infuse the vertical with the biopolitical. Maneuvers through orbit, air, and spectrum simultaneously have the potential to draw attention to vertical fields of history, power, and mediation, and affect daily life and material conditions in locations around the planet. As I will demonstrate, vertical mediation is manifest in such practices as the celebration of US air power in post-9/11 television broadcasts, the implementation of new security and screening protocols in the world's airports, the integration of geospatial imagery into US military interventions and reconstruction projects, and the use of drones to administer and secure territories and target suspects from above.

Cultural Atmospherics

As this book recasts the meanings of coverage and explicates processes of vertical mediation, it also considers their participation in the production of cultural atmospherics and media ecologies. The etymology of the word *atmosphere* comes from the modern Latin *atmosphaera*, which was derived from the Great *atmos* (vapour) and *sphere* (ball or sphere). By the seventeenth century the term was used to refer to "the mass of aeriform fluid surrounding the earth; the whole body of terrestrial air." Its more figurative definition as a "surrounding mental or moral element, environment. . . . prevailing psychological climate; pervading tone or mood; characteristic mental or moral environment . . ." surfaced during the eighteenth century. To describe something as atmospheric is to refer to it as "Existing, taking place, or acting in the air."[49] The war on terror became atmospheric not only in the sense that it was initiated within and through the air, as Virilio and Sloterdijk argue,[50] but also in the sense that it became part of a "pervading tone or mood" as it circulated within everyday media cultures.

In this book I approach the practices of coverage and vertical mediation as part of a broader field of cultural atmospherics—everyday social relations that take shape as media and communication move, quite literally, through the atmosphere (air, airwaves) to various sites on earth. Analyzing the war on terror, Peter Adey develops the concept of "security atmospheres" to account for the way "security starts to become an enveloping, overlapping, and immersive world," and suggests, "by attuning to atmospheres we may gain a far thicker and immersive sense of security's deployment."[51] Building upon his prior work on "affective atmospherics," Adey argues that atmospheres have the potential to "crystallise worlds": they "suffuse subjects, materials, discourses, and practices" but can also "push back against their management. . . ."[52] The capacity to imagine and experience affective and security atmospheres, I argue, is shaped by media and communication.[53] If coverage refers generally to media content and discourse and vertical mediation accounts for the materialization of power and communication through the air, orbit, and spectrum, then cultural atmospherics are the everyday social relations, structures of feeling, dispositions, and affects that emerge as consequences of vertical power.

The concept of cultural atmospherics highlights the unboundedness of media and communication and their constitutive relation to air and airwaves. Such a relation, of course, precedes the war on terror. As John Durham Peters has shown, the history of the idea of communication is materially contingent upon the air, which serves as a common carrier of everything from speech to broadcast signals.[54] Fred Turner's history of multimedia demonstrates how audiovisual technologies were organized after World War II to produce "democratic surrounds." Invoking Marshall McLuhan's idea that media are "extensions of man," Turner explains "the democratic surround was not only a way of organizing images and sounds; it was a way of thinking about organizing society. . . . [It] presented a powerful alternative to mass media and totalitarian society," even as it brought about new forms of control.[55] Building on such ideas, this book explores how orbit, air, and spectrum—vertical surrounds, if you will—have been used to communicate, mediate, and organize societies during the war on terror.

The concept of *cultural atmospherics* is invoked in a literal and figurative sense, literally to account for the way that cultural practices such as audiovisual communication move through (or beyond) the atmosphere in the process of their production, distribution, and/or, reception, and, figuratively, to account for the potential of such processes to generate affects and sensations, modulate moods, reorder lifeworlds, and alter everyday spaces. After the 9/11 attacks, the air and airwaves were filled with urgent messages and tragic spectacles. The strikes on the twin towers played over and over again in television news broadcasts. Security announcements blared through loudspeakers in airports, shopping malls, and public buildings, filling the air with frequent warnings. Color-coded terror alerts appeared on nightly news segments as if television weather reports. And airport security protocols were overhauled in ways that fundamentally altered what it felt like to fly.

Different social subjects have experienced post-9/11 cultural atmospherics in different ways. In the context of the war on terror, white Americans, political officials, and law enforcers have approached Arabs and other people of color, immigrants, Muslims, and those of non-Christian denominations as suspect. Such racial profiling has altered everyday relations and atmospherics in workplaces, schools, and neighborhoods, intensified discrimination, and created deep social divides. To mitigate future terror attacks law enforcers have developed terrorist watch lists and no-fly lists, re-normalizing racialized surveillance practices. As US surveillance has become more pervasive and extensive, it has especially affected Arabs, Muslims, and people of color, whose bodies and personal information have been captured, tracked, and analyzed for any number of reasons.[56] As Simon Browne crucially explains, "racializing surveillance is not static or only applied to particular human groupings, but it does rely on certain techniques in order to reify boundaries along racial lines, and, in doing so, it reifies race."[57] The techniques and boundaries of racializing surveillance have been intensified and extended along a vertical axis of power in the context of the war on terror.

As racist practices (and responses to them) circulate through the air, airwaves, and via satellite, they too shape cultural atmospherics. During the war on terror, racial differences have been used not only to structure and reinforce social hierarchies, but also to restructure the materialization of power in and through the vertical field. Satellites have been used to "orbit hate," according to Monroe Price. Drones, according to Keith Feldman, have been used to enact "racialization from above."[58] Flashlights, Simone Browne explains, have been carried to "illuminate blackness" in the night air.[59] As power circulates through the vertical field, media—whether satellite relays, drone imagery, or reflected light—help to make its embodied affects intelligible and thus make them matter. Cultural atmospherics involves attempting to understand how systems of social stratification, affective relations, and vertical domains intersect.

Because the concept of cultural atmospherics also tries to account for the intra-actions of media and their environs, the concept is closely related to that of media ecology. Since 1968 media and communication scholars have used this term to account for the "study of media environments."[60] One strand of media ecology research builds upon the work of Marshall McLuhan, Neil Postman, Walter Ong, and others, and conceptualizes the world of culture as an extension of the natural environment, suggesting that it must be protected and preserved and, in some cases, purified. As Postman has explained, the main concern of media ecology is "how media of communication affect human perception, understanding, feeling and value; and how our interaction with media facilitates or impedes our chances of survival."[61] Some media ecologists have assumed the role as a moral guardian or watchdog in an effort to regulate or "clean up" media cultures, particularly those characterized by excessive violent and sexual content. As Eric McLuhan writes, "Media ecologists have the duty to warn the public of the toxic side effects of new media/environments on the world's cultures and societies, including our own."[62] Much of this work can be characterized as making taste and morality-based judgments about the quality of media culture.

Another strand of media ecology research has been defined by Matthew Fuller. His book *Media Ecologies* builds upon the work of post-structuralist philosophers including Gilles Deleuze and Felix Guattari, Michel Foucault,

Antonio Negri, and others to explore the relationship of media to an array of objects and processes. Fuller uses the term ecology "because it is one of the most expressive [that] language currently has to indicate the massive and dynamic interrelation of process and objects, beings and things, patterns and matter."[63] His approach to media ecology queries established knowledges about media systems and investigates the radical dynamisms that constitute them, demonstrating how even the most seemingly "immaterial" components of media are, in fact, deeply rooted in particular material formations. In this way, Fuller's media ecological practice is invested less in moral outrage over the quality of media and more in the political, subjective and ethico-aesthetic dimensions of media systems.

While my project is much more closely aligned with Fuller's account of media ecology, the concept of cultural atmospherics differs from media ecology in multiple ways. First, it is intended not so much as a general theory of media or culture, but rather as a concept that can be used to reflect upon changing relations between media and environs within the historical conjuncture of the war on terror (from 2001 to 2017), and especially, in the context of the struggle to control the vertical field, including orbit, air, spectrum, and ground. Second, cultural atmospherics is concerned less with morality and more with materiality. It is especially focused on analyzing coverage to demonstrate how vertical strategies and mediations, involving aero-orbital platforms, take shape and become intelligible. Finally, cultural atmospherics recognizes the multiple assemblages of media that are possible—the hybridization and mixing of different technologies, platforms, and formats on and beyond the earth's surface, whether airplane broadcasting, satellite imaging, or drone sensing, and adopts a more materialist, infrastructural approach.[64]

Building upon research on vertical power and media ecologies, the concepts of *coverage*, *vertical mediation*, and *cultural atmospherics* are companion terms that emphasize respectively the changing media discourses, power relations, and affects of the war on terror. As I argue throughout this book, different kinds of coverage—from television shows to drone strike scenes—have made US practices of vertical mediation intelligible to publics and, in the process, produced cultural atmospherics where these practices become embodied and felt. Media and the war on terror cannot be understood only as stories and screens; they are also more dispersive and dynamic material processes involving the ownership, control, and use of aero-orbital technologies and domains. The shock of the 9/11 attacks compelled US forces to reorganize these technologies and domains to reassert their global power. Coverage brings these practices into focus and signals the vertical mediations and cultural atmospherics that have emerged in their wake.

Concept Sketching

To demonstrate how coverage, vertical mediation, and cultural atmospherics function in the context of the war on terror, I use a mixed methodology that combines discourse and textual analysis, industry research, and visualization. I developed an archive of coverage that includes US state and defense department records, commercial television news broadcasts, international press reports, declassified satellite and aerial imagery, Powerpoint presentations, Google Earth layers, airport security scans, viral videos, websites, and more. Rather than conduct a study of media organizations or institutions, I rethink the meanings of coverage from the perspective of a consumer-citizen-viewer encountering different media in the process of trying to make sense of historical events of the war on terror. This approach has involved television viewing, web navigation, site visits, close readings, and conversations. It also included the creation of *concept sketches* that serve as synthesizing responses to this research. These sketches, which open each chapter, are designed to visualize the vertical mediation processes that I conceptualize and critically delineate throughout this book. I present these drawings not so much as illustrations but as visual demonstrations or creative mediations of the technologies, practices, and fields used to reassert US vertical dominance in the context of the war on terror.[65]

While these sketches appear as primitive drawings, the act of creating them has the potential to generate something more substantive.[66] Drawing enabled me to map a political critique of the vertical field from a critical media studies perspective. Putting objects of my analysis on paper forced me to recognize the different players, strategies, and technologies that have been combined and mobilized in US efforts to control vertical space after 9/11. It allowed me to imagine the material conditions and affective relations of aero-orbital maneuvers and to consider how coverage infers the presence of these maneuvers even as it represents sites on earth. Drawing also challenged me to acknowledge the limits of my approach, which, for instance, does not address laws pertaining to vertical sovereignty or extraterritorial domains.[67] Nevertheless, by visualizing vertical power formations, these concept sketches also helped me to delineate operations that are imperceptible to most people and to determine the structural organization of this book. The sketches are reproduced in the book to guide readers through different domains of the vertical field—orbit, air, spectrum, and ground—and to visually delineate practices of airing, searching, monitoring, and targeting that structure the chapters. Drawings are especially useful when exploring phenomena that are distributed and imperceptible because they help to give abstract materialities intelligible forms.

Collectively, this book's chapters present analyses of war on terror coverage linked to processes of vertical mediation. Each chapter is organized in relation to a mediating practice that occurs through or in relation to the vertical field, including airing, searching, monitoring, and targeting. Chapters explore the airing or broadcasting of television signals after 9/11, the screening of airline passengers and their belongings, the monitoring of war zones with geospatial imagery, and the targeting of terror suspects using drones. These practices of vertical mediation are articulated through an analysis of various forms coverage.

Though the chapters are organized in approximate chronological order, they are also structured to chart a progression in vertical violence, beginning with the US commandeering of the airwaves after the 9/11 attacks and culminating in US targeted killings by drones. The chapters function both as discrete analyses of particular media coverage and as a composite or cumulative record that attests to a broader reorganization of vertical space, media, and power during the war on terror.

As I situate my analysis of media in the context of the war on terror, I also reflect upon the changing formats and spatial contexts of media and highlight their multiple and extensive locations. Media extend into domains far beyond the familiar sites of the screen, the home, or the nation, and into the amorphous domains of orbit, air, and spectrum. To support this point, I engage with scholarship across the fields of critical media and communication studies, science and technology studies, surveillance and security studies, cultural geography, and feminist theory. The book's chapters explore not only how media function as sites of discourse, power/knowledge, positioning, and meaning-making, but also how they are used to map, monitor, patrol, and secure spaces as they take shape through the vertical field. Finally, the book considers how vertical mediations are interwoven with biopolitics and power hierarchies organized around social difference.

Chapter 1, "Airing," marks a vertical turn in US television after 9/11 through analyses of network news segments, military psy-ops programs, and aerial assaults on foreign TV networks. Focusing first on network news coverage of the US war in Afghanistan from 2001–2002, the chapter explores how CNN and Fox News integrated satellite images, frontline reporting, and studio maps in ways that visualized and reasserted US vertical power, while the Oxygen network aired town hall meetings designed to carry international women's voices live-via-satellite as they questioned and critiqued US military action in Afghanistan. The second part of the chapter explores more coercive televisual formations such as US military PSY-OPS programs in Afghanistan and Iraq, which commandeered air and spectrum to disseminate broadcasts and leaflets from the sky. Such aerial broadcasting not only communicated with people on the ground, but also worked to establish systems of aerial control and administration in areas the US deemed connected to terrorists. The chapter closes with an analysis of the US military's unprecedented aerial assaults on commercial television facilities owned by the Arab-language network, Al Jazeera.

Chapter 2, "Searching," approaches US airport security after 9/11 as a practice of vertical mediation. Focusing on labor, technologies, and imagery at the checkpoint, the chapter first discusses the emergence of the Transportation Security Administration (TSA) and describes the working conditions of federal airport screeners tasked with keeping the skies safe. The labor of searching for something at the checkpoint involved material challenges ranging from injuries on the job to low pay, from undercover testing to objectionable racial profiling.

To carry out their work, TSA screeners use a combination of screening technologies including backscatter X-ray machines, millimeter wave body scanners, and pat-downs in efforts to secure the air. Despite a host of new screening technologies and increasing machine automation, I argue that practices of close sensing, which establish continuities between vision and touch, are crucial to securing the air. Finally, the chapter analyzes the types of coverage generated by the X-ray belt, revealing how the checkpoint is used not only to scrutinize travelers' possessions but also to preserve and protect consumer capitalism at the site of air travel. Only by giving up personal information, including views, scans, and X-rays of their bodies and belongings, can travelers enter the air.

Chapter 3, "Monitoring," explores US strategic use of geospatial images after 9/11. Building on my previous research on satellite remote sensing practices, I argue in this chapter that geospatial images not only *document* or *represent* conditions on earth, but can also be used to enact and bring about material transformations. The chapter begins with an analysis of US Secretary of State Colin Powell's use of satellite images in making the case for war against Iraq before the UN Security Council in 2003. In this globally televised presentation, Powell demonstrated how to read satellite images like a state and prompted public recognition of the capacity for satellite images to be spun. In an effort to formulate a cultural critique of image data gathered through the vertical field, I then explore the *microphysics of geospatial imagery*—the socio-technical and power-laden processes by which electromagnetic radiation traveling through the atmosphere is detected and turned into imagery. Drawing upon work in the fields of object-oriented ontologies and new materialisms I consider the *surplus matter of satellite images*, explicating how overhead views function as a backdrop for graphic inscriptions. I suggest that a focus on this backgrounded content can activate materialist imaginaries and alternate uses of geospatial imagery. Finally, I explore how state, military, and corporate entities have used geospatial imagery to advance strategic campaigns in Afghanistan and Iraq in the context of the war on terror. Focusing on processes of mediascaping, natural resource speculation, reconstruction, and predictive analytics, I show how geospatial images transform the territories of sovereign nation-states into US intellectual property that can be stored, shared, acted upon, and/or traded in the global digital economy. This is another way US forces have worked to reassert vertical power after 9/11.

Chapter 4, "Targeting," explores grounded dimensions of the US drone wars in Pakistan (2001–present) and the Horn of Africa region (2004–present) through an analysis of coverage that includes drone attack photos, aerial assault videos, drone protest media, drone infrastructure maps, infrared images, and drone crash scene photos. This coverage ranges from views on the ground to views from above, from visible light to infrared images, from documentary evidence to parodic commentaries, and emerges from sources as diverse as the US government, YouTube, and Pakistani activists. As I argue throughout this book, vertical mediation is a process that far exceeds the screen and involves the capacity to register the dynamism of occurrences within, upon, or in relation to myriad materials, objects, sites, surfaces, or bodies on earth. To demonstrate this in the context of drone warfare, I organize this chapter into two sections. The first focuses on the US drone war in the Federally Administered Tribal Areas (FATA) region of Pakistan and explores how drone attack photos, aerial assault videos, and protest media draw attention to grounded dimensions of drone war and registered peoples' objections and resistance to US vertical power. The chapter's second section shifts focus to the US drone war in the Horn of Africa and explores how drone media help to bring the infrastructural, perceptual, and forensic materialities of drone warfare to the surface. Combined, these two sections demonstrate how drone coverage draws attention to and maps a vertical field of biopower, exposes the logics of speculation and uncertainty that underpin drone warfare, and makes legible a new disenfranchised class that I refer to as "the targeted"—people who are the intentional or incidental victims of drone violence.

In the book's epilogue I discuss continuities in vertical power across the administrations of Presidents George W. Bush, Barack Obama, and Donald Trump. I also describe the steps Trump has taken to bolster US vertical power. During his short time in office, Trump has intensified US drone wars, waged aerial assaults on Syria and Afghanistan, accelerated the deregulation and commercialization of orbit and outer space, and implemented a controversial Muslim ban at US airports. While many have focused on Trump's use of Twitter as the defining characteristic of his leadership, I argue that his vertical maneuvers are equally important. Synthesizing the book's critical interventions, I conclude with an analysis of vehicle-ramming attacks on the streets of Western cities as a response to drone wars, and suggest the need for complex understanding of power, technologies, and publics.

Notes

1 "Text of George Bush's Speech," *The Guardian*, September 21, 2001, accessed May 8, 2016, www.theguardian.com/world/2001/sep/21/september11.usa13
2 Gore Vidal, *Perpetual War for Perpetual Peace: How We Got to Be so Hated* (New York: Thunder's Mouth Press/Nation Books, 2002); Dexter Filkins, *The Forever War* (New York: Alfred A. Knopf, 2008); Derek Gregory, "The Everywhere War," *The Geographical Journal* 177, no. 3 (2011): 238–250.
3 Sarah Kember and Joanna Zylinska, *Life after New Media: Mediation as a Vital Process* (Cambridge, MA: MIT Press, 2012).
4 James Der Derian, *Virtuous War: Mapping the Military-industrial-media-entertainment Network* (Boulder, CO: Westview Press, 2001).
5 John Durham Peters, *The Marvelous Clouds: Toward a Philosophy of Elemental Media* (Chicago, IL and London: University of Chicago Press, 2015); also see Jussi Parikka, *A Geology of Media* (Minneapolis, MN: University of Minnesota Press, 2015) and Janet Walker and Nicole Starosielski, Eds., *Sustainable Media: Critical Approaches to Media and the Environment* (New York: Routledge, 2016).

6 *Oxford English Dictionary*, second ed., 1989, accessed July 1, 2008.
7 Roger Stahl, *Militainment, Inc: War, Media, and Popular Culture* (New York: Routledge, 2010), 140.
8 Ibid.
9 Fraser MacDonald, Rachel Hughes, and Klaus Dodds, *Observant States: Geopolitics and Visual Culture* (London: I.B. Tauris, 2010), 3.
10 Nicholas Mirzoeff, Watching Babylon: the War in Iraq and Global Visual Culture (New York: Routledge, 2005), 74.
11 Caren Kaplan, "Precision Targets: GPS and the Militarization of U.S. Consumer Identity," *American Quarterly* 58, no. 3 (2006): 708.
12 Rey Chow, *The Age of the World Target: Self-Referentiality in War, Theory, and Comparative Work* (Durham, NC and London: Duke University Press, 2006), 34. According to Chow, "Our daily uses of the light switch, the television, the computer, the cell phone, and other types of devices are all examples of [a] . . . paradoxical situation of scientific advancement, in which the portentous . . . disappears into the mundane, the effortless, and the intangible. We perform these daily operations with ease, in forgetfulness of the theories and experiments that made them possible. Seldom do we need to think of the affinity between these daily operations and a disaster such as the atomic holocaust. To confront that affinity is to confront the terror that is the basis of our everyday life" (30).
13 Megan Boler, *Digital Media and Democracy: Tactics in Hard Times* (Cambridge, MA: MIT Press, 2008); Rita Raley, *Tactical Media* (Minneapolis, MN: University of Minnesota Press, 2009); Ramesh Srinivasan, "What Tahrir Square Has Done for Social Media: A 2012 Snapshot in the Struggle for Political Power in Egypt," *Information Society* 30, no. 1 (2013): 71–80.
14 See, for instance, Jodi Dean, *Publicity's Secret: How Technoculture Capitalizes on Democracy* (Ithaca, NY: Cornell University Press, 2002); Jack Z. Bratich, *Conspiracy Panics: Political Rationality and Popular Culture* (Albany, NY: SUNY Press, 2008); Trevor Paglen and AC Thompson, *Torture Taxi: On the Trail of the CIA's Rendition Flights* (Brooklyn, NY: Melville House Publishing, 2006); Trevor Paglen, *I Could Tell You But Then You Would Have to Be Destroyed by Me: Emblems from the Pentagon's Black World* (Brooklyn, NY: Melville House Publishing, 2008).
15 Giuliana Bruno, *Atlas of Emotion: Journeys in Art, Architecture, and Film* (London: Verso, 2002).
16 Martin Heidegger, "The Age of World Picture," in *The Question Concerning Technology and Other Essays*, trans. William Lovitt (New York: Harper and Row, 1977), 115–154. Nicholas Mirzoeff, *How to See the World: An Introduction to Images, from Self-Portraits to Selfies, Maps to Movies, and More* (New York: Basic Books, 2016).
17 Denis E. Cosgrove, *Apollo's Eye: A Cartographic Genealogy of the Earth in the Western Imagination* (Baltimore, MD: Johns Hopkins University Press, 2001).
18 Lisa Parks, Satellite Views of Srebrenica: Televisuality and the Politics of Witnessing, *Social Identities*, 7:4, 2001, 585-611; Digging into Google Earth: An Analysis of 'Crisis in Darfur,' *Geoforum* 40, no. 4 (July 2009): 535–545; "Zeroing In: Overhead Imagery, Infrastructure Ruins, and Datalands in Afghanistan and Iraq," in *Communication Matters: Materialist Approaches to Media, Mobility, and Networks*, Jeremy Packer and Stephen Wiley, Eds. (London: Routledge, 2011), 78–92.
19 Trevor Paglen, *Blank Spots on the Map: The Dark Geography of the Pentagon's Secret World* (New York: Penguin, 2009); also see Paglen and Thompson, *Torture Taxi*.
20 Brian Massumi, "Potential Politics and the Primacy of Preemption," *Theory and Event* 10, no. 2 (2007); Massumi, "The Primacy of Preemption," in *Ontopower: War, Powers, and the State of Perception* (Durham, NC and London: Duke University Press, 2015), 3–20.

21 Armand Mattelart, *The Globalization of Surveillance*, trans. Susan Taponier and James A. Cohen (Cambridge, UK: Polity Press, 2010), 198. As Mattelart writes, "A security society is centrifugal; it opens up; its mode of communication broadens the physical and moral horizon," 9.

22 David Lyon, *Surveillance after September 11* (Cambridge, UK: Polity Press, 2003), 8.

23 Lisa Parks, "Drones, Vertical Mediation, and the Targeted Class," *Feminist Studies* 42, no. 1 (2016): 227–235.

24 Pippa Norris, Montague Kern, and Marion R. Just, Eds., *Framing Terrorism: The News Media, the Government, and the Public* (New York and London: Routledge, 2003); Andrew Hoskins and Ben O'Loughlin, *Television and Terror: Conflicting Times and the Crisis of News Discourse* (Basingtoke, UK: Palgrave, 2007); Roger Stahl, *Militainment, Inc: War, Media, and Popular Culture* (New York and London: Routledge, 2010); Stacy Takacs, *Terrorism TV: Popular Entertainment in Post-9/11 America* (Lawrence, KS: University Press of Kansas, 2012); Philip Seig and Dana M. Janbek, *Global Terrorism and New Media* (New York and London: Routledge, 2011); Des Freedman and Daya Kishan Thussu, Eds. *Media & Terrorism: Global Perspectives* (Los Angeles, CA: Sage, 2012).

25 James Hay, "The Invention of Air Space, Outer Space, and Cyberspace," in *Down to Earth: Satellite Technologies, Industries, and Cultures*, Lisa Parks and James Schwoch, Eds. (New Brunswick, NJ: Rutgers University Press, 2012), 19–41.

26 John W. Dower, Cultures of War: Pearl Harbor/Hiroshima/9–11/Iraq (New York: W. W. Norton & Company, 2010): 4–10, 22–41; Gloria Ladson-Billings, "It's Your World, I'm Just Trying to Explain It," in *9/11 in American Culture*, Norman K. Denzin and Yvonna S. Lincoln, Eds. (Walnut Creek, CA: AltaMira Press, 2003): 255; Emily S. Rosenberg, *A Date Which Will Live: Pearl Harbor in American Memory* (Durham, NC and London: Duke University Press, 2003): 2–3, 174–190; Geoffrey M. White, "Pearl Harbor and September 11: War Memory and American Patriotism in the 9–11 Era," *The Asia-Pacific Journal* 1, no. 4 (2003): 1–21.

27 Stuart Croft, *Culture, Crisis and America's War on Terror* (Cambridge, UK: Cambridge University Press, 2006): 124.

28 Walter A. McDougall, *The Heavens and the Earth: A Political History of the Space Age* (New York: Basic Books, 1985).

29 Kevin Robins, "Sights of War," in *Into the Image: Culture and Politics in the Field of Vision* (New York: Routledge, 1996), 61–82.

30 Paul Virilio, *Strategy of Deception* (London: Verso, 2007), 51–52.

31 Ibid.

32 Ibid, 31.

33 Ibid, 33.

34 Ibid, 14.

35 Ibid, 31.

36 Eyal Weizman, "Control in the Air," *Open Democracy*, May 2, 2002, accessed May 8, 2016, www.opendemocracy.net/ecology-politicsverticality/article_810.jsp

37 Lisa Hajjar, "Lawfare and Targeted Killing: Developments in the Israeli and US Contexts," *Jadaliiya*, January 15, 2012, accessed February 15, 2014, www.jadaliyya.com/pages/index/4049/lawfare-and-targeted-killing_developments-in-the-I

38 Stephen Graham, "Vertical Geopolitics: Baghdad and After." *Antipode* 36, no. 1 (2004): 12–23. Also see, Stephen Graham, *Vertical: The City from Satellites to Bunkers* (London: Verso, 2016).

39 Peter Sloterdijk, Amy Patton, and Steve Corcoran. *Terror from the Air* (Los Angeles, CA: Semiotext(e), 2009), 109.

40 Ibid.

41 Ibid, 84.

42 Media and communication scholars who have explored "air conditions" include: John Durham Peters, *Speaking into the Air: A History of the Idea of Communication* (Chicago, IL: University of Chicago Press, 1999); James Schwoch, *Global TV: New Media and the Cold War, 1946–69* (Champaign-Urbana, IL: University of Illinois Press, 2008), which addresses the issue of the extraterritoriality; Hay, "The Invention of Air Space"; Fred Turner, *The Democratic Surround: Multimedia & American Liberalism from World War II to the Psychedelic Sixties* (Chicago, IL: University of Chicago Press, 2013); Anna McCarthy *Ambient Television: Visual Culture and Public Space* (Durham, NC and London: Duke University Press, 2001).

43 Chow, *The Age of the World Target*, 12.

44 Ibid.

45 Ibid, 26.

46 See Laura Kurgan, *Close Up At a Distance: Mapping, Technology, and Politics* (New York: Zone Books, 2013).

47 For further discussion of these dynamics see Inderpal Grewal, *Saving the Security State* (Durham, NC and London: Duke University Press, 2017).

48 Diana H. Coole and Samantha Frost, *New Materialisms: Ontology, Agency, and Politics* (Durham, NC and London: Duke University Press, 2010); Jane Bennett, *Vibrant Matter: A Political Ecology of Things* (Durham, NC and London: Duke University Press, 2010).

49 *Oxford English Dictionary.*

50 Virilio, *Strategy of Deception*; Sloterdijk, *Terror from the Air.*

51 Peter Adey, "Security atmospheres or the crystallization of worlds," *Environment and Planning D: Society and Space* 32 (2014): 835, 838.

52 Ibid, 846.

53 For a discussion of the relationship between ambient media, atmospheres and subjectivation see Paul Roquet, *Ambient Media: Japanese Atmospheres of Self* (Minneapolis, MN: University of Minnesota Press, 2016).

54 John Durham Peters, *Speaking into the Air: A History of the Idea of Communication* (Chicago, IL and London: University of Chicago Press, 1999).

55 Turner, *The Democratic Surround*, 9, 10.

56 Sunaina Maira, "Surveillance Effects: South Asia, Arab, and Afghan American Youth in the War on Terror," in *At the Limits of Justice: Women of Colour on Terror*, Suvendrini Perera and Sherene H. Razack, Eds. (Toronto: University of Toronto Press, 2014), 86–106; Arun Kundnani, *The Muslims are Coming! Islamophobia, Extremism, and the Domestic War on Terror* (London: Verso, 2015); Louise Amoore, "Biometric Borders: Governing Mobilities in the War on Terror," *Political Geography* 25 (2006), 336–351.

57 Simone Browne, *Dark Matters: On the Surveillance of Blackness* (Durham, NC and London: Duke University Press, 2015), 17.

58 Monroe Price, "Orbiting Hate? Satellite Transponders and Free Expression," in *The Content and Context of Hate Speech: Rethinking Regulation and Responses*, Eds. Michael Herz and Peter Molnar (Cambridge, UK: Cambridge University Press, 2012), 514–538; Keith Feldman, "Empire's Verticality: The Af/Pak Frontier, Visual Culture, and Racialization from Above," *Comparative American Studies* 9, no. 4 (2011): 325–341.

59 Browne, *Dark Matters*, 25.

60 Neil Postman, 1968. See Kate Milberry, "Media Ecology," *Oxford Bibliographies*, accessed August 18, 2017, www.oxfordbibliographies.com/view/document/obo-9780199756841/obo-9780199756841-0054.xml

61 Lance Strate, *Echoes and Reflections: On Media Ecology as a Field of Study* (New York: Hampton Press, 2006), 17.

62 "Those engaged in teaching 'media literacy' and other media-training course are actually engaged in the business of peddling toxic and addictive things to naïve users/

addicts-to-be." See Eric McLuhan, "Concerning Media Ecology," in *Valuation and Media Ecology: Ethics, Morals, and Laws*, Corey Anton, Ed. (New York: Hampton Press, 2010), 84-85.

63 Matthew Fuller, *Media Ecologies: Materialist Energies in Art and Technoculture* (Cambridge, MA: MIT Press, 2005), 2.

64 Lisa Parks and Nicole Starosielski, Eds. *Signal Traffic: Critical Studies of Media Infrastructures* (Urbana, IL and Chicago, IL: University of Illinois Press, 2015).

65 Kember and Zylinska, *Life after New Media*, 201–205.

66 For further discussion of the relationship between drawing and thinking see, Bernhard Siegert, "White Spots and Hearts of Darkness: Drafting, Projecting, and Designing as Cultural Techniques," *Cultural Techniques: Grids, Filters, Doors, and Other Articulations of the Real*, Geoffrey Winthrop-Young, trans. (New York: Fordham University Press, 2015): 122–146; Mike Biddulph, "Drawing and Thinking: Representing Place in the Practice of Place-Making," *Journal of Urban Design* 19, no. 3 (2014): 278–297; Michael Taussig, "What Do Drawings Want?," *Culture, Theory and Critique* 50, no. 2 (2009): 263–274.

67 For a discussion of these issues see, Ricky J. Lee and Sarah L. Steele, "Military Use of Satellite Communications, Remote Sensing, and Global Positioning Systems in the War on Terror," *Journal of Air Law and Commerce* 79, no. 1 (2014).

1

AIRING

US Television's Vertical Turns

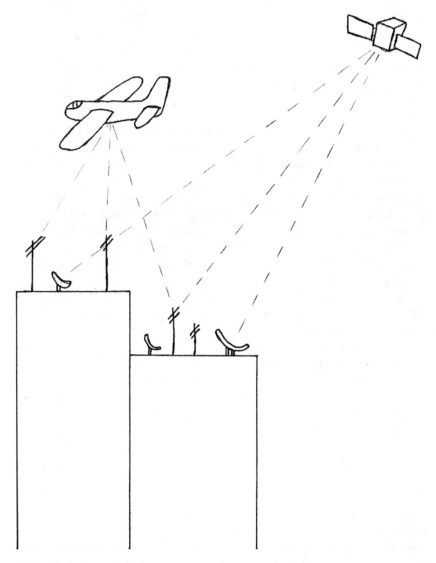

FIGURE 1.1 "Airing." Concept sketch by Lisa Parks.

Source: The author

On May 1, 2003 President George W. Bush landed on the USS *Abraham Lincoln* aircraft carrier near San Diego upon its return from the Persian Gulf. Decked out in full flight gear, Bush arrived in a small S-3B Viking jet. After his dramatic tail hook landing, Bush saluted and shook hands with the vessel's crew. A short while later Bush put on a suit, jumped on a platform, and delivered a live television address to the nation. In it he announced that major combat operations in Iraq had ended, standing beneath a massive banner that declared "Mission Accomplished." Though the costly stunt was critiqued by some congressional leaders, the press celebrated this unusual Presidential performance calling Bush a "high-flying jet star" and "a one-time fighter dog." Chris Matthews quipped, "he looks like he flew the plane" and Brian Williams admitted, "He looked terrific and full of energy in a flight suit."[1] Ann Coulter applauded Bush's ability to "land on a boat at 150 miles per hour" and jabbed, "It's hard to imagine any Democrat being able to do that . . . It's stunning."[2] David Sanger of *The New York Times* described Bush's entrance as a "*Top Gun* moment."[3]

Bush's dramatic landing became a media event that crystallized US efforts to reclaim control of the vertical field after 9/11. Orchestrated less than two years after the attacks, and the year before the 2004 Presidential election, the event worked to restore a world order based on US aero-orbital dominance established during the Cold War. If the 9/11 attacks spectacularly ruptured this dominance by commandeering US satellites, airplanes, and airwaves, then Bush's dramatic fighter jet performance set out to forcefully reassert it, replacing horrific views of hijacked airplanes crashing into the World Trade Center's twin towers with scenes of the President jetting down from the skies victorious. This chapter analyzes a series of post-9/11 televisual formations leading up to this moment and demonstrates how US forces used coverage to reclaim, visualize, and exercise US control over orbital, aerial, and spectral domains at home and abroad, including in Afghanistan and Iraq.

Since the 9/11 attacks occurred before the era of broadband Internet, social media, and the smart phone, most Americans experienced these events via television. While there is a vast scholarly literature on media and terrorism, relatively few scholars write explicitly about television.[4] Leftist scholars and public intellectuals who have written about "the media" and "the war on terror" often dismiss television out of hand without ever watching it, lumping it into what James Der Derian calls a military-industrial-information-entertainment complex.[5] To understand US *television's* specific relation to the war on terror, it is helpful to consider work by television scholars who take the medium's content and form seriously. In her study of the US television industry's response to 9/11, Lynn Spigel suggests this historic event interrupted the normalcy of television and made TV executives nervous and uncertain about what kinds of programming to air.[6] Their solution to this uncertainty was to reorganize the textual and narrative logic of TV programs from *Oprah* to *West Wing* to *South Park*, among others, to promote nationalist myths that "channeled the nation back to commercial TV 'as usual.'"[7] Building on this work, Stacy Takacs explores how US television entertainment organized public thinking about and endorsed militaristic agendas of the war on terror. "U.S. television representations," Takacs argues, "helped to 'maintain' the discourse of national security and 'hold together' a national consensus favoring the use of war to achieve peace during the Bush years."[8] As television entertainment mainstreamed the language of war, Takacs suggests, other possible responses such as diplomacy, modes of legal redress, or programs to alleviate the frustrations that engender acts of terrorism became unthinkable.[9]

As these television scholars demonstrate, historic events such as 9/11 and the war on terror have provided occasions for reassessing and recalibrating television's "normalcy" in light of these changing political conditions. Building on this idea, this chapter explores shifts in the material arrangement and potentials of television technology. After 9/11, I argue, US television took a *vertical turn*. As television technologies were mobilized simultaneously to restore order on the home front and wage a war on terror in Afghanistan and Iraq, they revealed what is at stake in controlling the vertical field. On the one hand, US commercial television news segments drew attention to the vertical in unprecedented ways, using satellite images, frontline reporting, and cartography to stage and reassert US dominance over the orbital, air, and airwaves. On the other hand, the US military deployed aircraft to commandeer the air space and airwaves of Afghanistan and Iraq and, in the process, destroyed and reconfigured the media infrastructures of both countries.

To account for these divergent practices, I conceptualize television not solely as commercial entertainment or military monitoring, but as a flexible set of socio-technical potentials that can be organized into different assemblages which shape and determine what is "covered" and "aired." This approach builds from critical conceptualizations of television that have emerged throughout the twentieth century. In 1935, Rudolph Arnheim described television as a hybrid medium, "a relative of motorcar and airplane: . . . [as] a means of cultural transportation. . . ."[10] Emphasizing its transformative potential, Arnheim recognized television's capacity to "give us a feeling for the multiplicity of what happens simultaneously in different places," yet insisted the technology "does not cause these beneficial changes by itself. It offers possibilities, which the public must seize."[11] Several decades later, Raymond Williams cautioned against fixed understandings of this "cultural technology." Recognizing television's convergence with satellites and cable systems, he wrote, "Just as television was coming to seem a determined cultural form or a determined technology, there are these radically alternative definitions and practices, trying to find their way through."[12] Today, television is integrated with vertical platforms (such as airplanes and satellites) at the level of content and form.

Since television is *of the airwaves* it arguably has an inherent relation to the vertical, but I argue this verticality became more intelligible and pronounced to publics after 9/11, due to particular practices of US television news networks and the US military. Rather than embrace commercial network or military definitions of television—systems of mass entertainment or strategic monitoring— I adopt a critical/conceptual approach and explore how televisual practices function as *vertical mediations*—as dynamic processes of audiovisual production and distribution that bring together and rely upon specific organizations, technologies, and resources (including the orbit, the air and airwaves) to communicate and/or affect material conditions and power relations from orbit to the ground.

This chapter analyzes post-9/11 television coverage that staged and enacted US dominance in and through the extraterritorial domains of the spectrum, air, and orbit.[13] The chapter's first section provides a critical analysis of US commercial TV news segments and live satellite broadcasts aired in the weeks after the 9/11 attacks. Focusing on commercial news networks' integration of satellite images, frontline reporting, and cartography, I explore how coverage worked to make the vertical field intelligible as a site of struggle and reinstate US "air power." The second half of the chapter shifts focus to televisual practices involving US military PSY-OPS (psychological operations) programs in Afghanistan and Iraq. During the early phases of the war on terror, the US military commandeered air space and airwaves above these countries to conduct aerial broadcasting and leaflet bombing campaigns. These practices were used not only to communicate with people on the ground, but also to establish new modes of aerial control and administration in areas the US deemed connected to terrorism. Chapter 1 closes with a discussion of the US military's more coercive efforts to control the vertical field, discussing its aerial assaults on facilities owned by the Arab-language television network, Al Jazeera.

Vertical Views in TV News

As post-9/11 television news reports replayed video of airplanes crashing into the twin towers of the World Trade Center to remind viewers of this traumatic event, they began to adopt an array of strategies to mitigate the devastating effects of these scenes. Post-9/11 news coverage differed across the networks, but CNN and Fox News established what might be considered a dominant paradigm. This paradigm can be understood as taking shape in the CNN show *Military Options*, which began after September 11th and lasted during early phases of the US war in Afghanistan. Anchored by owl-eyed correspondent Wolf Blitzer and also by Miles O'Brien, *Military Options* typically featured retired military commanders explaining new weapons systems and maneuvers in the Afghani war theater, CNN Pentagon and White House correspondents summarizing press conferences, and declassified US military intelligence interpreted by experts and officials. After 9/11 CNN added several military experts to its expert pool including retired Generals Wesley Clark, David Grange, George Joulwan and Major General Don

Shepperd, who made regular appearances in late 2001. Though the program's title seems to suggest a show dedicated to deliberation of various "military options," its formulaic assimilation of military spokespersons, vantage points, and rhetoric featured only one true option in response to the 9/11 attacks—a war against Afghanistan. The show, in other words, was not so much about "options" as it was a resounding endorsement of US military decisions made behind closed doors and without substantive public or congressional debate. Wolf Blitzer even went so far as to describe post-9/11 anti-war demonstrations as unpatriotic. This flagship program articulated an explicit pro-war stance and displaced longstanding ideals of journalistic objectivity, setting the tone for CNN's coverage of the war on terror.

In the weeks after 9/11, CNN coverage regularly integrated satellite images in ways that highlighted US vertical power. Television news producers used satellite images to remind viewers that the US has the capacity to monitor the Taliban and Al Qaeda from above. On September 21, 2001 *Military Options'* Wolf Blitzer and David Ensor aired three commercial satellite images acquired by Space Imaging a year earlier. In their discussion, Blitzer and Ensor used the images to pinpoint the kinds of sites the US might strike if the Bush administration decided to wage attacks on Afghanistan. The first satellite image showed the Duranta Lake Dam area, a hydroelectric facility constructed by Soviet Union companies during the early 1960s, 7 km west of Jalalabad. It was followed by a satellite image of the Abu Khabab Camp nearby, allegedly used by Osama Bin Laden's followers for chemical weapons and high explosives training. A third satellite image pointed to underground tunnel entrances near the Abu Khabab training camp as well as a helipad nearby. Ensor admits that since these satellite images were generated a year earlier, there is likely no one left at these bases. Nonetheless, he uses the images to symbolically stage US military retaliation and to spotlight the kinds of Afghani targets the US is likely to strike. By highlighting orbital platforms and emphasizing the fact that the US used them to monitor sites in Afghanistan prior to 9/11, the segment works to reassert US vertical power by implying that the US has been watching this area from above all along.[14]

A week later, on September 28, 2001, CNN aired a similar segment. In this one, former military commander Don Shepperd uses a commercial satellite image of Kandahar to explain how US troops are preparing for war in Afghanistan. As the satellite image is projected in the background, Shepperd indicates US troops are studying Afghani infrastructure including bridges, communication, and water systems and reviewing overhead imagery to prepare for "commando raids." Here the satellite image is used not only to celebrate the unique way satellites can make infrastructures visible from above, but also to emphasize the capacity to alter or destroy those infrastructures, invoking Rey Chow's important analysis of the age of the world target, a time when seeing is articulated with the capacity to destroy or kill.[15]

Reinforcing US orbital power, several days later, on October 4, 2001, CNN aired a special report on US spy satellites that featured declassified satellite images of alleged Al Qaeda facilities in Afghanistan.[16] The segment, anchored by David Ensor, indicated the US would use its arsenal of satellites and unmanned aerial vehicles (such as Predators) to locate Osama Bin Laden in Afghanistan's vast and jagged mountain ranges, which jutted 12,000 feet and higher. US satellites and drones, the reporter insisted, would enable troops to monitor this area without having to physically maneuver through it on the ground. The backbone of such strategies, CNN reported the next day, was a recently launched advanced K-11 spy satellite able to "see" things as small as 6 inches in diameter. Emphasizing the spy satellite's material relationship to objects and activities on the ground, its image data, reporter Ann Kellan explained, would be used to create 3-D models of Afghanistan's terrain before US troops ever set foot on its soil. Highlighting US satellite technology, the segment shifted from a discussion of the power of the K-11 spy satellite to US signal intelligence (SIGINT) satellites, which were used to intercept conversations and conduct eavesdropping in Afghanistan.

CNN segments construct aero-orbital views as continuous with the capacity to alter and destroy sites on Earth—as part of a vertical field of material relations, or what I call vertical mediations. In an October 29, 2001 CNN "War Room" report, Jamie McIntyre presented "before and after satellite photos" released by the US Defense Department, revealing "a complex of military maintenance buildings near Kabul reduced to rubble by US smart bombs . . . one of dozens of targets hit in recent days." The segment's visual track shifts from static satellite views to aerial video of targets being struck in Afghanistan followed by massive plumes of smoke.[17] It establishes a visual vertical trajectory from the satellite in orbit to aircraft in the sky to targets on the earth's surface, and, in doing so, recalls material elements of the 9/11 attacks while visualizing a forceful retaliation against them.

Aired in the weeks after 9/11, these CNN segments established particular patterns for perceiving and interpreting the war on terror, and reasserted US vertical hegemony in multiple ways. First, the segments flattened and compressed the vertical field into two-dimensional views of the earth's surface that could be integrated within the flow of commercial television and used to highlight US military dominance in areas of surveillance, logistics, and targeting. Second, CNN's use of satellite images enabled the news network to visually extend its reach upward and lay claim to orbital platforms so that its viewers could, like military officers, monitor Afghanistan from above and zero in on potential or actual targets. While such practices emerged earlier in coverage of the US Persian Gulf War (1991) and wars in Bosnia (1993–1995) and Kosovo (1998–1999), vertical views were integrated more extensively and frequently in post-9/11 news, and were normalized as a result. Third, by integrating satellite images in post-9/11 reporting, CNN implicitly endorsed the capacity of US corporations and military organizations to use orbital platforms to acquire and circulate, at their discretion, high-resolution views of Others' sovereign territories, as will be discussed further in Chapter 3. Finally, CNN's presentation of declassified "before and after" satellite images interpellated viewers as part of a civic verification system used to confirm and, in effect, authorize the ongoing destruction of targets in Afghanistan. The frequent airing of such "before and after" segments in the context of the war on terror socialized publics to read satellite images as demonstrations of US vertical power rather than as scenes for critical inquiry. Collectively, these CNN's news segments worked to mitigate the traumatic effects of 9/11 media coverage, which replayed hijacked US commercial airplanes striking the twin towers, by pointing to US aero-orbital platforms and their capacities to see and destroy sites and people on earth.

Machismo in the Mountains

In addition to using satellite imagery to showcase US vertical power, post-9/11 US television coverage adopted other strategies, including live reporting from the frontlines of the war in Afghanistan. Just as CNN's *Military Options* valorized the top-down views of military officials and satellite images, Fox News used *Geraldo Rivera Reports* to spotlight acts of US military retaliation in Afghanistan and deliver front row views of it. While CNN and Fox News have different styles of reporting and are competitors, their post-9/11 coverage converged around their active endorsement of war. Geraldo's segments offered a cranked-up militarized masculinity, one that reveled in gonzo-style reporting, unapologetic revenge, and macho vigilantism. In his Tora Bora coverage, Geraldo monitors B52 bombers and F-16s crisscrossing the sky, crawls around the desert in military garb, befriends Afghani rebels, and fends off flying bullets caught in the crossfire, functioning more like an extreme sports enthusiast than a war correspondent. Rivera's frontline reporting was designed to whip up vengeful sentiment, endorse US retaliation, and confirm that US bombs were indeed falling from the sky and striking Al Qaeda hideouts near Tora Bora. Days after US aircraft attacked the caves near Tora Bora, Geraldo and his crew wandered inside them to expose what he called the "rats' nest." In an interview with Fox News reporters Sean Hannity and Alan Colmes nearly a year later, on October 4, 2002, Rivera boasted that he was proud to spend a couple of nights in Osama bin Laden's caves because, as he put it, it was "symbolic of what I think is a tremendously underappreciated victory." Later, when asked why bin Laden and his cohort had still not been found, Rivera explained, "I believe that these guys are all hunkered down, like the sissies they are, hiding under some one's skirt in Pakistan." Acting as if a soldier of words, Rivera (and others on the Fox News channel) consistently feminized the enemy, referring to Taliban and Al Qaeda as sissies, wimps, and rats. But Rivera was not limited to the sword of his tongue. He positioned himself as one of TV journalism's rare warriors, insisting, "I'm very fit. I still box

. . . I'd like to find a reporter who can outdistance me . . . Courage has never been my problem. Brave men run in my family."[18]

In Rivera's frontline coverage, Fox News encourages viewers to experience US military retaliation through a camera aligned with a nationalist American masculinity that is proudly racist and sexist. Rivera not only celebrates his and the US military's "tremendous victory" in getting inside bin Laden's caves, offering a view even satellites cannot capture, but also emphasizes his superiority at every juncture. As he belittles Al Qaeda and the Taliban as "sissies" and refers to their hideouts as "rats' nests," Rivera describes himself as "fit" and "brave." While Rivera did not get to drop any bombs himself, his inflammatory rhetoric offered a way for viewers to participate in violence and militancy using hate and discrimination.

In November 2001, Fox News sent Geraldo Rivera back to Afghanistan to cover the US air campaign. Rivera, who claimed he could not bear to stay on the sidelines during a big story, left his job at CNBC on November 16, 2001, and flew to Afghanistan three days later. As Rivera explained at the time, "the war on terrorism is the biggest story of our times [and] I've got to get out there. And when you're an anchor, you're literally anchored. I had to break the chain."[19] From December 5–18, 2001 Rivera sent live satellite transmissions from outposts in the White Mountains near Tora Bora where US "daisy cutters" were reportedly trying to "flush Al Qaeda fighters out of the caves." Hired as Fox News's "hot spot" correspondent, Rivera was assigned to capture footage of Osama bin Laden the moment he emerged from the caves defeated. Rivera positioned himself as the perfect man for the job, stating, "I'm feeling more patriotic than at any time in my life. Itching for justice, or maybe just revenge."[20]

Much of Rivera's Tora Bora coverage emphasized the brute force of US military airpower as it was unleashed on alleged Al Qaeda and Taliban hideouts in the Tora Bora mountains of Afghanistan. A report transmitted live on December 6, 2001 from the White Mountains on the road to Tora Bora showed Rivera caught in the crossfire, ducking and taking cover as missiles and bullets darted through the air around him. Rivera used the occasion to emphasize the dangerous nature of his work and risks he was willing to take to pursue bin Laden.[21] In other reporting that day, Rivera identifies "a B-52 coming in live" and proclaims, "You see it right now. We just had one of the fighter-bombers come in and drop one of the precision munitions. Now comes the big B-52. This guy's going to unload big-time on the Tora Bora terrorist base right behind us in the White Mountains. We're watching virtually from underneath the bomb bay, actually, happily just clear of it. He's going to drop any minute."[22] In another segment, Geraldo appears in a Pashtun hat and military jacket standing on a hilltop near Tora Bora. He has organized and timed his report so that he can present live views of US aircraft just as they drop their payloads on nearby caves. Rivera looks up at the sky and explains that he has been watching similar flyovers all day and wants to reveal to US viewers what aerial retaliation looks like up close. He orders his camera operator to shoot the sky and, as a plane circles above, Rivera excitedly proclaims, "He's just about to do it! He's gunna unload it any second. I've been watching this all day! They're gunna unload it right now and destroy all the bad guys' hideouts in that mountain over there!" The segment continues for more than a minute as the camera pans and strains to keep US aircraft in view, but the attack never happens. Rivera, demoralized, assures his audience that the air raids have been happening all day and are bound to happen again, just not right now. In a segment from Tora Bora on December 14th Rivera reports "furious bombing" by the "US air armada" throughout the area. Pointing to a massive cloud of smoke on the mountain peak behind him, he boasts, "a bomb just exploded there not more than 45 seconds ago!" Rivera explains that the US military strategy is to scorch the forest on top of the mountains to eliminate the "terrorists' cover." When asked by the anchor whether Osama bin Laden would face challenges making an escape through the snow on those mountains, Rivera responds, "If they try to escape they're going to stand out like little black dots against the white blanket." He continues, "You've seen the gun-camera video of the scurrying 'arabs' as the planes bear down on them at night or day. It will be very unpleasant."[23]

If televised satellite images looked down upon the earth to spotlight potential targets, Rivera's segments offered the opposite perspective as his camera operator tilted up and scanned the skies to showcase US aircraft unloading bombs and missiles. These segments conjoined television and the vertical field in different ways, drawing attention to downward-looking views of earth's surface and upward looking views of maneuvers through the sky. In doing so, this coverage constructed the vertical field as a space uniquely accessed via US television news as multiple technologies of observation (satellite sensors, aircraft pilots, hand-held cameras, and human eyes) and vectors of action (orbit and flight paths, ground logistics, and sightlines) are brought together and rendered in its frames as part of broader US hegemonic agendas. In the wake of 9/11, television news became a key site for making the vertical intelligible and palpable as a field of US conquest and struggle. Television coverage exemplified a vertical turn by using satellite images and frontline reporting to emphasize US control of vertical domains—orbit, the air, and airwaves—in Afghanistan and elsewhere. To contend with the spectre and uncertainty of terrorism—where it was and where it might strike next—television news coverage constructed a language of vertical control, immediately following the 9/11 attacks, suggesting that the enemy could be monitored via satellite and targeted from above and that renegade TV reporters and their viewers could witness and celebrate US retaliatory air strikes on enemy targets in Afghanistan from the frontlines.

Walking on Maps

Another way television news advanced this discourse of vertical control was through the use of cartographic projections on the studio floor. Though US television news networks have used maps for decades,[24] in its coverage of the war in Afghanistan CNN experimented with new cartographic techniques, frequently projecting world or regional maps onto the studio floor, news desks, and walls. CNN's cartographics constructed the vertical as a field of reportage and military engagement, as a domain that demonstrated the global reach of US military and commercial TV networks. On multiple occasions, CNN anchors not only walked across massive maps projected on the floor while discussing the post-9/11 world order, but also held and manipulated graphic icons designed to represent military equipment and personnel. CNN anchor Joie Chen may not have been deployed to the warfront like Geraldo Rivera, but she regularly meandered through an immersive map of Afghanistan projected on the studio floor while interviewing former commanders in "the War Room" about the US military's strategic maneuvers. Like the satellite image and sky watching coverage already discussed, these cartographic projections symbolically asserted US control over the vertical field by transforming it into a framed and flattened site of military strategy. As these cartographic projections were used to help viewers "locate" terrorism, the maps also inscribed neocolonial impulses in CNN's news coverage, reinforcing US efforts to identify new sites of conquest and spheres of influence in the changing conjuncture of the war on terror.

In one segment, Chen interviews retired Major General Don Shepperd about US attacks on Kandahar and Jalalabad. As Chen politely asks questions pointing to various sites on the map. Shepperd, the authoritative white male expert, explains the strategy behind US assaults, detailing the direction of the attacks, artillery used, and anticipated effects. Here broadcast correspondence and military command are brought to the cartographic interface in a way that is fully gendered. The repetition of such sequences on CNN commandeers Asian American femininity as a complicit partner in US militarism as opposed to an active investigator of conditions that might necessitate it. As Lisa Nakamura suggests, such representations should be analyzed not only as new media forms or interfaces, but also in relation "to a matrix of lived cultural practices, identities, geopolitics, and postcolonial, racial, and political positions."[25] In this news segment, Chen is figured in a gendered hierarchy of discourse as Shepperd's expert explanations determine how and where she moves across the map and what questions she asks.[26] The two stand upon and crouch around the floor map of Afghanistan as if playing a strange hybrid of *Twister* and *Risk*. As they step all over the map of Afghanistan and place graphic icons (tanks, airplanes, troops, etc.) to illustrate US occupation of its air and ground space, they performatively enact US vertical hegemony in the TV news studio, showing US military technologies and personnel inscribed all over the map as if they had dropped in, like George W. Bush, from the air. After 9/11 Chen and other female journalists often found themselves aligned with white militarized masculinity even when they sought to question it. Those who stepped out of line, so the logic went, risked being subject to the same kind of aggression staged on the map.

In another segment Chen went into CNN's map room to provide a look inside the caves in Tora Bora.[27] As Chen enters the room, she describes the "very steep" white mountains of the Nangarhar province, where Tora Bora is located, as "one of the most dangerous places on earth right now." Chen then interviews Professor Thomas Gouttirre, an Afghan Studies expert, about this area's geology and terrain. Their conversation emphasizes the historical use of this same area by Afghan mujahedeen as a refuge and training area when they were fighting against the Soviet Union. This area, "riddled with caves," Chen explains, is one of the suspected hideouts of Osama Bin Laden, yet given its unique geological features, the two conclude, it will be very difficult to find them. Here Chen uses cartography to take viewers underground and inside mountains, constructing subterranean dimensions of the vertical field. By walking on the map and using it to optically penetrate the insides of caves, this CNN segment constructs television as a kind of geological survey technology that can isolate obscure underground facilites used by the Afghan mujahedeen and Osama bin Laden.

The TV news segments of CNN and Fox News discussed thus far constructed the vertical as a field visualized by US satellites, occupied by US aircraft, and monitored by US reporters. This vertical field became intelligible to viewers when Blitzer and Ensor presented satellite images of "terrorist hideouts" in Afghanistan, when Geraldo Rivera pointed up at the sky to US bombers unloading bombs on "enemies" on the ground, and when Chen and Shepperd towered over and treaded across a cartographic projection of the Afghanistan war theater to explain US military strategies. These segments visually asserted US control over the vertical field by discursively mobilizing the satellite image, the frontline report, and the map to support US military retaliation as the only viable response to 9/11. While these practices were not new to television, their use took on heightened significance after 9/11 as the US sought to reclaim its control over satellites in orbit, planes in the air, and communication through the airwaves. News segments confirmed that the world was being monitored by US satellites, military aircraft were dominating the skies above Afghanistan (and later Iraq), and US journalists were filling the airwaves with news of US military capacity and power. Such segments negotiated public anxieties brought on by the 9/11 attacks by publicly reasserting US hegemony over the vertical field.

Feminist Verticality

While CNN and Fox News segments adopted various strategies to assert US vertical hegemony after 9/11, the Oxygen network's coverage differed. This US cable network was launched in February 2000 by some of the most powerful women in television, including Marcy Carsey, Geraldine Laybourne, Caren Mandabach, and Oprah Winfrey. Since its headquarters were in Battery Park, near the World Trade Center, the network was knocked off the air on 9/11. Rather than transmit vertical views that emphasized US military dominance,

Oxygen used live satellite links and cablecasts to air programs featuring diverse groups of women debating and evaluating possible US responses to the 9/11 attacks, including military options. Women on Oxygen's live shows consistently called for peaceful resolutions at time when most Americans and US news networks did not dare do so. Rather than use television air time to celebrate US aero-orbital platforms, women who appeared on Oxygen's live 9/11 specials ardently questioned and critiqued the prospect of US aerial bombardments and military responses in Afghanistan.

The first live satellite program, *United We Stand: National Town Hall Meeting*, aired on September 17 from Oxygen's studio in New York, just six days after 9/11. The (90 min?) program, broadcast without commercial interruptions, featured a panel of US feminists including Gloria Steinham, Kim Crenshaw (sociologist), Cheryl Mills (former Clinton advisor), Eve Ensler (author of *Vagina Monologues* and political activist), among others. Hosted by former CNN International correspondent May Lee and comedian Stephanie Miller, the discussion ranged widely. After mentioning that Bush thought the Taliban was a rock band during his presidential campaign, Steinham discussed the phenomenon of blow-back and the fact that the US had given Osama bin Laden $3 billion over the past decade. Crenshaw explained how racial profiling and civil rights violations were impacting Arab Americans, and asked "After the Oklahoma City bombing did FBI go around arresting young white men and Persian Gulf War veterans?" Women in the studio audience had a chance to voice their opinions as well. A young Afghan American woman stood up and emotionally cautioned, "If we retaliate we better be willing to be accountable for those who die in the attacks! We better realize that Afghani women and children will die! Let's not pretend! Let's talk about it in the media!" And an Israeli woman explained that after having served the Israeli army, she fully supported US military retaliation since terrorism must be stopped at all costs. The panelists and audience were seated against a backdrop of American flags, which blanketed this televised feminist dialogue in a diorama of red, white, and blue. On the one hand, such iconography conjoined feminism with patriotism, blending these sometimes incommensurable positions and making them part of a broader national agenda. On the other hand, it suggested that feminist anti-war sentiments had to be mired in a visual field of flag-waving in order be aired and taken seriously.

Oxygen's discussion of the US war against Afghanistan continued in a live international satellite broadcast called *World Wide Women Responding to the Crisis*, aired from London on October 4, 2001. This 90-minute special, hosted by well-known British talk show host Kaye Adams, featured prominent guests such as writer and human rights activist Isabelle Allende, human rights lawyer Asma Jahanghir, Zinzi Mandela, businesswoman and daughter of Nelson Mandela, and Rabbi Julia Neuberger. It also included live feeds from Sarajevo, Moscow, Paris as well as New York as May Lee, host of the network's flagship show *Pure Oxygen*, chimed in. The program aired only in the US. Oxygen wanted its viewers to have an opportunity to hear what women from around the world had to say about the 9/11 attacks and the prospect of US military retaliation. Again, the perspectives ranged widely. Jasmine, a British Indian woman born in Uganda, stressed again and again how the events of 9/11 were adversely impacting Muslim communities worldwide, insisting "I want no revenge I want justice!" An Irish journalist who had covered IRA terrorist attacks in the UK compared them to 9/11 to suggest that such violence has occurred recently in other Western countries as well. Both Zinzi Mandela and Asma Jahanghir urged viewers to consider possibilities other than military retaliation. The program also integrated pre-recorded segments revealing how 911 was impacting the lives of Muslim women in North London, and what life was like in Sarajevo after the war in Bosnia. In other words, the Oxygen special allowed women from different countries, ethnic backgrounds, and occupations to discuss alternatives to US military intervention and encouraged US viewers to think twice before adopting the nationalistic party line.

Reactions to the live satellite program spilled over onto Oxygen's website and numerous viewers posted comments triggered by the broadcast. Responses to Oxygen's special programming ranged widely as well.

> I want to know why everyone flies an American flag when people from 80 countries were killed . . .

> I have been waiting for some news program to openly discuss some very uncomfortable truths about American Governmental policies world wide for the past 50 years . . .

> since I was a little girl . . . all I heard was Bomb Iraq . . . Bomb Iran . . . or damn raghead . . . or sandniggers . . . PLEASE . . . Leave me out of YOUR hate . . . THIS American Does NOT support the attacks to Afghanistan and NO I don't back up Bush . . . he's an ignorant hick who is leading YOU to hate . . .

> What's up with this show going past it's scheduled time lot. I wanted to see Xena. . . .

As Oxygen used live satellite transmission to publicize women's discussions of 9/11 and the war in Afghanistan, the new network sustained itself during this precarious time with conventional programming geared toward women. What resulted was a bizarre flow of originally scheduled shows, implying that women should carry on with business as usual, interspersed with 9/11 public service announcements, video memorials, and panicky tickers. During the yoga program, *Inhale*, viewers were encouraged to breathe deeply and assume postures while a ticker ran across the bottom of the frame encouraging them to visit Oxygen.com for tips on how to handle the 9/11 tragedy. The Oxygen website encouraged women to make "patriotic purchases" and listed 20 ways to spend $20, suggesting this was a way to tell the terrorists, "Ha! You can't dictate our lives." Items on the list included 20 lottery tickets, a share of stock, a bottle of wine, a doll, split a membership to Costco, a jump rope, a box of truffles, and lipstick.[28] To cope with 9/11 Oxygen encouraged viewers to "soothe their souls" with "grief and forgiveness rituals" and to "rebuild the USA one share at a time." New links appeared on the site such as "caring for kids" and "help and healing." While these traumatic events no doubt required a healing process, Oxygen addressed women in conventionally feminine ways as neoliberal consumers and mothers as opposed to political activists and policymakers, implying women could shop or jump rope their way out of this global political quagmire. Thus even as Oxygen created vital public forums for feminist political speech, its flow structure and website content interpellated female viewers as "feel-good feminists" who were more concerned about making good investments and making flags fashionable than resisting US militarization. Oxygen's live satellite programs circulated feminist political dissent in a climate of intensifying US nationalism, but since the network was new, producers did not want to alienate sponsors or viewers and ended up mitigating or tempering anti-war feminisms to sustain the network.[29]

Nevertheless, Oxygen's live post-9/11 satellite programs were significant in the ways they challenged US vertical hegemony. Not only did several speakers in these broadcasts explicitly question or oppose US military retaliation and air strikes as a response to the 9/11 attacks, the live satellite transmission of these forums pushed feminist anti-war discourses into the airwaves, crafting a temporary media space in which US militarization could be contested. Rather than use satellite images, live frontline reports, or maps like CNN and Fox News to simulate US media-military control over vertical domains, Oxygen's coverage brought women together in the same room to discuss and deliberate world political events without fancy graphics or frontline sensations. Though the perspectives of the discussants varied there was a general consensus that the US should not race into war in Afghanistan. The act of transmitting such an event into the airwaves (up to a satellite, down through cable systems, and across national territories) was itself a significant feat, and, I want to suggest, a challenge to US vertical hegemony, which, given its patriarchal and militaristic forms, tends to reduce, minimize, quash, flatten, and bury the anti-war voices of women and feminism. It is extremely rare for a US cable network to allocate an entire hour of uninterrupted airtime exclusively to women's perspectives on a world political event. Oxygen did this twice in the two weeks after 9/11. Though this practice did not stick, it resonated with later programming by Al Jazeera, which became known for using international satellite transponder space and talk show formats to directly address Arab women's political issues that were ignored or sidelined by conservative or authoritarian political regimes in the Middle East.[30]

Despite the challenges Oxygen's coverage presented to US military retaliation, in general post-9/11 US television news coverage worked to reassert US vertical hegemony. Television news reports featured high-resolution commercial satellite images that pinpointed Taliban training camps and hideouts and used graphics to turn them into targets. They featured vigilante reporters on location in Afghanistan watching the skies as US bombers unloaded weapons upon "terrorist enemies" in the Tora Bora mountains. And they showed anchors and former commanders in the studio mapping retaliatory US military maneuvers through the air, ground, and sea. This type of coverage made the vertical field intelligible and palpable to viewers by making the overhead views of satellite imagery and cartographic projections and reporters' ground-up views of the sky part of television news flow. This vertical turn in television news coverage coincided with a broader concern about the permeability of the air and airwaves and brought urgency to calls to tighten security in related sectors such as the airport, as discussed in Chapter 2. The struggle for US vertical hegemony also resulted in US military "air raids" on Afghanistan and Iraq, which ranged from aerial PSYOPS campaigns to aerial assaults on the transmission facilities of commercial TV networks such as Al Jazeera. The 9/11 attacks and the resulting television news coverage helped to create a discursive environment in which any number of strategic US maneuvers could be pursued, rationalized, and justified.

Aerial Broadcasting and Leafleting: US Military PSY-OPS

The US response to the 9/11 attacks extended far beyond the frames and discourses of television news and into circumterrestrial space. This too became part of television's vertical turn. After 9/11 the US military ran aerial PSY-OPS (psychological operations) programs in Afghanistan and Iraq.[31] These programs used military aircraft to broadcast radio and television signals and drop leaflets while flying through Afghan and Iraqi air space. Combining technologies of flight, navigation, broadcasting, and printing, these PSY-OPS generated vertical mediations that differed from those of television news reports discussed earlier. Rather than stage or enact vertical power within the discourses and frames of network TV news, this televisual assemblage mobilized US military aircraft to commandeer the air and spectrum, jam the ruling regime's telecommunications systems, and transmit media content produced by the US military and commercial entertainment companies. As such, these practices enacted vertical forms of power that were based upon the integrated control of satellite, aircraft, and telecommunication infrastructures, and this control was projected through multiple media forms.

Airplane broadcasting began as part of US military PSY-OPS in Afghanistan on October 3, 2001, two days before combat operations began. The 193rd Special Operations Wing's EC-130J aircraft known as Commando Solo (see Figure 1.2)—a plane described as "never seen always heard"—flew over Afghanistan transmitting US military radio broadcasts.[32] As this "flying radio station" maneuvers through the air in figure eight patterns at altitudes up to

FIGURE 1.2 As the EC-130J Commando Solo airplane flies through the air, US troops onboard conduct psychological operations via the broadcast airwaves. Such operations occurred in Afghanistan and Iraq as part of the war on terror.

Source: https://commons.wikimedia.org/wiki/File:EC-130J_Commando_Solo.JPG—public domain, via Wikimedia Commons

20,000 feet,[33] an 850-foot spool wire antenna drops from the belly of the plane to broadcast the aircraft's 10,000-watt transmissions.[34] Commando Solo's squadron had conducted similar PSY-OPS during previous conflicts in Kosovo, Bosnia, Panama, Grenada, and the Gulf War. This time Army specialists trained in Pashto and Dari languages (and regional customs) prepared radio broadcasts transmitted on three frequencies while the plane flew across different parts of Afghanistan between October 2001 and March 2002.

One of the frequencies used in Afghanistan was 1107, which had been operated as a Taliban station called Radio Voice of Shariah. After this Kabul-based station was knocked out of service by a missile strike, the US military commandeered this frequency and used it to broadcast radio messages to Afghanis from airplanes. A goal of these US military airplane radio broadcasts was to establish solidarity with Afghani civilians. To entice Afghan people to listen to the radio, US military broadcasts integrated local music, which the Taliban had condemned.[35] One US military broadcast announced: "We have no wish to hurt you, the innocent people of Afghanistan . . . Stay away from military installations, government buildings, terrorist camps, roads, factories, or bridges."[36]

Another broadcast blamed the Taliban for the war and encouraged Afghanis to resist stating, "Noble people of Afghanistan, the Taliban has tarnished the name of your proud nation by making it a haven for criminals and terrorists. . . . Their actions are bringing war to your homes. Is this what you want? Is this the kind of future you want for your children? Speak out! Stand up and let your voice be heard! Resist, and encourage your friends and neighbors to resist!"[37] Other broadcasts addressed the Taliban directly with statements such as: "Attention Taliban! You are condemned. Did you know that? The instant the terrorists you support took over our planes, you sentenced yourselves to death. . . . Our forces are armed with state of the art military equipment. What are you using, obsolete and ineffective weaponry? . . . Our bombs are so accurate we can drop them right through your windows. Our infantry is trained for any climate and terrain on earth. United States soldiers fire with superior marksmanship and are armed with superior weapons."[38] Though these psy-ops messages sounded like exchanges from a children's playground or a bad science fiction movie, US troops consulted with Army specialists who had been born in Afghanistan to develop the messages' content and tone. These specialists knew Dari, Pashto, Farsi, and Urdu, and were familiar with the region's cultural contexts.[39]

These airplane radio messages functioned as vertical mediations as they set out to change material conditions on the ground, instructing Afghans to stay away from their own infrastructure, urging them to resist Taliban control, and highlighting the power, precision, and flexibility of US military equipment and personnel. When the US military began transmitting these radio broadcasts in October 2001, very few Afghans owned radio sets as the Taliban had banned radio and it was a crime to possess a receiver. As a result, the US military airdropped thousands of radio receivers into Afghan cities and villages in 2001 and 2002 so that people could listen to these US military broadcasts. Airdropped radio models included the Freeplay wind-up radio, which was locked onto a frequency that automatically tuned in US military broadcasts, and the KAITO 220-volt AC radios powered by battery, solar, or crank (dynamo).[40] Crank radios were particularly useful given that many Afghans lived without electrical access and could not afford batteries.[41] Thus the US military not only commandeered the air and spectrum to transmit airplane radio broadcasts, but used the vertical field as a distribution corridor as US troops parachuted bulk crates of radio sets down to earth along with food and humanitarian aid packages.

To supplement and reinforce airplane broadcasting, the US military used another practice of vertical mediation known as leafleting. Military aircraft flew above targeted areas and unloaded "leaflet bombs" containing thousands of pieces of paper imprinted with simple illustrations and text in Pashto and Dari. Video documentations of leafleting runs reveal US troops in aircraft cargo bays opening boxes filled with leaflets as they are sucked into the sky as swarms of paper that scatter in multiple directions. In Afghanistan the first two leaflets were dropped from a B-52 on October 14, 2001,[42] when US troops dropped at total of 385,000

FIGURE 1.3 This leaflet features a coalition soldier shaking hands with an Afghan citizen and proclaims (in Pashto and Dari), *"The partnership of nations is here to help."*

Source: www.psywarrior.com/Herbafghan.html—screen capture used under the Fair Use Doctrine

leaflets over the eastern town of Ghazni, the northwestern town of Sherberghan, and in the area between Sherberghan and the western city of Herat. In the first leaflet a coalition soldier shakes hands with an Afghan citizen and text proclaims (in Pashto and Dari), "The partnership of nations is here to help." Its backside similarly states, "The partnership of nations is here to assist the people of Afghanistan" (see Figure 1.3). While the first leaflet constructs coalition troops as the Afghanis' humanitarian partners, the second one focuses on communication and features a drawing of a broadcast tower emitting radio waves to two boom boxes. It encourages recipients to tune in to "Information radio" during two daily broadcast periods (0500–1000 and 1700–2200) and on three radio frequencies (864, 1107, 8700 kilohertz). Finally, a third leaflet, dropped on October 29, 2001, provided instruction about humanitarian airdrops in four color illustrations that depict an airplane dropping humanitarian daily rations (HDR) food packets into a remote landscape, an Afghan man discovering a yellow packet imprinted with the letters HDR, the man tearing the packet open next to the word "Halal," which signals the food was prepared in accordance with the Koran, and the man sitting with four other people, presumably family or friends, eating food from the yellow HDR packets (see Figure 1.4).

While cable TV news coverage on the home front displayed vertical views in ways that emphasized US aero-orbital power, in Afghanistan coverage included radio broadcasting and leafleting performed by US troops. These practices generated a different kind of televisual assemblage, one that brought GPS satellites, military aircraft, and audiovisual transmission together. Satellites guided US military aircraft through Afghani air space so that personnel could transmit signals and drop messages to receivers and people on the ground below. These maneuvers marked a different kind of vertical turn in the televisual. Rather than spotlight

FIGURE 1.4 This leaflet provides instructions about accessing humanitarian daily ration (HDR) food packets.

Source: www.psywarrior.com/Herbafghan.html—screen capture used under the Fair Use Doctrine

US vertical power only at the level of content and representation, US PSY-OPS personnel commandeered the air and spectrum to transmit radio signals and drop leaflets from aircraft so that they could reach as many people as possible in a country with extremely limited terrestrial infrastructure. The vertical organization of audiovisual communication—coverage—enabled the US military to beam information and propaganda into Afghani territory while also monitoring those who received it.

While the first leaflets were humanitarian in tone, the US military unloaded other leaflets that intended to threaten and intimidate members of the Taliban and Al Qaeda and their supporters. For instance, one, which resonates with the US satellite images discussed earlier, warns, "Watching you," and illustrates how the US and its coalition use remote-sensing satellites to scan the earth and spot

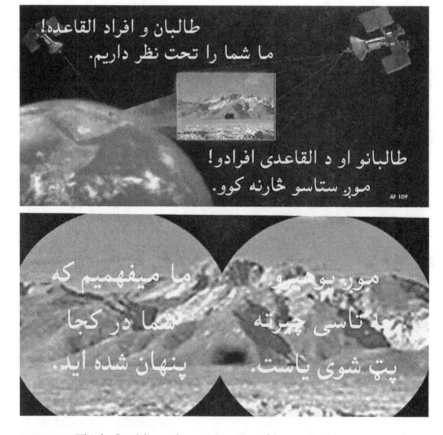

FIGURE 1.5 This leaflet delivers the warning, "watching you" to insurgents, and asserts US control over the full range of vertical space, from satellites in orbit, to intelligence stakeouts on the ground, to the insides of caves.

Source: www.psywarrior.com/Herbafghan.html—screen capture used under the Fair Use Doctrine

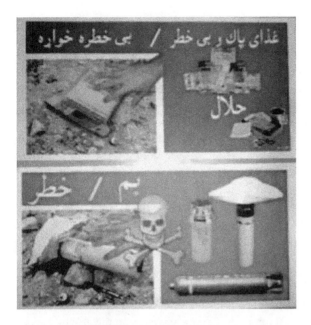

FIGURE 1.6 The leaflet warns civilians not to confuse HDR food packets with
cluster bombs, which look similar.

Source: www.psywarrior.com/Herbafghan.html—screen capture used under the Fair Use Doctrine

enemy hideouts such as caves. The leaflet's backside frames the cave from a closer
vantage point through a pair of binoculars, and works to communicate US
control over the full range of vertical space, from satellites in orbit, to intelligence
stakeouts on the ground, to the insides of caves (see Figure 1.5). By September
2, 2002, the US military had distributed 90,000 copies of this leaflet using M129
"leaflet bombs."[43] Other leaflets emphasized the US hunt for specific enemies.
On November 2, 2001 the Pentagon announced it had dropped an oversized
leaflet featuring photographs of Taliban leader Mullah Mohammed Omar's face
and the license plate of one of his vehicles in the crosshairs of a gun scope. The
Mullah had apparently forbidden any photos of himself. On the left are three
pairs of the same stern-looking white male's eyes with the phrase "We are
watching!" repeated beneath them. The Pentagon indicated it printed 16 million
copies of this leaflet and dropped batches at intervals. Another leaflet emphasized
US air power and surveillance and features a photo of an AC130U Spectre
gunship firing tracers downward through the night sky. The leaflet's backside
shows three Taliban fighters' faces in the crosshairs while Osama bin Laden and
Mullah Omar lurk in the background. Text at the bottom reads: "Taliban and
Al-Qaida—We know where you are hiding."

US military leafleting in Afghanistan sent contradictory messages. On the one
hand, these vertical mediations appropriated Aghani air and spectrum to forge a

partnership with civilians, transmitting friendly messages and offering humanitarian aid. On the other hand, leaflet drops highlighted US air power and issued warnings to "enemies" and others, indicating that coalition forces could see, target, and destroy anything on the ground. The use of the vertical field for these contradictory agendas had the affect of confounding and confusing people on the ground and created uncertainty about what would be falling from the skies—signals, leaflets, food, or bombs? Revealing the potential for confusion, one leaflet illustrated the difference between a yellow HDR packet and a yellow cluster bomb, which looked very similar.[44] The leaflet shows an HDR packet on top with a green backdrop and a hand touching it and the contents of the aid package appear to the right. The image beneath it is a cluster bomb set against a red background also touched by a hand, but has a skull and crossbones stamped upon it as a warning not to touch it. Images of the bomb's explosive components appear to the right (see Figure 1.6).

Since the vertical field was used for such divergent purposes as aerial bombardment, leafleting, broadcasting, and humanitarian airdrops, it was difficult for civilians to discern when US and coalition air presence would be aggressive or lethal and when it would be peaceful, and thus these practices of vertical mediation altered peoples' disposition to the sky. Civilians on the ground had to learn which US military aircraft fired weapons and which unloaded aid packages. They had to figure out where and how to hide so they would not be seen and targeted by those above. And they had to determine how to read and respond to the messages in radio broadcasts or leaflets. In other words, the US military's assertion of control over aero-orbital space brought about a particular kind of vertical biopolitics as the power to control the air and airwaves was articulated with the power to move bodies and affect minds—to reorder lifeworlds on the ground. Vertical mediations also generated a new set of interpretive practices from the ground up. Rather than examine views from above and determine where to strike, civilians looked up at aircraft and attempted to "read" them by virtue of the way they appeared, sounded, and moved. Such practices are also vertical mediations, but they take shape from positions on the ground and involve attempts to interpret objects, movements, and events above based on patterns over time. For instance, a video on YouTube, reveals that one person was tracking leafleting as he collected 66 coalition leaflets in Afghanistan. Those on the ground were watching and tracking US aerial activities too.[45]

These practices of vertical mediation and coverage in Afghanistan serve as a reminder that the war on terror is an information war, and that the vectors of information flow extend in multiple directions, including from top down and the ground up. The US military used coverage not only to construct and threaten its Taliban and Al Qaeda enemies; its aerial PSY-OPS campaigns also projected a sinister kind of aerial humanitarianism that forced civilians to learn the logics, language, and nuances of US military violence in order to avoid it. Such campaigns brought civilians further into the folds of war and created a vertical field of occupation, communication, and administration in which bombs alternated with broadasts, firefighting mixed with food drops. In this context, the capacity for civilians to decipher not just broadcasts and leaflets but *material conditions in general*—what is that in the sky? what is that on the ground? who is my friend or enemy?—became a vital tactic of survival. Grounded sensing, interpretation, and action in the material world by civilians also function as practices of vertical mediation as they too can render vertical forms of power intelligble and subject to intervention.

The US military and coalition not only commandeered the air and spectrum to transmit airplane radio broadcasts and leaflets—to control which signals and information were in the air—but also used the vertical field as a distribution corridor to parachute bulk crates of radio sets down to earth along with food and humanitarian aid packages. As pieces of paper and food packets flutter to the earth (see Figure 1.7) and are found, they have the potential to affect thought and behavior. Leaflets were designed to redefine systems as functional or non-functional, objects as friendly or threatening, and sites as safe or dangerous. They provided instruction regarding everyday activities ranging from radio listening to food consumption. Such practices not only altered Afghans' disposition to the sky, encouraging awareness of maneuvers and messages from above, but also,

FIGURE 1.7 Black Hawk helicopters, such as this, and other aircraft have distributed Psyops leaflets in Afghanistan and Iraq throughout the war on terror. Photo by Pfc. Richard Jones Jr.

Source: www.pri.org/stories/2017-07-10/how-us-military-uses-behavioral-economics-fight-isis—public domain

over time, changed the ground beneath their feet as these maneuvers and messages were part of a broader administrative campaign to reorder life on earth.

This strategy of aerial broadcasting continued in Iraq in 2002 as the US began preparing for war against Saddam Hussein's regime. Fixated on Hussein's possession of "weapons of mass destruction"—especially chemical and atomic weapons—which could have profound effects on circumterrestrial space, the US used satellite images, discussed in Chapter 3, and aerial PSY-OPS in order to prepare for a war against Iraq. Commando Solo began flying PSY-OPS missions on December 12, 2002, airing radio broadcasts on a range of FM, AM, and shortwave frequencies from 6–11pm each night.[46] On December 16, US military aircraft dropped 480,000 leaflets over the southern no-fly zone to inform civilians how to tune in to "Information Radio."[47] These radio broadcasts and leaflets, which were created by the 4th Psychological Operations Group (Airborne) at Fort Bragg in North Carolina,[48] tried to dissuade Iraqis from supporting Saddam Hussein's regime.

Referred to as "weapons of mass persuasion,"[49] the PSY-OPS messages portrayed Hussein as a reckless leader in possession of chemical weapons, long-range missiles, and unmanned aerial vehicles—all air-based weapons—and suggested his actions were putting Iraqis in danger. While PSY-OPS messages alleged Saddam Hussein intended to use the sky to kill people, the US military used the sky to send "life-saving" information. Radio broadcasts typically started with a combination of Arabic and Western music.[50] According to research at Ft. Bragg, songs by Celine Dion, Sheryl Crow, and Santana are popular among Iraqis so they get "air time."[51] One radio broadcast declared, "While there are many dangers in the world, the threat from Saddam Hussein is unique. He possesses the most deadly arms of our age and has not hesitated in the past to use them to destroy those he perceives as his enemies. His use of chemical weapons has been unprovoked, without restraint or modern precedent, and completely violates the conventions of war followed by every civilized country."[52] Another radio message warned Iraqis to turn against Hussein insisting, "History has shown that appeasement of brutal domineering regimes only brings greater tragedy. Saddam, too, has a lust for power, and the world will stand up and put an end to the terror he imposes on others, before he destroys Iraq and crushes the hopes of its proud people."[53] These radio broadcasts aired at night, which PSY-OPS personnel describe as "prime time,"[54] and these messages were reiterated through other media such as leaflets and the Bush administration's speeches and statements, which were also aired in Iraq."[55] As Des Freedman and Daya Thussu suggest, "By virtue of its unprecedented capacity for global surveillance, as well as its domination of global communication hardware and software (from satellites to telecommunication networks; from cyberspace to 'total spectrum dominance' of real spaces and the messages which travel through these), the US is able to disseminate its image of terrorism to the world at large."[56]

FIGURE 1.8 This leaflet warns Iraqi civilians and insurgents to stop repairing fiber optic cable in Iraq as it is a relic of the old regime that is "targeted for destruction."

Source: www.iwar.org.uk/psyops/resources/iraq/PsyOps-Iraq15.htm—screen capture reproduced under the Fair Use Doctrine

As Commando Solo transmitted radio and television broadcasts into Iraqi spectrum, fixed-wing aircraft and Blackhawk helicopters dropped millions of leaflets into Iraqi air space between 2002–2003.[57] Many of these leaflets addressed Iraqi soldiers and members of the Republic Guard and encouraged them to defect. The messages of airdropped leaflets told soldiers how to surrender, not to harm civilians, and discouraged them from using weapons of mass destruction and urged them not to set oil fields on fire. Leaflets reinforced these messages. For instance, on January 31, 2003, coalition forces dropped 840,000 leaflets over southern Iraq.[58] Among the various leaflets dropped, two emphasized coalition air power. One featured an image of three fighter jets flying above an exploded fiber optic line buried beneath the ground. It warned "Stop repairing military fiber optic cable," indicating "You are risking your life." The lines, the leaflet continued, are used to "suppress the Iraqi people by Saddam Hussein and his regime" and are being "targeted for destruction" (see Figure 1.8).[59] Another leaflet urged Iraqis to respect the no-fly zone, and features a photo of a fighter jet dropping several missiles, declaring, "Coalition Air Power can strike at will. Any time, any place."

Aerial leafleting and broadcasting campaigns were part of the US military's strategy of "full spectrum dominance," which involves use of land, air, maritime, and outer space assets in an effort to control all dimensions of the physical battlespace, including the air, surface, subsurface, extraterrestrial, electromagnetic spectrum, and information space.[60] In addition to radio broadcasting, by 2003 Commando Solo beamed content from US commercial television networks into Iraq as part of its PSY-OPS campaign. A five-hour per day program called "Toward Freedom" transmitted news programming from the major US commercial TV networks into Iraqi airwaves, including ABC World News Tonight, CBS Evening News, PBS News Hour with Jim Leherer, NBC Nightly News, and Fox News Special Report with Brit Hume. The show also integrated Pentagon press briefings by Defense Secretary Donald Rumsfeld and General Myers that were translated into Arabic, and snippets of British TV content.[61] US Press Secretary Ari Fleisher indicated the program was a transitional effort designed to fill an information vacuum until Iraqi news media were established. Putting news segments from US commercial TV networks into Iraqi air space and became a way of modeling a "free press," which was ironic given the fact that such networks were far from "free" and resoundingly supported the US war in Afghanistan as discussed earlier. "Every week," Rumsfeld declared, "General Myers and I stand in the Pentagon in front of independent journalists—professionals—and try to answer their questions. Some of the questions are tough, many are insightful and all add to the information available to the American people and the people of the world."[62] Rumsfeld explained that he wanted his briefings broadcast into Iraq "because the truth matters" especially given that Hussein's regime is built on "terror, intimidation and lies."[63]

Aerial broadcasting and leafleting not only delivered PSY-OPS messages into Iraqi airspace and airwaves, but also initiated a broader strategy of media restructuring by the US in Iraq, which is also discussed in Chapter 3. By March 2003, during the first phase of a US military invasion known as "shock and awe," aerial PSY-OPS programs were coordinated with more aggressive actions, such as the bombardment and destruction of Iraqi broadcast and telecom infrastructure.[64] Taking over the airwaves, disabling telecom facilities controlled by Sadam Hussein, and replacing and restructuring Iraqi media infrastructure was an explicit US military strategy. To supervise this restructuring in January 2003 the Pentagon created a "Rapid Reaction Media Team," which would serve as a "quick start bridge" between Hussein's state-run Iraqi media and a longer term "Iraqi Free Media" network.[65] The mission of this team was to "inform the Iraqi public about USG/coalition intent and operations, to stabilize Iraq . . . and to provide Iraqis hope for their future."[66] Among the team's major tasks was to design and air television programming twelve hours a day seven days a week and radio twenty four hours a day seven days a week. The team also had to develop a plan for infrastructure access and spectrum allocation that involved coordination with CENTCOM. One result of this process was the formation of the Iraqi Media Network, which began TV broadcasting from Baghdad in May 2003, a month after Hussein's regime fell.[67] Plagued with internal problems and criticism, the network was thought to be more of a US propaganda tool than an independent media outlet.[68] The network was renamed Al Iraqiya, which means "the Iraqi One"—in November 2003 and has since operated as a public service station owned by the Iraqi government. Thus the transmission of US voices and programs into the Iraqi airwaves and the fluttering of leaflets to the ground were part of a broader initiative to fundamentally reform or vertically reorganize the structure, allocation, and use of spectrum in Iraq. One challenge in launching new US-supported radio and television networks and establishing their success was the reality that most Iraqis were already tuning in to other Arab-language satellite television networks whose signals were also falling into Iraq such as Al Jazeera and Al Arabiya, networks that US officials perceived as threats.

US Bombing of Al Jazeera

The US struggle for vertical hegemony involved staging US air power in television news and commandeering the air space and airwaves of Afghanistan and Iraq, but it assumed more violent forms as well. While US officials rationalized the destruction of telecom and broadcast infrastructures operated by the Taliban and Saddam Hussein, they took unprecedented action when they authorized aerial assaults on the facilities of commercial broadcaster Al Jazeera (and other Arab television networks) in Afghanistan and Iraq. Although Al Jazeera emerged in 1996, five years before 9/11, most Westerners became familiar with the Arab-language satellite television network after it first broadcast videotapes from Osama bin Laden in 2002. Partly financed by the Emir of Qatar, Al Jazeera, which means "island" or "peninsula" in Arabic, generated coverage of wartime events in ways that differed from those of US cable networks, in part because of reporters' familiarity with and deeper understanding of Muslim countries and their histories. Further, since Al Jazeera's reporters speak and read Arabic languages they could engage with militias, communicate with civilians, and venture into conflict zones to expose grim scenes of US invasion and occupation.

Over time media consumers perceived Al Jazeera as the Arab world's equivalent to the BBC or CNN. After the satellite network broadcast a series of video messages from Bin Laden and Al Qaeda, the Bush administration publicly condemned Al Jazeera as the "mouthpiece of Osama bin Laden" and insisted the network was being used by Al Qaeda to distribute coded messages to it cells and supporters around the world.[69] This allegation was ironic given that immediately after 9/11 both CNN and Fox News had served a similar role for the Bush administration. Despite such accusations, it is important to note that Al Jazeera had become popular throughout the Arab world in the years before 9/11 because the network exposed human rights abuses, showed live coverage of political events, discussed women's rights under Islam, and criticized government parties in a region where the broadcast media are largely under state control.[70] Al Jazeera's early motto was "the opinion and the counter opinion" and its management claimed to be committed to free debate, the elimination of taboos, and the awakening of rigid societies.[71]

Despite Al Jazeera's reputation for trying to educate the Arab world about democratic principles, the network became a US military target two months after 9/11. On November 13, 2001 the US military dropped a 500-pound bomb into the network's Kabul station just before the Afghan Northern Alliance, an anti-Taliban contingent, seized the city. Although no employees were killed, the network's broadcast facilities were destroyed along with some employees' homes. As BBC reporter William Reeve covered the event live from his nearby office he was loudly interrupted by the explosions. Footage of Reeve ducking beneath his desk to avoid fallout from the blast aired again and again on BBC TV, signaling the precarious position of broadcast journalists in the war on terror.[72] The attack was also covered live by Al Jazeera reporter Taysur Allumi, one of the network's few correspondents on the ground when the US invaded Afghanistan in 2001.

On April 8, 2003, the US military engaged in a similar attack in Baghdad not only striking Al Jazeera's broadcast facilities, but those of another Arab network, Abu Dhabi TV (of the United Arab Emirates), as well as the Palestine hotel where many international correspondents were known to have been staying. The US military killed three journalists that day including Tariq Ayoub of Al Jazeera, Taras Protsyuk of Reuters, and Jose Cuso of Spanish network, Telecino. The events culminated in a press conference during which Tariq Ayoub's wife, Dima Tareq Tahboub, implored the international community to investigate the attacks and to "please tell the truth," as her husband, she explained, had "died trying to reveal the truth to the world" as a journalist.[73] In addition to speaking at the press conference via phone, she published an editorial in the *Guardian* six months after her husband's death describing her traumatic loss and condemning the US attacks:

> . . . In Bagdhad during the war, the coverage of al-Jazeera again focused mainly on the daily suffering and loss of ordinary people; and again the Americans wanted their crimes and atrocities to pass unnoticed. The two bombs they dropped on al-Jazeera's Baghdad office were the ones that killed my husband. Then the Americans opened fire on Abu Dhabi television, whose identity was spelled out in large blue letters on the roof. The next target was the Palestine hotel, the headquarters of world media representatives—an American tank fired a shell and two more journalists were killed. Thus the US tried to conceal evidence of its crimes from the world and kill the witnesses . . . My husband and the others were killed in broad daylight, in locations known to the Pentagon as media sites.[74]

Dima Tareq Tahboub's appeal for a thorough investigation was accompanied by critiques from members of the international press community, including Reporters without Borders, and the Committee to Protect Journalists.[75] Just as troubling as the physical destruction of Arab networks' broadcast facilities, was the unexplained arrest and detention of Al Jazeera's employees by US troops.

Taysur Allumi reportedly served time in a Spanish prison after being charged, with US pressure, by a Spanish court as being a member of Al Qaeda.[76] In December 2001 a Sudanese cameraman, Sami Muhyideen al-Haj working for Al Jazeera was apprehended by US military and eventually taken to detention facilities in Guantanamo Bay, where, according to his lawyer Clive Stafford Smith, he was beaten, denied treatment for throat cancer, and subjected to shifting allegations by US officials.[77] In November 2003, Al Jazeera employees Salah Hassan and Suheib Badr Darwish were detained and tortured in Abu Ghraib prison and then released more than a month later.[78] In January 2006 US troops arrested Al Jazeera's Kabul correspondent Waliullah Shaheen, cameraman Nasir Hashimi, and driver Mahmood Agha in Afghanistan for allegedly filming too close to US military headquarters and reportedly confiscated five telephones and a camera.[79]

The US military attacks on Al Jazeera's stations and staff attempted to terminate the network's war coverage and impede its circulation in the global media economy. Just as US military forces commandeered the vertical field in efforts to shape PSY-OPS and state television in Afghanistan and Iraq, by bombing Al Jazeera the US sought to regulate whose languages, perspectives, and networks could cover the wars in Afghanistan and Iraq. Since Al Jazeera reporters often questioned the rationales and effects of US foreign policies and military interventions (often attracting substantial audiences as a result), the US used the occasion of the war on terror to reassert its primacy over the global airwaves, and violently knocked these competitor stations off the map. The US bombings of Al Jazeera articulate vertical mediation as a violent practice that sought to reaffirm the global dominance of US commercial networks and prevent alternative views of US wars from coming into being by destroying the property, killing and detaining the journalists, and seizing the equipment of competitor networks.

In addition to bombing Al Jazeera, the US has also developed media strategies to compete with the flagship Arab satellite TV network. After the war in Iraq began, the US began beaming the nightly newscasts of US networks ABC, CBS, NBC, Fox News, and PBS from aircraft into Baghdad as bombs fell from the sky.[80] As Christian Parenti suggests, the US hostility toward Al Jazeera "is best viewed in the context of the escalating, multimillion-dollar regional media war between Al Jazeera and the US government."[81] Parenti goes on to note that, in an effort to combat Al Jazeera's popularity, the US government allocated $62 million in 2004 to launch a Virginia-based Arab language satellite television network called Al Hurra ("the free one"). The *Washington Post* called the new satellite network the "most expensive effort to sway foreign opinion over the airwaves since the creation of Voice of America in 1942."[82] Al Hurra's signal reaches a potential audience of 120 million in 22 countries. In 2004 USAID also funded the development of the first commercial television network in Afghanistan, Tolo TV, which airs Western-style programming influenced by MTV and reportedly caused much controversy among Muslim officials.[83]

The struggle to reassert US vertical hegemony after 9/11 involved a multi-pronged approach. With regard to the televisual, it included highlighting US air power in homefront news coverage, commandeering the air and airwaves of Afghanistan and Iraq for PSY-OPS, establishing new US-supported state television organizations, and bombing the stations of competitor TV networks. Since US officials insisted continuously that terrorism could be anywhere and everywhere, attempts to combat it took all kinds of forms, ranging from cable TV news segments to airdropped leaflets, from radio broadcasts to the killing and detention of TV journalists. These televisual practices enabled US forces to materialize their vertical power by making it legible and felt. This approach had to be so multi-dimensional not only because US officials imagined terrorism as a constant potential, but also because the 9/11 attackers had so flagrantly infiltrated multiple vertical systems—satellites, airlines, and telecommunication networks—thought to be under US control. These televisual practices functioned as vertical mediations in the sense that they used aero-orbital technologies to dynamically communicate about, project, and materialize vertical power relations in screens and spectrum, leaflets and lifeworlds.

US military officials first claimed that neither of the attacks on Al Jazeera was intentional, but evidence to the contrary emerged. In 2005 Great Britain's *Daily Mirror* leaked a five-page transcript detailing a conversation between Tony Blair and George Bush. In it Bush made explicit his intention in April 2004 to order the military bombing of Al Jazeera headquarters in Doha, Qatar in the midst of the US campaign in Fallujah.[84] Even though Blair managed to persuade Bush against such an attack, the leak revealed it was certainly plausible that the Bush administration would have ordered prior attacks on Al Jazeera in Kabul and Baghdad. After interviewing top US officials for his book *The One Percent Doctrine*, investigative journalist Ron Suskind confirmed that the US bombings of Al Jazeera were deliberate.[85] Such information has provided families of Al Jazeera employees and other journalists killed or injured in US attacks the incentive to proceed with lawsuits against the US government.

The documentary film *Control Room* (2004) details Al Jazeera's reporting on the invasion of Iraq and addresses the US bombing of the network's Baghdad station as well as the increasingly precarious position of war correspondents. The film features footage of Tariq Ayoub perched on the station's rooftop surrounded by sandbags piled several feet high and wearing a bullet-proof vest and a safety helmet as another unseen correspondent communicates with a senior producer, Samir Khader, moments before Ayoub's death. They informed Khader they noticed a plane circling above. Ten minutes later it dove down and fired several missiles at them. The explosions killed Ayoub and ripped out the Al Jazeera office's windows and doors and lit it on fire. Khader described the US attack as "a crime that should be avenged, or at least investigated," (in doc.) and Al Jazeera Baghdad correspondent, Majed Abdel Hadi, insisted, "We were targeted because the Americans don't want the world to see the crimes they are committing against the Iraqi people."[86] Similar to cable TV news coverage discussed earlier, such footage makes palpable the vertical forms of power that have come to define the war on terror.

The US bombings of Al Jazeera are significant for several other reasons as well. First, the attacks establish a troubling precedent in that the US has singled out a media corporation and its employees as military targets. Never before have private transnational media companies and their workers been subject to a series of overt US military assaults and detentions. This is particularly disturbing to journalists whose livelihoods depend on a modicum of security when covering military conflicts. BBC anchor Nic Gowing insists that reporters have every right to cover wars and peacekeeping operations, yet points to a disconcerting trend whereby "a lot of the military—particularly the American and the Israeli military—do not want us there . . . security forces in some instances feel it is legitimate to target us with deadly force and with impunity."[87] Just as CNN and Fox News failed to distinguish between civilian and military views of the war on terror, former US Secretary of Defense Donald Rumsfeld insisted there is no distinction between civilian and military targets in a total war against terrorism.[88] This means that any target is a fair target: any journalist can be detained or killed, any television station destroyed. At a press conference after the attack on Al Jazeera, CNN correspondent Tom Mintier indicated that the press has received the same line from the US military when asked about attacks on journalists: "The battlefield is a dangerous place. The only nearly safe position is of embedded reporters with coalition troops." After probing about whether journalists could hang white flags to surrender and protect themselves, US officials declared, "You simply shouldn't be in this location."[89] US attacks on commercial TV networks are not only fatal assaults on the livelihoods of correspondents and property of their employers; they impede the free and diverse expression of journalists trying to make sense of the war on terror from different perspectives.[90]

Second, the attacks on Al Jazeera make clear that the war on terror is intertwined with the global media economy. After bombing Al Jazeera, in 2004 the US launched its own Arab satellite television network, Al Hurra, and has supported the formation of a commercial network in Afghanistan, TV Tolo.[91] Thus, in addition to destroying Al Jazeera facilities and apprehending its employees, the US has developed its own enterprises to compete with Arab media corporations, even if Al Hurra is, as one journalist put it, "widely regarded as a laughingstock in the middle east."[92] The US positioning of Al Hurra in the Arab media market was initially deemed so audacious that it led one political satirist to describe it with the headline, "Fox News Buys Al-Jazeera."[93] Despite a series of blunders at the outset, Al Hurra has been available in 22 countries for more than a decade where it competes with 550 Arab-language satellite TV channels.[94]

Third, Al Jazeera bombings have serious implications with respect to gender issues. Al Jazeera not only employs many Arab women, but regularly airs programs such as *Only for Women*, *Everywoman*, *The Opposite Direction*, and *Religion and Life*, which address gender and sexual issues that are of interest to Arab women and men alike.[95] Like the live Oxygen satellite broadcasts discussed earlier, Al Jazeera has aired news features that assess how the wars in Afghanistan and Iraq have uniquely impacted women's lives. After 9/11, Bush administration officials often invoked women's treatment under Islam and in the Arab world as one of the rationales for US military intervention, yet it has managed to destroy facilities of the Arab satellite television network consistently committed to discussing such issues. One effect of the US bombing of Al Jazeera, then, was to exhibit a disregard for the voices and experiences of Arab and Muslim women and to threaten the publicization of their concerns in the global mediascape. Though Arab women appear on the US-funded networks Al Hurra and Tolo TV, there is a difference between representing women and actually supporting them.

Finally, the bombings of Al Jazeera exposed the Bush administration's cynicism about the relationship between television and democracy. How can the airwaves be imagined as spaces of free deliberation, debate, dissent, evaluation, and opposition if the networks used to circulate news and information are targeted in military assaults? If the only legitimate stance is that of CNN and Fox News supporting US military actions, then the relationship between television and democracy demands recalibration. As the editors of *The Nation* boldly put it, "If a President who claims to be using the US military to liberate countries in order to spread freedom then conspires to destroy media that fail to echo his sentiments, he does not merely disgrace his office and soil the reputation of his country. He attacks a fundamental principle, freedom of the press—particularly a dissenting and disagreeable press—upon which that country was founded."[96] The Bush administration was more interested in demonizing and replacing Arab media networks with US-controlled ones than in supporting existing networks in the Middle East such as Al Jazeera, which were working to support principles of free speech and diversity.

Some Middle Eastern political leaders consider satellite channels like Al Jazeera to function as "off-shore democracies" because they offer unique platforms to communicate with policymakers and publics in countries where TV channels are usually tightly controlled by the state. In this context, satellite television networks operate as deterritorialized and transnational entities that pose difficult and challenging questions to leaders of authoritarian states and fundamentalist societies throughout the world.[97] The point here is not necessarily to celebrate Al Jazeera over CNN or Fox News, but rather to push for further consideration of the different ways in which "television" and "democracy" are being redefined in different parts of the world in relation to the war on terror. The US struggle for vertical domination was not limited to ownership of aero-orbital platforms; it also involved the capacity to control the global media market. The expanding world audience of Al Jazeera, its decision to air Al Qaeda videos, and its investigative reporting on the war on terror from the field in Arabic and English led US officials to increasingly perceive the commercial TV network as a threat.

This chapter has explored how coverage including commercial TV news segments, live satellite programs, airplane broadcasting and leafleting, and bombings of commercial TV networks—articulated a vertical turn after 9/11 by drawing attention to aero-orbital space and US efforts to reassert its dominance over and through it. The vertical turn in post-9/11 coverage involved a pre-occupation with the capacity to observe from, operate within, and maneuver through aero-orbital domains in ways that generated the power to control activities on the ground. CNN and Fox News' news segments used satellite images, frontline reporting, and cartography in ways that visualized and per-formatively enacted US control over the vertical domains. While Geraldo Rivera's monitored the skies above Tora Bora and Joie Chen roamed across world maps discussing military strategy with former commanders, Oxygen's live satellite programs aired content and voices that questioned whether US military airstrikes were an appropriate response to 9/11 and placed women on the leading edge of such deliberations. As US television news segments deployed various strategies to reclaim the vertical, US military aircraft did so more audaciously and coercively, broadcasting radio and television signals in the spectrum and dropping leaflets into the air space of Afghanistan and Iraq. Such military PSYOPS programs were only the beginning, however, as they were followed with violent US aerial assaults on Afghani and Iraqi state telecom and broadcast facilities and on those of commercial TV networks Al Jazeera and Abu Dhabi TV as well.

The vertical turn in post 9/11 television coverage was not only articulated with US efforts to reassert its hegemony, it also worked to publicize and normalize militant US aero-orbital presence and set the stage for other practices of vertical mediation in the decades that followed. The introduction of new passenger screening and airport security protocols, the expansion of the geospatial imaging industries and their use to monitor conflicts around the planet, and the devel-opment of drone warfare and targeted killing programs all became other practices of vertical mediation related to the war on terror. Like the televisual assemblages described in this chapter, these other projects involved the use of technologies of flight, imaging, and targeting to reassert US dominion and control over the spectrum, air, and orbit and pre-empt further terrorist attacks. Reinforcing a generalized preoccupation with "air conditions," including broadcast trans-missions, psychological operations, and aerial bombardments, this constellation of television worked to redress the breech of vertical space on 9/11 and draw attention to new sites and forms of political struggle.

Notes

1 These quotes appear in Pat Caddell, "May 1–4, 2003: Many in Media Give Enthusiastic Endorsement to Bush's 'Mission Accomplished' Event," *History Commons*, undated, http://historycommons.org/entity.jsp?entity=pat_caddell_1
2 Ann Coulter, "Mission Accomplished: A Look Back at the Media's Fawning Coverage of Bush's Premature Declaration of Victory in Iraq," *Media Matters for America*, April 27,

2006, accessed July 18, 2017, http://mediamatters.org/research/2006/04/27/mission-accomplished-a-look-back-at-the-medias/135513

3 David E. Sanger, "Aftereffects: The Scene; In Full Flight Regalia, the President Enjoys a 'Top Gun' Moment," *The New York Times*, May 2, 2003, www.nytimes.com/2003/05/02/world/aftereffects-scene-full-flight-regalia-president-enjoys-top-gun-moment.html

4 Nitzan Ben-Shaul, *A Violent World: TV News Images of Middle Eastern Terror and War, Critical Media Studies: Institutions, Politics, and Culture* (Lanham, MD: Rowman & Littlefield, 2006); Christopher Flood et al., Islam, security and television news (Basingstoke, UK: Palgrave Macmillan, 2012); Andrew Hoskins and Ben O'Loughlin, *Television and Terror: Conflicting Times and the Crisis of News Discourse,* New Security Challenges (Basingstoke, UK: Palgrave Macmillan, 2007); Tal Samuel-Azran, Al-Jazeera and US War Coverage (New York: Peter Lang, 2010); Philip Hammond (Ed.). *Screens of Terror: Representations of War and Terrorism in Film and Television since 9/11* (Suffolk, UK: Arima Publishing, 2011).

5 James Der Derrian, *Virtuous War: Mapping the Military-Industrial-Media-Entertainment Network* (Boulder, CO: Westview Press, 2001).

6 Lynn Spigel, "Entertainment Wars: Television Culture after 9/11," *American Quarterly* 56, no. 2 (2004): 235–270.

7 Ibid, 239.

8 Stacy Takacs, *Terrorism TV: Popular Entertainment in Post-9/11 America* (Lawrence, KS: University of Kansas Press, 2012), 20.

9 Ibid.

10 Rudolph Arnheim, "Television," 1933, 194.

11 Ibid.

12 Raymond Williams, *Television: Technology and Cultural Form* (New York: Schocken Books, 1974), 137.

13 For a precursor study, James Schwoch, *Global TV: New Media and the Cold War, 1946–69* (Urbana, IL and Chicago, IL: University of Illinois Press, 2009).

14 Wolf Blitzer, "Military Options," *CNN,* Vanderbilt Television News Archive, September 21, 2001, http://tvnews.vanderbilt.edu/diglib-fulldisplay.pl?SID=20130826 67108154&code=tvn&RC=644119&Row=1

15 Rey Chow, *The Age of the World Target: Self-Referentiality in War, Theory, and Comparative Work,* Next Wave Provocations (Durham, NC and London: Duke University Press, 2006).

16 David Ensor, "Target: Terrorism," *CNN Evening News,* CNN, Vanderbilt Television News Archive, October 4, 2001.

17 Wolf Blitzer, "War Room," *CNN Evening News,* CNN, Vanderbilt Television News Archive, October 29, 2001, http://tvnews.vanderbilt.edu/diglib-fulldisplay.pl?SID= 20130826109832763&code=tvn&RC=644233&Row=6

18 Gail Shister, "Rivera on a Mission as Fox News War Correspondent," *Philadelphia Inquirer,* November 6, 2001, http://inq.philly.com/content/inquirer/2001/11/06/magazine/SHIS06.htm

19 "Geraldo Rivera Goes from CNBC to Fox," *foxnews.com,* November 2, 2001, accessed July 18, 2017, www.foxnews.com/story/0,2933,37898,00.html.

20 Jim Naureckas, "Fox at the Front: Will Geraldo Set the tone for future war coverage?" FAIR website, January 2002, accessed July 18, 2017, https://fair.org/extra/fox-at-the-front/

21 Some questioned the veracity of Rivera's Tora Bora reporting. For instance, Rivera reported he became choked up near a "friendly fire" incident on December 6, but he was actually 300 miles away from the location where it occurred. Rivera admitted later that it was an honest mistake made in the "fog of war." See http://articles.baltimoresun.com/2001-12-27/features/0112270154_1_geraldo-rivera-friendly-fire-

honest-mistake; www.cbsnews.com/news/geraldo-hit-by-unfriendly-fire/; www.nyc.indymedia.org/en/2001/12/9132.shtml; www.facebook.com/GeraldoRivera/posts/689344001098623

22 "Political Headlines," *Hannity & Colmes* (21:00), Fox News transcript, December 6, 2001.

23 "Osama bin Laden on the Cusp of Capture/Termination in 2001 Tora Bora," YouTube video, 5:33, from a live broadcast televised by Fox News Channel, posted by "dreamlandnightmare," January 7, 2013, www.youtube.com/watch?v=CoxYm53nwic

24 Mark Monmonier, *Maps with the News: The Development of American Journalistic Cartography* (Chicago, Il: University of Chicago Press, 1989); Robert Henson, *Weather on the Air: A History of Broadcast Meteorology* (Boston, MA: American Meteorological Society, 2010).

25 Lisa Nakamura, *Digitizing Race: Visual Cultures of the Internet* (Minneapolis, MN: University of Minnesota Press, 2008), 204.

26 In August 2013 Joie Chen took an anchor position with Al Jazeera America, CNN's competitor.

27 "Afghanistan Terrain Remains Challenge for Troops," transcript, *CNN Live Today*, CNN, December 5, 2001, accessed July 18, 2017, www.cnn.com/TRANSCRIPTS/0112/05/lt.24.html

28 The full list of items included 20 lottery tickets, take a friend to the movies, magazine subscription, a share of stock, a bottle of wine, a doll, split a membership to Costco, two candles, a jazz cd, a box of truffles, a jump rope, mascara, lip balm, a manicure. The list was featured next to an image of a woman with closed eyes in a bubble bath. For further discussion of 9/11 and consumerism, see Dana Heller (Ed.), *The Selling of 9/11: How a National Tragedy Became A Commodity* (Basingstoke, UK: Palgrave Macmillan, 2005); and Marita Sturken, *Tourists of History: Memory, Kitsch, and Consumerism from Oklahoma City to Ground Zero* (London and Durham, NC: Duke University Press, 2007).

29 This strategy combined with other programming measures managed to keep the network alive and NBC Universal purchased the company for $925 million in 2007. See Michael Learmonth, "NBC U Sucks in Oxygen," *Daily Variety*, October 10, 2007, 1.

30 Naomi Sakr, *Satellite Realms: Transnational Television, Globalization and the Middle East* (London and New York: I.B. Tauris, 2002).

31 Matt Sienkiewicz delineates what he calls the "soft-psy" approach to media intervention in his excellent study of US efforts to reshape radio and television systems of the Middle East after 9/11. He explains this approach involves "the melding of market-oriented, neoliberal 'soft power' strategies with the more rigid and content-oriented ideas typified by military 'psy ops.'" Cleverly referring to these efforts as "the other air force," Sienkiewicz details the remodeling of television in Afghanistan, Iraq, and Palestine. See, Matt Sienkiewicz, *The Other Air Force: U.S. Efforts to Reshape Middle Eastern Media Since 9/11*, reprint ed. (New Brunswick, NJ: Rutgers University Press, 2016), 3–4.

32 Jim Garamone, "U.S. Commando Solo II: Takes Over Afghan Airwaves," October 29, 2001, accessed July 18, 2017, www.bouwman.com/911/Operation/SoloII.html

33 Scott Simon, "Good Morning, Afghanistan: Flying Radio Stations Broadcast Coalition's Message," *Weekend Edition Saturday*, NPR, October 20, 2001, accessed July 18, 2017, www.npr.org/programs/wesat/features/2001/psyops/011020.psyops.html; "Lockheed Martin EC-310 Commando Solo Specs," *NPR.org*, accessed July 18, 2017, www.npr.org/programs/wesat/features/2001/psyops/011020.psyops.ec130.html

34 Tracy Wilkinson, "Military's 'Weapon of Mass Persuasion,'" *Los Angeles Times*, March 20, 2003, accessed July 18, 2017, http://articles.latimes.com/2003/mar/20/news/war-sway20

35 Herbert A. Friedman, "Psychological Operations in Afghanistan," *Home of the Psywarrior*, accessed July 18, 2017, www.psywarrior.com/Herbafghan.html

36 www.defense.gov/news/newsarticle.aspx?id=44603

37 Jean Marbella, "U.S. Radio Broadcasts, Pamphlets Tell Afghans They Aren't the Enemy," *The Baltimore Sun*, October 16, 2001, accessed July 18, 2017, http://articles. baltimoresun.com/2001-10-16/news/0110160072_1_taliban-broadcasts-bin

38 Jamie McIntyre, "U.S. Propaganda to Taliban: 'You Are Condemned,' " *CNN*, October 18, 2001, accessed July 18, 2017, http://asia.cnn.com/2001/US/10/17/ret.us. propaganda/index.html; Marbella, "U.S. Radio Broadcasts"; Julian Borger, Rory McCarthy, and Richard Norton-Taylor, "The US Message to the Taliban," *The Guardian*, October 19, 2001, accessed July 18, 2017, www.theguardian.com/world/ 2001/oct/20/afghanistan.terrorism7; Another broadcast told the people of Afghanistan why the United States is attacking the Taliban and Al Qaeda. "On Sept. 11, 2001, thousands of people were killed en masse in the United States," it reads. "Among them was a two-year-old girl. Barely able to stand or dress herself. Did she deserve to die? Why was she killed you ask? Was she a thief? What crime had she committed? She was merely on a trip with her family to visit her grandparents. Policemen, firefighters, teachers, doctors, mothers, father, sisters, brothers all killed. Why?"

39 Charles Brisco et al., *Weapon of Choice: US Army Special Operations Forces in Afghanistan* (Fort Leavenworth, KS: Combat Studies Institute Press, 2003), 257–259. Also see Douglas Waller, "Opening Up the Psyops War," *TIME*, October 16, 2001, accessed July 18, 2017, http://content.time.com/time/nation/article/0,8599,179827,00.html

40 For further discussion of the later Radio in a Box initiative in Afghanistan, see Monroe E. Price and Sam Jacobson, " 'Radio in a Box': Psyops, Afghanistan and the Aesthetics of Low-Tech," *USC Center on Public Diplomacy*, June 23, 2011, accessed July 18, 2017, http://uscpublicdiplomacy.org/blog/radio_in_a_box_psyops_afghanistan_and_the_ aesthetics_of_the_low-tech

41 Mark Thompson, "Radio Afghanistan," *TIME*, November 12, 2012, accessed July 18, 2017, http://nation.time.com/2012/11/12/radio-afghanistan/#ixzz2C2far864

42 Friedman, "Psychological Operations."

43 Ibid.

44 The US changed the color of the HDR packets to blue to try and prevent people from mistaking them for cluster bombs. See U.S. Changes Color of Food Aid," *CNN.com*, November 1, 2001, http://edition.cnn.com/2001/US/11/01/ret.afghan.fooddrops/

45 "My Complete Collection of Leaflets Dropped in Afghanistan 2001," YouTube video, 3:22, posted by "dOvetastic," March 29, 2010, www.youtube.com/watch?v=_- M4lHdJvts

46 Commando Solo fleet is based in Doha at Camp Snoopy, and shares runway with Qatar Airways planes at the Doha International airport: Mika Mäkeläinen, "Shock and Awe on the Air: US Steps Up Propaganda War," *DXing.info*, April 5, 2003, accessed July 18, 2017, www.dxing.info/profiles/clandestine_information_iraq.dx

47 "Commando Solo Radio Messages Over Iraq," *Home of the Psywarrior*, accessed July 18, 2017, www.psywarrior.com/CommandoSoloIraqScripts.html

48 Mäkeläinen, "Shock and Awe on the Air."

49 Charles Portman, "Commando Solo II: Weapons of Mass Persuasion," *The Information Warfare Site*, accessed July 18, 2017, www.iwar.org.uk/psyops/resources/commando- solo/wmp.htm

50 Wilkinson, "Military's 'Weapon of Mass Persuasion.' "

51 Portman, "Commando Solo II."

52 "Commando Solo Radio Messages over Iraq."

53 "U.S. Drops Leaflets for Iraqi People," *CNN.com*, January 2, 2003, accessed July 18, 2017, www.cnn.com/2003/WORLD/meast/01/02/sproject.irq.leaflet.drop/

54 Wilkinson, "Military's 'Weapon of Mass Persuasion.' "

55 Jean Marbella, "A Battle Waged Over Iraqi Airwaves," *The Baltimore Sun*, March 22, 2003, accessed July 18, 2017, http://articles.baltimoresun.com/2003-03-22/news/0303220021_1_war-in-iraq-psychological-operations-commando-solo

56 Des Freedman and Daya Kishan Thussu (Eds.), *Media & Terrorism: Global Perspectives* (London: SAGE Publications, 2012), 4.

57 By March 20, 2003, 17 million leaflets were dropped into Iraq, Wilkinson, "Military's 'Weapon of Mass Persuasion.'"

58 United States Central Command, "Coalition Forces Drop Leaflets in Southern Iraq," news release, *The Information Warfare Site*, January 31, 2003, accessed July 18, 2017, www.iwar.org.uk/psyops/resources/iraq/PsyOps-Iraq15.htm

59 Ibid.

60 Rahul Mahajan, *Full Spectrum Dominance: U.S. Power in Iraq and Beyond* (New York: Seven Stories Press, 2003).

61 CNN refused to join the project, and a spokesman said, "We didn't think that as an independent, global news organization it was appropriate to participate in a United States government video transmission." Henry Michaels, "American 'Free Press' in Action: US Networks Agree to Serve as Pentagon Propaganda Tool in Iraq," *World Socialist Web Site*, April 15, 2003, accessed July 18, 2017, www.wsws.org/en/articles/2003/04/med-a15.html

62 Secretary of Defense, Donald H. Rumsfeld, News Transcript, Briefing at the Foreign Press Center, January 22, 2003, accessed April 2, 2018, archive.defense.gov/Transcripts/Transcript.aspx?TranscriptID=1330

63 Ibid.

64 Michael Knights, "Infrastructure Targeting and Postwar Iraq," *The Washington Institute*, March 14, 2003, accessed July 18, 2017, www.washingtoninstitute.org/policy-analysis/view/infrastructure-targeting-and-postwar-iraq. On March 26, 2003 the US military bombed Iraqi television stations in Baghdad after Hussein had used the station to express his defiance and show the bodies of captured or slain US soldiers. Hussein used the television station to suggest he was still in power. See Greg Miller, "Iraqi Station Down, Not Out," *Los Angeles Times*, March 26, 2003, accessed July 18, 2017, http://articles.latimes.com/2003/mar/26/news/war-tv26; On March 24 Fox News Channel's Bill O'Reilly said, "I think they should have taken out the television, the Iraqi television . . . Why haven't they taken out the Iraqi television towers?" CNN's Aaron Brown said, "a lot of people wondered why Iraqi TV had been allowed to stay on the air, why the coalition allowed Iraqi TV to stay on the air as long as it did." Henry Michaels, "American 'Free Press' in Action."

65 "White Paper: 'Rapid Reaction Media Team' Concept," *The National Security Archive*, accessed July 21, 2017, www2.gwu.edu/~nsarchiv/NSAEBB/NSAEBB219/iraq_media_01.pdf

66 Ibid.

67 Joyce Battle (Ed.), "Iraq Media Timeline," *The National Security Archive*, May 8, 2007, accessed July 18, 2017, www2.gwu.edu/~nsarchiv/NSAEBB/NSAEBB219/#timeline

68 In June 2003 independent press watchdog groups called for it to be dismantled since it was unclear whether it was supposed to be independent media or a propaganda tool.

69 "Al Jazeera Kabul Offices Hit in US Raid," *BBC News*, November 13, 2001, accessed July 18, 2017, http://news.bbc.co.uk/2/hi/south_asia/1653887.stm

70 For further discussion of these issues see Hugh Miles, *Al Jazeera: The Inside Story of the Arab News Channel That Is Challenging the West* (New York: Grove Press, 2005).

71 For more nuanced and detailed perspectives about Al Jazeera see Miles, *Al-Jazeera*; see also Philip Seib, *The Al-Jazeera Effect: How the New Global Media are Reshaping World Politics* (Washington, DC: Potomac Books, 2008); Mohamed Zayani and Sofiane Sahraoui, *The Culture of Al-Jazeera: Inside an Arab Media Giant* (Jefferson, NC: MacFarland, 2007); Rick Zednik, "Perspectives on War: Inside Al Jazeera," *Columbia*

Journalism Review 40, no. 6 (2002): 46–47; see also the documentary film *Control Room* directed by Jehane Noujaim (2004; Magnolia Pictures).

72 Matt Wells, "How Smart Was This Bomb?" *The Guardian*, November 19, 2001, accessed July 18, 2017, www.guardian.co.uk/waronterror/story/0,1361,597067,00. html. Lindsay Palmer, *Becoming the Story: War Correspondents after 9/11* (Urbana, IL and Chicago, IL: University of Illinois Press, 2018).

73 This footage was available on YouTube in a clip: "The Murder of Tarek Ayub (A US War Crime)," YouTube, posted by "Halifaxion," June 23, 2006, www.youtube. com/watch?v=c-u7ZL-gsw8. It was excerpted from the documentary film *Control Room* (see note above). See: "US War Crime: The Murder of Tarek Ayub," DailyMotion video, 8:34, posted by "BadKitty," March 10, 2007, www.dailymotion. com/video/x1em68_us-war-crime-the-murder-of-tarek-ay_news

74 Dima Tareq Tahboub, "The War on Al-Jazeera," *The Guardian*, October 4, 2003, accessed July 18, 2017, www.guardian.co.uk/print/0,,4767201-103677,00.html

75 "Reporters without Borders Outraged at Bombing of Al-Jazeera office in Baghdad," *Reporters without Borders*, April 8, 2003, updated January 20, 2016, accessed July 18, 2017, http://en.rsf.org/iraq-reporters-without-borders-outraged-08-04-2003,05945.html

76 John Cherian, "Bombing out Dissent," *Frontline* 23, no. 2 (2006), www.flonnet.com/fl2302/stories/20060210001305600.htm

77 For a detailed discussion of al-Haj see Joel Campagna, "Sami al-Haj: The Enemy?" *Committee to Protect Journalists*, accessed July 20, 2017, www.cpj.org/Briefings/2006/DA_fall_06/prisoner/prisoner.html

78 Christian Parenti, "Al Jazeera Goes to Jail," *The Nation*, March 29, 2004, accessed July 18, 2017, www.thenation.com/article/al-jazeera-goes-jail

79 "Al Jazeera Employees Arrested in Afghanistan," *Radio Free Europe Radio Liberty*, January 1, 2006, accessed August 16, 2013, www.rferl.org/content/article/1064338. html; and "Al Jazeera Crew Arrested Photographing Security Features of US Base in Kabul," *The Jawa Report*, January 1, 2006, accessed August 16, 2013, http://mypetjawa. mu.nu/archives/148932.php

80 Karen DeYoung and Walter Pincus, "US to Take Its Message to Iraqi Airwaves," *Washington Post*, May 11, 2003, A17.

81 Parenti, "Al Jazeera Goes to Jail."

82 Ellen McCarthy, "Va.-Based, U.S.-Financed Arabic Channel Finds Its Voice," *Washington Post*, October 15, 2004, A01.

83 Ben Arnoldy, "Kabul's Must-See TV Heats Up Culture War in Afghanistan," *The Christian Science Monitor*, May 10, 2005, accessed July 18, 2017, www.csmonitor.com/2005/0510/p01s03-wosc.html. For further information on the development of Tolo TV see "Tom Freston—Afghanistan," interview by the Media Industries Project, Carsey-Wolf Center, UC Santa Barbara, August 9, 2011, www.carseywolf.ucsb.edu/mip/tom-freston-afghanistan. See also the documentary film about Tolo TV, *The Network*, directed by Eva Orner (2012; FilmBuff, 2013), and the Tolo TV website: http://tolo.tv/

84 Kevin Maguire and Andy Lines, "Exclusive: . . . Ally," *Daily Mirror (UK)*, November 22, 2015, https://web.archive.org/web/20051128012515/http://www.mirror.co.uk/news/tm_objectid%3D16397937%26method%3Dfull%26siteid%3D94762%26headline%3Dexclusive--bush-plot-to-bomb-his-arab-ally-name_page.html. Also see, Memo: Bush wanted Aljazeera bombed, *Aljazeera.com*, November 22, 2005, www.aljazeera. com/archive/2005/11/2008410151627996559.html

85 Ron Suskind, *The One Percent Doctrine* (New York: Simon and Schuster, 2006), 138. Suskind confirmed this finding in an interview with CNN's Wolf Blitzer on June 20, 2006: "Interview with Author Ron Suskind," transcript, *The Situation Room*, CNN, June 20, 2006, accessed July 18, 2017, http://transcripts.cnn.com/TRANSCRIPTS/0606/20/sitroom.02.html

86 Associated Press, "US Bombs Al-Jazeera Baghdad Office—Kills Cameraman," *Rense.com*, April 8, 2003, accessed August 16, 2013, http://rense.com/general36/camm.htm

87 Quoted in Steven Weissman, "Dead Messengers: How the U.S. Military Threaten Journalists," *Truthout*, June 22, 2005.

88 Quoted in Cherian, "Bombing Out Dissent."

89 Scene in *Control Room*.

90 For further discussion of the increasingly precarious position of journalists reporting on the war on terror, see Lindsay Palmer, *Becoming the Story*.

91 "Tom Freston—Afghanistan," interview by the Media Industries Project, Carsey-Wolf Center, UC Santa Barbara, August 9, 2011, www.carseywolf.ucsb.edu/mip/tom-freston-afghanistan

92 Abigail Lavin, "Fair and Balanced? Al Jazeera is Planning to Bring English-Language News to an American Audience," *The Weekly Standard*, September 20, 2006, accessed July 18, 2017, www.weeklystandard.com/Content/Public/Articles/000/000/012/722 udgca.asp

93 Andy Borowitz, "Fox News Buys Al-Jazeera," *Newsweek*, February 1, 2005, accessed July 18, 2017, www.borowitzreport.com/2005/02/01/fox-news-buys-al-jazeera/

94 Craig Whitlock, "U.S. Network Falters in Mideast Mission," *Washington Post*, June 23, 2008, accessed July 18, 2017, www.washingtonpost.com/wp-dyn/content/article/2008/06/22/AR2008062201228.html?sid=ST2008062302295/

95 This coverage has been especially important to a diverse, international Arab community that has felt its representations and positions misconstrued, caricatured, and gravely reduced in historical and contemporary Western news media. For a broader history of these issues, see Edward W. Said, *Orientalism* (New York: Random House, 1979).

96 Jeremy Scahill, "The War on Al Jazeera," *The Nation*, December 19, 2005, accessed July 18, 2017, www.thenation.com/article/war-al-jazeera.

97 For a discussion of this point see Sakr, *Satellite Realms*, Miles, *Al Jazeera*; Marc Lynch, *Voices of the New Arab Republic: Iraq, Al Jazeera, and Middle East Politics Today* (New York: Columbia University Press, 2006); and the 2004 documentary film *Control Room* (see note above).

2

SEARCHING

Screening Practices at US Airport Security Checkpoints

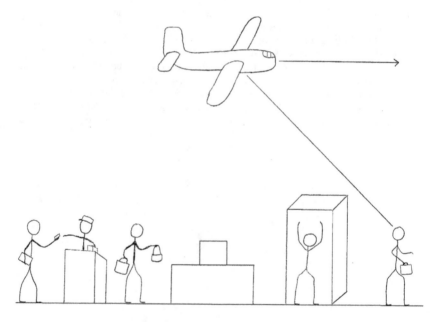

FIGURE 2.1 "Searching." Concept sketch by Lisa Parks.

Source: The author

As television took a vertical turn after 9/11, US officials were revamping the nation's airports. Terrorists' flagrant violation of US airport security systems on 9/11 prompted a major overhaul of security checkpoints and protocols. Two months after the attacks, the US government passed the National Transportation Security Act, establishing the Transportation Security Administration (TSA) to secure the nation's airports, railways, bridges, and highways. Since then the TSA has engaged in a laborious transformation of airport security, expanding and bolstering checkpoints, installing new screening technologies, and deploying large staffs. The TSA has boldly declared its presence in airports, occupying and branding space as aggressively as McDonald's and Starbucks. TSA information boards cover airport walls and marquees. Flocks of uniformed TSA agents appear everywhere, some wearing special tags that read, "I am TSA!" And every few minutes TSA public service announcements blare through loudspeakers warning passengers to keep baggage in sight at all times and to report any abandoned luggage to authorities. The US reacted to the 9/11 attacks by transforming airport security as part of its efforts to reclaim control over the vertical field.

This process occurred not only in the US, but also extended to airports around the world. A dominant player in the global commercial airlines industry, the US government leveraged this moment and worked with the International Civil Aviation Organization (ICAO) to implement more stringent airport security for international airlines flying to and from the US.[1] These protocols involved more intensive passenger and luggage screening, using magnetometers, body scanners, chemical sensors, luggage X-ray and inspection, and body pat-downs, restricted access to cockpits, and use of sky marshals. Such measures were put into place in airports from London to Doha, from Tokyo to Johannesburg. By asking nations to implement such practices, the US exerted a powerful influence upon the daily operations of airports, airlines, and air space of other nations. Changes in airport security protocols not only regulated which bodies and matter could fly through US air space, but also through that of other nations around the world.

The post-9/11 reorganization of airport security became a practice of vertical mediation as it reshaped experiences of air travel and materialized particular kinds of "aeromobilities"—power-laden movements through the air.[2] Labor, technologies, and imagery have been organized at the airport checkpoint to screen passengers and their belongings before they board airplanes and, in doing so, to determine who and what can enter the air. This process produces new social hierarchies as screeners project the threat of terrorism onto travelers of color such that their bodies and belongings are scrutinized more frequently and aggressively than those of whites. A leaked 2008 TSA manual indicates such racial profiling is standard operating procedure. The administration requires checkpoint staff to conduct enhanced screening on all travelers from Cuba, Iran, North Korea, Libya, Syria, Sudan, Afghanistan, Lebanon, Somalia, Iraq, Yemen, and Algeria, countries whose majority populations are non-white ethnic/racial groups.[3] This and other TSA screening practices discussed throughout this chapter reinforce reductive assumptions about national origins and racialized bodies, and create a culture of state violence against "Muslim-looking" travelers, using the checkpoint to draw attention to, question, and control their aeromobilities.[4] Though white passengers pass through the checkpoint too, they are comparatively invisible. Airport screeners question or pat down white passengers more to create the appearance that everyone is treated equally under the gaze of TSA surveillance—to perform what Simone Browne calls "security theater"—than to impede or raise doubts about them.[5] Whites are not hassled, touched, or questioned at the checkpoint in the same way as people of color.

The screening process at airport security checkpoints is deeply political and affects bodies unevenly. Given this "surveillance of the minority," Didier Bigo argues that airport security checkpoint functions as part of a broader system of power he calls the *ban-opticon*. Altering the concept of the panopticon and panopticism to account for the shifts in the conjuncture of the war on terror, Bigo explains that the ban-opticon is "characterized by the exceptionalism of power . . ., by the way it normalizes the non-excluded through its production of normative imperatives, the most important of which is free movement. . . ."[6] The checkpoint normalizes non-exclusion through the imperative of movement —it invites free movement only to use it as a mechanism for scrutinizing and sorting racialized bodies in the name of their future potential behavior. In this way, the checkpoint is both a thoroughfare and a wall. As a site of flexible surveillance, it functions both as a democratic gateway that every traveler must enter in order to fly and a trap for those with certain profiles, attributes, or backgrounds. Because of this, the checkpoint, quite literally, produces racialized social hierarchies—the TSA invokes the norm of "free movement" precisely to keep certain bodies out of the air.

Beyond reinforcing racialized hierarchies at the site of air travel, the state has used the checkpoint to simultaneously bolster federal security presence and experiment with privatization. After 9/11 the TSA hired a new class of federal employees—airport screeners—to serve on the "frontlines"[7] of the war on terror and supplied them with millions of dollars' worth of screening equipment from private contractors. As public sector employees use checkpoints to screen travelers, they also support processes of privatization. Not only does the X-ray belt enable the flow of travelers' private commodities, the TSA has sold advertising space in the belt's grey bins to fund equipment purchases. And the administration has collected enormous amounts of travelers' biometric data, the location and ownership status of which are unclear. Given such conditions, the checkpoint can be understood as a test bed for privatization. Airport screening impacts a host of economic issues, ranging from the ownership and value of body scans to the cost of bottled water beyond the checkpoint, from worker compensation to the resale of confiscated objects. Much more than a security border, the airport checkpoint has become a site of experimental capitalism that extends US vertical hegemony by proliferating value from the ground into the air.

To explicate how airport screening functions as a practice of vertical mediation, this chapter analyzes labor conditions, technologies, and images at the checkpoint. First, I explore the working conditions of TSA screeners, noting the physical demands of their work and the persistence of manual labor despite the technologization of the checkpoint. Second, I discuss the implementation of new screening technologies such as backscatter X-ray machines and millimeter wave body scanners at checkpoints and describe "close sensing" practices, which structure relations between looking and touching. Third, I examine uses of the X-ray belt and describe how they reassert the power and reach of capitalist privatization at the site of air travel. The X-ray belt uses the electromagnetic spectrum to make travelers' belongings/consumer goods visible and valuable and has become a site of commercialization as well. I discuss the object-oriented visual economy that takes shape at the checkpoint, and I suggest that the X-ray sequence ultimately exposes the state's inability to regulate the flow of objects and matter in the age of globalization. Throughout each section, I critically examine various forms of coverage related to airport screening, whether documentaries produced by TSA whistleblowers, body scans, or X-ray belt simulations. Despite a host of new screening technologies and increasing machine automation, I argue that the hands of TSA screeners ultimately determine what enters the air.[8] Machines can detect liquids, metals, or chemical traces, but TSA screeners must push buttons to get them to do so. Machines can also identify a gun or knife in a bag, but TSA screeners must visually confirm its presence and physically remove or confiscate it. Such hand–eye coordination is integral to vertical mediation at the checkpoint and enables the TSA to extend its reach into the air. Vertical mediation at the checkpoint, then, involves the coordination of labor, technology, and imagery to "secure the air."

Checkpoint Labor

Airport screeners were first implemented in US airports during the 1970s after a series of skyjackings around the world aroused concerns about airline security. In 1972 the Federal Aviation Administration (FAA) made it mandatory for airlines to search passengers and their carry-on bags and magnetometers were installed in US airports. After the 1988 bombing of Pan Am flight 103 over Lockerbie, Scotland, airport security intensified and the FAA began to screen computers and radios more carefully on flights coming from Europe and the Middle East. These changes were implemented because a bomb had been placed in a radio given to a young woman and it was programmed to explode in mid-air. Despite bolstered security measures, by the end of the 1990s members of the US Congress began to express concern about airport screeners. At a Congressional hearing on March 16, 2000, political leaders identified the airport screener as the "weak link" in airport security because of poor training, high job turnover, uncompetitive compensation and benefits, and a failure among private contractors to conduct rigorous background checks and random drug testing.[9] From the 1970s until 2001, commercial airlines paid private contractors to operate and staff airport security checkpoints in the nation's airports. A comparative study with the UK, Belgium, the Netherlands, Germany, and Canada found that US airport screeners were outclassed by better-trained, higher-paid, and professionalized screeners in other countries.[10]

In 2000, US airport screeners were making between $5.25 and $6.75 USD per hour, often leaving their jobs just after being trained to take higher paying jobs flipping burgers at fast food outlets in the same airport. The job turnover rate at some airports including Chicago O'Hare was 400%. Screeners worked long hours—often twelve-hour days—scrutinizing 20 year-old black and white monitors that were very difficult to see.[11] The labor of the airport screener was described at a congressional hearing as a "repetitive, monotonous and stressful task that requires constant vigilance."[12] A year before 9/11, the consensus in the

FIGURE 2.2 The TSA bolstered airport security checkpoints and screening practices after 9/11 as seen in this photo of the Denver airport. Photo by Danjo Paluska.

US Congress was that "inadequate training and low morale among screeners threaten safety and security in the skies. . . ."[13]

After 9/11, President George W. Bush signed the National Transportation Security Act and the number of screeners surged from 8,000 private workers in the year 2000 to 55,000 federal employees in 2003.[14] During this period there was a concerted effort to standardize training, increase salary and benefits, and produce a professionalized class of airport screeners. The regime of screening and scrutiny at the checkpoint became more intrusive as passengers were not only asked to pass through magnetometers and place their baggage on an X-ray machine, but over time were asked to remove belts, coats, and shoes, empty their pockets, and submit to wand sweeps or pat-downs by TSA officials. Some passengers were also randomly selected for further searching and questioning.

The protocols and interpersonal dynamics at airport checkpoints changed dramatically after 9/11, and have generated friction for many reasons. Passengers are annoyed by the invasiveness of the new procedures. Long lines cause delays and sometimes travelers miss their flights. Personal items are regularly and increasingly confiscated and never returned. The TSA has earned nicknames such as "Tourism Suppression Agency" and "Thousands Standing Around."[15] TSA screeners have even entered the business of mood control. As of 2004, TSA officers can fine passengers for "non-physical interference." If "attitude" becomes an "aggregating factor" the TSA is authorized to issue civil penalties ranging from $150–10,000.[16] Such violations can include verbally threatening a TSA screener, refusing to submit to additional screening, or entering the sterile area before screening is finished.[17] A newlywed woman bringing a wedding cake knife in her carry-on as a memento was fined $150.[18] Cecelia Beaman, A 57-year-old middle school principal and grandmother from Seattle taking care of 37 kids on a field trip to California, put a bread knife that she made sandwiches with in her bag en route to the airport and forgot to take it out before the checkpoint. She was fined $500 and put on the terrorism watch list.[19] Other passengers with names that resemble those on the no-fly list were treated as suspect, detained, and/or denied transit such as Catherine Stevens, wife of US senator Ted Stevens whose name is like singer/songwriter Cat Stevens, who was alleged to have ties to Muslim fundamentalists and denied entry into the US.

As checkpoint tensions have escalated, public discussions of them tend to privilege the civil liberties of travelers over those of this new class of federal employees, many of whom have high school educations and come from working class and non-white ethnic backgrounds. Alongside a flurry of congressional hearings, surveys have been conducted regarding the morale, working conditions, and effectiveness of TSA airport screeners, revealing widespread discontent among them. A 2006 report included comments from 11,000 TSA screeners that were so negative that the federal government, despite several requests, refused to make them public and only released the quantitative parts of the study.[20] For instance, TSA screeners sustained more injuries on the job than all other federal employees and were injured four times as often as construction workers and seven times as often as miners.[21] Another study found that TSA workers handling checked luggage lifted one bag every seven seconds, and most of these weighed more than fifty pounds.[22] Not surprisingly, the most common injuries are muscle and back strains due to heavy lifting, tendonitis, hernias, and cuts and lacerations sustained while reaching into bags for sharp objects. Between 2002–2004, US taxpayers paid $67 million in expenses related to airport screeners injured on the job. In 2005, their injuries and lost wages cost the federal government $52 million.[23] That year 29% of all airport screeners were injured on the job, missing 250,000 days of work, which caused staff shortages and heightened security concerns.[24]

While US taxpayers have subsidized billions of dollars' worth of screening equipment since 9/11, airport screening still relies upon manual labor requiring workers to carry heavy bags, check tickets, shuffle plastic bins, search carry-ons, confiscate items, frisk passengers, and operate machinery. The frequency of injuries on the job was so high between 2001 and 2005 that it prompted the TSA to create an occupational safety and health program to "build a culture of safety" among screeners, which included workplace hazard assessments, posted employee notices, and an injury hotline. From 2005 to 2012 reported TSA injuries on the job dropped 80%.[25] Reducing physical injuries at the checkpoint was articulated with mitigating terror in the air.

Beyond physical injuries, airport screeners often face ontological confusion at the checkpoint. TSA workers are regularly subject to a variety of secret tests by undercover officers and experiments by citizen vigilantes. The so-called Red Team is a band of undercover officers that arrives at checkpoints to covertly evaluate operations and often attempts to pass through with illegal objects, whether guns, bombs, or knives. In one exercise a woman secured a gun to her upper thigh under a thick bandage and after it was detected through wanding, she was asked about it and claimed she had staples from a recent surgery and was allowed to pass through.[26] James McNeil of the security firm McNeil Technologies smuggled a gun past the gates in Rochester and then testified to Congress about his stunt to make the case that security experts do not even know what screeners need to be trained for.[27] Twenty-year-old college student Nate Heatwole managed to get prohibited items including box-cutters, knives, and liquid bleach past airport screeners and onto aircraft, claiming he was intending to test TSA procedures. After doing this successfully on several flights, he emailed the TSA to notify the administration of his experiment and was subsequently fined $500 and put on probation.[28] If official TSA Red Team tests were designed to evaluate and improve screeners' job performance at the checkpoint, citizen tests were intended to determine whether new checkpoints and TSA protocols were effective in keeping banned objects off of airplanes. Given the fine line between testing and breaching airport security, the state discouraged travelers from participating in such practices.

In efforts to keep the skies secure, TSA screeners had to learn how to read a variety to shapeshifting threats that were both real and unreal. Each day on the job airport screeners posted at the X-ray belt monitor must decipher between "actual" and "fake" threats. The Threat Image Projection (TIPS) program, which has been used at all airports, arbitrarily superimposes simulated images of contraband, bombs, and other dangerous materials onto X-ray images of passengers' carry-on bags as they pass through the machine. The system randomly selects from an archive of 4,000 images of threatening objects and automatically inserts them into X-ray views. Rapiscan Systems, a developer of this publicly run, privately made program, explains, "an 'escape' is recorded if the checkpoint operator does not respond to the virtual threat projection within the allotted time period."[29] In some cases, TIPS has caused enormous confusion. A *Seattle Times* investigation found numerous incidents in which threat images were identified by screeners, but bags "escaped" without being physically searched and thus entire terminals filled with passengers had to be evacuated and re-screened.[30]

In addition to deciphering real and fake threats at the checkpoint, airport screeners have faced pressure from supervisors in connection with Red Team visits. Former TSA screeners featured in the documentary film *Please Remove Your Shoes* (2010) indicate that failure rates on Red Team tests are above 90% and claim the TSA "falsifies operational tests left and right" so that checkpoint staff will appear trained and proficient in their jobs. These former screeners state that in some cases the arrival of Red Teams at airports was leaked in an attempt to improve scores. When TSA administrators rig test results to produce the impression of checkpoint effectiveness, they cover up and ignore the challenging labor conditions of TSA screeners. In June 2015 these challenges became more apparent when TSA screeners' test failures made national news headlines. Screeners failed to detect explosives and weapons in 95% of tests conducted by an undercover Red Team at airports across the country. Banned items made it through the checkpoint in 67 of the 70 tests.[31] Two years later, in June 2017, TSA screeners at the Minneapolis airport failed 94% of the tests administered there.[32] These dismal test results have generated growing concern among government officials and travelers.

TSA officials have responded to these test results insisting on the need to properly train staff to use new screening technologies and reduce the amount of material screeners are required to memorize. For instance, TSA screeners are expected to memorize 3,100 separate tasks and 88 different pat-down techniques.[33] Others link poor checkpoint performance to misconduct issues among airport screeners. A 2016 congressional report found on-the-job issues ranging from smuggling to molestation to cocaine use by TSA workers.[34] And a 2017 investigation found that 858 TSA screeners had failed random drug and alcohol tests between 2010 and 2016.[35] Searching for terror threats day in and day out places unique kinds of pressures upon workers leading to physical injuries, test failures, and addiction.

While such scenarios are concerning, so too are the Red Team's operations. These undercover tests constitute a kind of stateside PSY-OPS as they can generate profound confusion among screeners and travelers about the status of "the real" at the very moment when determining it could be a matter of life or death. Just as airplanes transmitted PSY-OPS messages via leaflets and airwaves that instructed people how to think about regime change and war in their countries, as discussed in Chapter 1, airport security checkpoints retrained people how to think about and prepare for air travel. Since 9/11, the checkpoint has been used to stage the state's struggle to define, test, and regulate changing security threats. TSA workers are paid to partake in a state-sponsored guessing game orchestrated by security experts and TSA administrators who concoct all kinds of potential violations which screeners on the frontlines are charged day after day to detect. Even though each day dangerous objects pass through without incident and each day actual attacks are imagined that are not carried out, the state-led trickery, gaming, and managed chaos at the checkpoint normalizes skepticism about the status of all people and things for screeners and travelers alike.

Such working conditions have generated high attrition among TSA screeners. Nearly 4,000 TSA screeners left their jobs between 2006 and 2016, while traveler volume through checkpoints jumped from 708 million to 740 million people during this period.[36] This situation of having 4,000 fewer screeners and 32 million more travelers has compounded already demanding and stressful working conditions at the checkpoint, contributing to poor performance on Red Team tests and low morale.[37] Commercial airlines' changing baggage policies have added to these problems. In 2008 airlines began charging passengers $25 to $35 for every checked bag. Travelers seeking to avoid extra fees began carrying their bags through checkpoints, resulting in increased workload for TSA screeners. Every bag must move through the X-ray belt and sometimes requires a physical search as well. The increase in travelers and bags, combined with reduced staffs created checkpoint congestion and frustration. These fraught conditions peaked during late spring and summer 2016. National news outlets reported "epic" checkpoint lines with "insane" wait-times, which the TSA attributed to higher passenger volume and a shortage of 5,800 TSA workers.[38] On top of this, in 2016 TSA screeners serving on the "frontlines" of the war on terror were being paid $15–22 per hour and earning an average of $25,000–30,000 a year, close to the poverty line for a family of four.[39] Such overall conditions have made checkpoint labor less appealing as a career path, prompting many TSA screeners to leave their jobs.

As checkpoint labor is configured so that fewer screeners process a higher volume of travelers, it has also become more racialized. In 2011 Hispanic and African American organizations recognized the TSA for its diverse hiring practices as 42% of TSA screeners are non-white.[40] While some perceive the diversity of TSA screeners as a sign of ethnic integration in the federal workforce, it is equally concerning that US people of color are entering airport security positions characterized by poor working conditions and low pay. If that were not enough, such TSA screeners have been tasked to participate in racial profiling practices at the checkpoint. To keep airlines and travelers secure, the state relies on an ethnically diverse class of airport screeners to operationalize racial profiling practices with which they are likely all too familiar. Some TSA screeners have called out such practices. For instance, in 2012 TSA officers participating in a "behavior detection" program at Boston Logan International submitted written complaints objecting to the ways certain passengers such as Hispanics traveling to Miami or African Americans wearing baseball caps backward were stopped, searched, and questioned for "suspicious behavior."[41] Though leaked TSA documents from 2008, discussed earlier, indicate racial profiling is standard operating procedure, the TSA has announced more recently that it has a "zero tolerance" policy with regard to "unlawful profiling."[42] Yet in 2016 a TSA officer from Minneapolis complained that higher-ups instructed him to profile Somali-Americans, a community that has claimed a long history of TSA mistreatment at that airport.[43] In 2017 the American Civil Liberties Union wrote a scathing report on a TSA "behavior detection" program run by plainclothes officers from 2007–2012 that cost taxpayers at least $1.5 billion. The report substantiated public allegations of racial and religious profiling at airports in Newark, Miami, Chicago, and Honolulu.[44] Thus, TSA screeners of color, who are often structurally disenfranchised within the US socio-economic system and treated unequally within the dominant racial formation, have disproportionately been tasked to secure the air.

The racialization of checkpoint labor scripts particular groups of color as defenders of the security state and, at the same time, differentiates them from other groups of color designated as "risks" or "threats" based on their relation to certain countries or regions of the world, religious beliefs, or physical appearance. The checkpoint, in other words, produces new racialized social hierarchies and reorganizes ethnicities-in-relation at the site of air travel.[45] In the process, surveillance technologies that historically have been mobilized against domestic black populations in the US are redirected to target "Muslim-looking" bodies.[46] Thus, the checkpoint is used, on the one hand, to celebrate a liberal politics of inclusion by showcasing "diversity and integration" of the TSA work force. On the other hand, those workers—often people of color—are tasked to conduct racially charged and divisive screening practices against other people of color. Such racialized arrangements of checkpoint labor appear to "democratize" surveillance by positioning racialized groups as the perpetrators and subjects of surveillance.

Vertical mediation—the struggle to control the air—involves the reassertion of socio-economic and racialized hierarchies at the checkpoint. Airport screeners may receive federal benefits, but they also endure difficult working conditions in low-paid jobs, positioning them as part of a growing working class in the security sector. As TSA screeners use the checkpoint to mediate and regulate what goes into the air, they function within a post-9/11 system Naomi Klein defines as "disaster capitalism," which mobilizes neoliberal economic principles of deregulation and outsourcing to address crises ranging from terrorist attacks to hurricanes.[47] In this context, the racialized labor of the working class has been redirected away from assembly lines and farms—since many of these jobs have been outsourced globally—into state security jobs that exploit workers' manual and ocular labor to "secure the air," or as the TSA puts it: "to protect the nation's transportation systems to ensure freedom of movement for people and commerce."[48] Airport screeners not only apply racial profiling to travelers of color; TSA "diversity" hiring practices have selected people of color to conduct this work. This *racialization of the practice of racial profiling* positions it within a post-civil rights framework.[49] When screeners of color approach travelers of color as "suspect," white power becomes muted so that airport screening can be read by citizens of a democracy as "fair" or "acceptable." The boundaries of whiteness are always shifting in relation to changing political and economic needs. Such conditions produce what Stuart Hall calls "inferential racism" as they conceal the unequal, structural conditions—the racialization of working class labor and terrorism—that create such an encounter in the first place.[50] As US vertical hegemony relies upon these encounters to reclaim the air, an array of checkpoint screening technologies support this power struggle as well.

Close Sensing

After the US government established the TSA, it fortified airport checkpoints with an armada of new screening technologies. Metal detectors, body scanners, X-ray machines, and chemical sensors are just some of the technologies that airport screeners have used to scrutinize passengers and their belongings in the wake of 9/11. Though magnetometers and X-ray machines were used prior to 9/11, models were upgraded and made more sensitive. In addition, the TSA intensified and regimented checkpoint protocols resulting in the coordinated use of multiple screening technologies as well as physical searches. When travelers and their belongings passed through checkpoints, machines generated various kinds of coverage used by TSA screeners to determine whether they were eligible to fly. Magnetic signaling, X-rays, body scans, and chemical tracings were often combined with physical searches as travelers and their belongings passed through the checkpoint. I refer to these practices as *close sensing* because they attend to the personal, intimate, and minute rather than the earthly, distant, and panoramic perspectives of remote sensing (or geospatial imaging) discussed in Chapter 3. Close sensing involves the combined use of screening technologies and physical searching to scrutinize travelers' bodies and belongings as they move through the checkpoint. In this way, close sensing is an extension of the kinds of screening practices Lisa Cartwright discusses in her history of scientific imaging where film, X-ray, and other technologies were combined to make the body publicly visible in new ways.[51] What distinguishes close sensing from scientific imaging is the authority the state has granted airport screeners to supplement machine vision with touch. According to TSA guidelines, all belongings or bodies that are handled must be scanned with a machine first.

Given this, close sensing is also a practice of "haptic visuality"—a way of seeing that is linked to touching. Laura Marks develops this concept to expand theoretical conceptualizations of visual media, and, in particular, to highlight the potential of images to touch, but the concept is useful in the airport security context as well since it posits material continuities between looking and touching. Unlike optical visuality, "haptic visuality," according to Marks, engages "other forms of sense experience, primarily touch and kinesthetics."[52] She offers the concept to foreground "a flow between the haptic and the optical" and "explore how a haptic approach might rematerialize our objects of perception. . . ."[53] Approaching the checkpoint as a site of haptic visuality or close sensing, as I elaborate in this section, emphasizes the ways labor and technologies are combined at this site to operationalize continuities between imaging and touching. This checkpoint process "rematerializes" perceptions of travelers' bodies and belongings through multi-modes of visual and tactile inspection. The results of the magnetometer, X-ray machine, body scanner, or chemical sensor often prompt manual interventions that prevent bodies or matter from entering the air.

To perform this work, TSA screeners rely on "screener assistant technologies" such as "Target," which use software to search X-ray images for dangerous materials—"the algorithm analyzes the mass, size, and atomic number of items in the image against preset thresholds; objects that match the defined criteria are identified for the operator."[54] TSA screeners also use image-processing programs, such as Crystal Clear, which enable them to zoom in for a closer view and/or perform organic–inorganic stripping. Given that screener assistant technologies can isolate suspicious areas or materials on the body and display them as imagery on monitors, the primary function of the TSA officer is to view this imagery and apply his/her manual labor to bodies and objects identified as suspect. It is impossible, then, to distinguish this coverage—X-rays and body scans—from pat-downs and physical searches, which are often conducted with conspicuous blue latex gloves, the iconic signature of the TSA. To foreground their manual interventions, TSA workers also leave "notices of baggage inspection" in checked luggage that is scanned and physically searched. The TSA extends its reach into the air as luggage subject to its manual inspection is carried to destinations around the world.

The combination of technologized and manual searching—or close sensing— has altered traveler behavior too. The checkpoint has become a physically charged site at which travelers hurriedly strip off layers of clothes, remove their shoes and belts, empty out their pockets, and lay all belongings on the X-ray belt to avoid further inspection.[55] These acts of disrobing are performed while in transit and in public view, not only in front of TSA screeners, but other passengers as well.

Because of this, gender and sexuality are often invoked as sites for the assertion of authority. The TSA implemented more aggressive pat-down policies in September 2004 after two Chechen women carrying explosives allegedly caused two plane crashes in Russia.[56] After these incidents, TSA officers were instructed to perform more intrusive pat-downs and to look for "irregularities in a person's natural shape or contour." As they did so, letters to newspaper editors and articles re-telling stories about TSA screeners looking down the back of women's pants, cupping their breasts, or groping body parts during physical searches emerged. One woman reported having her breasts touched as the TSA agent loudly asked, "Are those real!?" The agency received 250 formal complaints in the month after the 2004 pat-down policy went into effect.[57] TSA agents also have been encouraged to target gender-nonconforming people. As Toby Beauchamp explains, the government category of "female-appearing" is often applied in US surveillance contexts in ways that reinforce transphobic and racist imaginaries, turning checkpoints into sites used to police deviant bodies.[58]

Ethnic and religious differences have been used as rationales for close sensing as well. Muslims, Sikhs, and Arabs who wear turbans, *hijabs*, or robes for religious purposes are often subject to physical scrutiny, and must often step aside to dismantle turbans or remove hijabs to enable pat-downs by TSA screeners. The TSA set up makeshift stalls adjacent to checkpoints so that same-sex agents can ask a traveler to disrobe or perform a bodily inspection in "private." Some travelers have reported being questioned, searched, and detained for "looking Muslim" and indicate that such practices increased after terrorist attacks such as the 2013 Boston Marathon bombing or San Bernardino shootings in 2015.[59] Muslim Americans indicate they also are monitored on board planes by flight attendants and other passengers.[60] In 2016 four men, all US citizens in their 20s, filed a $9 million federal lawsuit against American Airlines claiming they were removed from a flight from Toronto to New York City for "looking too Muslim."[61] The same year two US citizens, married Muslims of Pakistani descent, were removed from a Delta flight because a flight attendant felt uncomfortable having them on board, according to the American Council on Islamic Relations, which requested a federal investigation into the incident.[62] Muslims and Sikhs are pat down and questioned so frequently that the Council on American–Islamic Relations, NAACP, and ACLU have become involved on multiple occasions.[63] These situations reveal that close sensing can exceed the check-point and result in passengers' removal from planes whenever airline staff deem necessary. Manual interventions persist even as screening technologies become more sophisticated.

African Americans have been subjected to intrusive close sensing as well. In 2011 *The New York Times* reported a series of complaints by African American women who had endured hair pat-downs by TSA agents. In some cases physical searches were performed even though body scans had not set off alarms.[64] In 2014 the ACLU filed a civil rights complaint against the TSA on behalf of

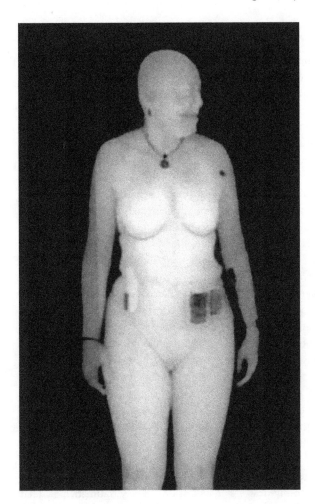

FIGURE 2.3 Director of the TSA security laboratory, Susan Hallowell, demonstrates how a backscatter x-ray machine detects the gun and bomb she had hidden under her clothing. By US Transportation Security Administration part of US Department of Homeland Security.

Source: https://commons.wikimedia.org/wiki/File%3ABackscatter_x-ray_image_woman.jpg—public domain, via Wikimedia Commons

Malaika Singleton, a neuroscientist with a PhD who was selected twice for a hair pat-down while traveling through LAX. According to the ACLU, on each occasion TSA officers "grabbed her hair and proceeded to squeeze it from top to bottom."[65] In a powerful analysis of such situations, Simone Browne suggests, "hair is named as a bodily marker that poses a barrier to passing through security for some."[66] Browne develops the concept of "racial baggage" to account for TSA pat-downs of pop music star Solange Knowles' afro, arguing that "certain acts and certain looks at the airport weigh down some travelers, while others travel lightly."[67] Close sensing brings screening and handling together in ways that are uneven and unjust, using the occasion of air travel to reassert bodily norms based on racialized power hierarchies.

The need for pat-downs is somewhat ironic given advances in machine vision and screener assistant technologies, mentioned earlier. One justification for the implementation of backscatter X-ray machines was that they would allow a "virtual strip search," enabling TSA screeners to see through passengers' clothes and detect someone carrying a gun or bomb, and thereby eliminate the need for more intrusive physical searches.[68] The TSA used the flood of traveler complaints about physical searches to legitimate the use of backscatter X-ray machines, claiming they perform a "virtual search" and make pat-downs unnecessary. Backscatter X-ray machines were first implemented in airports in Baltimore/Washington, Dallas/Fort Worth, Jacksonville, Florida, Phoenix, San Francisco, and London Heathrow.[69] Public concerns emerged about the high visibility of the body in backscatter images, which rendered breasts and genitalia in detail, earning them the nickname "x-rated X-rays." The Electronic Privacy Information Center and ACLU argued backscatter inspection constitutes a major privacy invasion and should be banned since it "compels passengers to submit themselves to a level of bodily exposure that almost everyone would consider is indecent and many find religiously or ethically offensive."[70] Such inspections also produce heightened concerns for gender-nonconforming and transgender travelers. To encourage the public to accept the technology, the director of the TSA security laboratory, Susan Hallowell, strolled through a backscatter machine to demonstrate its efficacy in detecting the gun and bomb she had hidden under her clothes (see Figure 2.3). Trying to minimize the issue of privacy encroachment, she suggested the only problem is that "it makes you look fat and naked."[71] Such a comment raises key questions for gender and racial analysis. For whom is being seen naked (or fat for that matter) "no big deal"? For whom is it deeply traumatizing? That a white female TSA administrator uses her own body to demonstrate how effortless it is to submit to a body scan reveals how whiteness becomes part of a hierarchy that is mobilized to shape checkpoint conditions for all. Most women would certainly not be alright with "looking fat and naked" in an airport, and such exposure might generate particular vulnerabilities for gender-nonconforming people or religious conservatives. Beyond such situations, there were other problems of exposure as well. Medical experts at UC San Francisco questioned whether these backscatter machines posed public health risks as they potentially exposed travelers to "dangerously high" levels of radiation, and pointed out their widespread use had not been evaluated by a neutral panel of experts.[72]

Backscatter X-ray machines and millimeter wave scanners participate in close sensing as they subject bodies to machine vision and touch. Louise Amoore and Rachel Hall argue that such technologies simultaneously enable the visual partitioning and projection of the body and, in doing so, establish a continuity between "digital dissection" and securitized visualization. They characterize the backscatter X-ray as a "form of technological vivisection, a digitised dismembering, through which bodies are 'somatically opened' and subjects erased simultaneously."[73] Given this capacity, they suggest there is more at stake at the checkpoint than invasions of privacy and bodily integrity. Backscatter X-rays and body scans bring into focus the collection of data as well as the prospect of its future use and circulation.[74] Contextualized in this way, close-sensing practices generate the potential to see and touch far beyond the checkpoint as the biometric data they produce may be stored and used in unanticipated ways in the future.

Despite concerns about privacy, public health, and big data collection, the TSA ramped up installation of backscatter X-ray machines after Umar Farouk Abdulmutallab, known as the "underwear bomber," attempted to detonate an explosive device in mid-air on December 25, 2009. Abdulmutallab managed to pass through the checkpoint in Amsterdam with explosives sewn into his underwear. The situation was used to rationalize further backscatter X-ray machine use, as security experts alleged the machines could have detected the

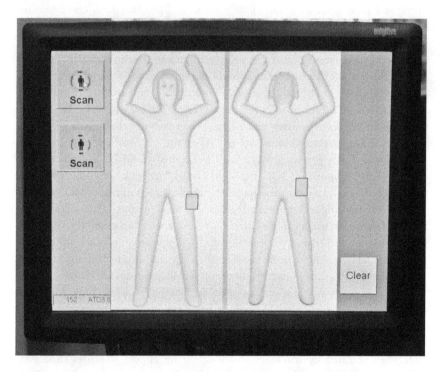

FIGURE 2.4 Use of a privacy algorithm with the millimeter wave scanner allows images to appear as bodily outlines with much less physical detail.

Source: https://s.hswstatic.com/gif/millimeter-wave-scanner-3-orig.jpg—screen captured used under the Fair Use Doctrine

white powder in his underwear. By 2012, the TSA installed 1,250 advanced imaging technology (AIT) units at the nation's 450 commercial airports, and 438 of those units were backscatter X-ray machines.[75] Yet almost as soon as they were installed, backscatter X-ray machines were removed from airports because they were not as efficient as millimeter wave body scanners.[76]

In efforts to refine checkpoint efficiency, the TSA also announced a new "layered approach" to passenger screening in 2012 based on a "risk-based system" which, TSA administrator Kelly Hoggan explained, allows airport screeners to "focus more attention on those travelers we believe are more likely to pose a risk to our transportation network while providing the opportunity for expedited screening to those we consider pose less risk."[77] This approach, which correlated with class and racial differences, coincided with the implementation of TSA Pre-check. This program enabled frequent fliers of certain US airlines or members of trusted travelers groups such as Global Entry, to be eligible for expedited screening at some checkpoints. The TSA also installed Automated Target Recognition (ATR) software on millimeter wave scanners "to enhance privacy by eliminating passenger-specific images."[78] As the traveler's body is scanned, the software detects items that could pose a threat and presents them on an outline of a body, allowing for more targeted pat-downs (see Figure 2.4). In such systems, machines generate images that are first read by other machines and then examined by humans. If a threat is suspected, human touch follows.

Despite the thousands of racial profiling and privacy invasion complaints against the TSA, the incident that went viral on November 17, 2010 involved a 31-year-old, white male software programmer. John Tyner used his mobile phone to record his encounter with a TSA officer during a checkpoint pat-down at the San Diego international airport. After the TSA officer explained the standard pat-down procedure and told Tyner he would be doing a "groin check," Tyner responded, "Ok, but if you touch my junk, I'm gonna to have you arrested." At that point the screener called a supervisor over who forbade Tyner from traveling and threatened him with a $10,000 fine.[79] The video Tyner recorded with his mobile phone went viral as it was broadcast on television news networks and shared via social media.[80] Significantly, when a white male professional is prevented from moving through the checkpoint the incident draws widespread public attention. Incidents involving people of color, whether African Americans or those with brown skin or hajibs who "look Muslim," occur much more regularly and generate less news media attention.

The institutionalization of close sensing at checkpoints in the US and abroad means that there are now more people in the world whose bodies and belongings have been scanned by machines and touched by airport screeners than ever before—the 9/11 attacks have been used to legitimate the production of a *closely sensed social class* at the site of airline travel. Those people who have passed through an airport security checkpoint since 9/11 share in common the experience of having their bodies and belongings scanned and touched as a condition of air travel. They have allowed the state to inspect their bodies and possessions in exchange for aeromobility. Their bodies and belongings have left traces, records, and data used by the TSA in efforts to assess, reorganize, and refine airport screening. And within this class the experience of screening can vary in degree, manner, and duration. It is important to note that those who are most closely sensed are not only screened by backscatter X-ray machines or closed circuit monitors, but are taken behind closed doors. Makeshift rooms exist for more intensive inspections and these spaces are cordoned off beyond public view. In such rooms, the visual is given over more fully to the tactile. In one sense, the checkpoint is a more protected place in terms of civil liberties because of the over-exposures that it affords, yet it also functions as a system for sorting those who are subject to even closer scrutiny, where seeing not only becomes touching but may become torture. Therefore, we cannot separate the practice of stateside close sensing at the airport checkpoint from the more excessive and violent versions of scrutiny and interrogation that have emerged in the midst of the US-led war on global terror. In some cases individuals have been apprehended and rushed through airport security gates only to be put on CIA "torture flights." In December 2005 new stories broke about hundreds of CIA flights that have funneled Islamist terror suspects from Europe and the US to the Middle East.[81] Close sensing, then, involves the hand–eye coordination of state power and may be articulated at checkpoints or in mid-air and may be applied to different bodies and to varying degrees. Airport screening practices might be understood as symptomatic, then, of a broader security regime in which looking authorizes touching and touching can become torture.

As backscatter X-rays and body scans activate touching and other manual interventions, they function not only as close sensing practices but also as vertical mediations as they shape who and what enters the vertical field. Various screening technologies are used at the checkpoint, but the hand remains vital to vertical mediation. For it is ultimately the TSA screener's hand—and the long arm of the law to which it is attached—that pushes buttons on machines to make them function, reaches into bags to remove banned items, pats down travelers' bodies, and prevents some from boarding or flying on airplanes. Close sensing at airport checkpoints thus foregrounds the ongoing significance of manual labor in US efforts to secure the air after 9/11. Over time manual efforts have been internalized by travelers themselves, who have learned to pre-emptively remove items from bags, place liquids in zip-locks, and empty their pockets before entering the checkpoint. Travelers have re-trained themselves to abide by security protocols that enable their entry into the air. Rachel Hall suggests, "As passengers become more comfortable with opening themselves up to the airport's wishes . . . it becomes important to ask how these developments within the culture of airport security are shaping the character of citizenship and public life in other contexts."[82] As travelers perform these actions they internalize and enact state security protocols through their embodied behavior and the kinds of objects they carry with them.

The X-Ray Belt

Beyond challenging labor conditions and practices of close sensing, vertical mediation at the checkpoint also involves scrutinizing an enormous number of travelers' belongings' as they pass through the X-ray belt. Developing a content-oriented or textual approach to this kind of coverage is a difficult proposition since TSA agents often prevent civilians from recording or standing near closed circuit monitors, even though such recordings are legal. As the agency's website indicates, "TSA does not prohibit the public, passengers or press from photographing, videotaping or filming at security checkpoints, as long as the screening process is not interfered with or slowed down. We do ask you to not film or take pictures of the monitors."[83] Yet there are numerous reports and videos online revealing instances in which TSA agents instruct travelers not to record the checkpoint, confiscate cameras, or order them to destroy their footage.[84]

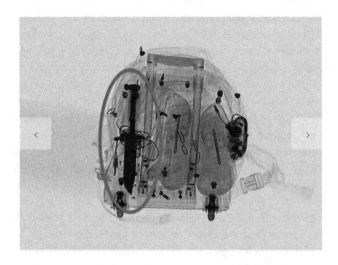

ALEX DAVIES TRANSPORTATION 12.22.15 7:00 AM

SHARE

CAN YOU SPOT THE CONTRABAND IN THESE AIRPORT BAGGAGE X-RAYS?

SHARE
3589

TWEET

COMMENT
29

EMAIL

FIGURE 2.5 Emphasizing the challenges of checkpoint screening, *Wired* published an interactive simulation that embedded knives and guns in different bags and challenged viewers to identify them.

Source: www.wired.com/2015/12/can-you-spot-the-contraband-in-these-airport-baggage-x-rays/—screen capture used under the Fair Use Doctrine

TSA officers are concerned that terrorists could use photos of checkpoint areas or X-ray monitors to subvert airport security systems.

The X-ray belt is a charged site because it is used by TSA screeners to search through all of travelers' carry-on items. At TSA checkpoints, X-ray machines are enclosed in boxes along conveyor belts. Travelers place their personal belongings in plastic bins that move along the conveyor belt, and these objects are X-rayed. Images appear instantly on closed-circuit monitors adjacent to the belt and TSA screeners examine them to determine whether a physical search of the bag or objects is necessary. If so, the screener notifies another agent and asks him/her to perform a manual search. A two-minute interactive simulation on an MSNBC website is instructive.[85] The interface invites the user to identify various threats that appear on a moving sequence of checkpoint X-ray images, including a gun, knife, and explosives, as passengers can be heard in the background telling the screener to hurry up. The user can pause and zoom in/out on the image or turn it from black and white into a color version that differentiates organic and inorganic matter. The simulation delivers a slide show of hypothetical X-rayed personal belongings splayed open for an airport screener's. When I tried the simulation myself I was overwhelmed by how difficult it was to identify the threatening objects placed in luggage and was struck by the odd application of such a high-stakes gaze to a stream of ordinary objects. Purses, briefcases, and backpacks rapidly pass by, containing objects such as pill bottles, coins, keys, and cell phones, but there are also knives, guns, and explosives that the screener is tasked to recognize. As the screener-in-training inspects the materials that pass, the voices of angry passengers can be heard on the soundtrack yelling, "This is taking for ever!" "My grandma could do a faster job than that!" or "Come on, I don't have all day!" In two minutes I screened 22 bags, 9 of which contained threats. I identified 77% of them correctly, earning a "C," and was warned at the end of my session, "Letting even one threat by would get a fully trained screener fired." Given that TSA screening agents have actually failed such tests quite frequently, as already discussed, this comment encourages the public to recognize the difficulty of screening and implies that TSA screeners are trained to be able to pass such tests.

A number of other simulations have appeared online revealing the difficulty of identifying banned objects amidst a plethora of personal belongings. For instance, *Wired* published a similar interactive project entitled "Can You Spot the Contraband in These Airport Baggage X-Rays?" embedding knives and guns in different bags and challenging viewers to identify them (see Figure 2.5).[86] A 2015 video entitled "X-ray images reveal just how eagle-eyed security staff have to be" emphasizes the challenging labor of airport screening, stating, "Next time you feel a pang of irritation, spare a thought for the long suffering employees who have to decipher every item in your bag through an X-ray machine." The video then presents a series of sample X-ray airport images from the Italian company SimulScan, including a knife, a large jar of body cream, and a gun in different bags.[87] Simulscan offers its own password-protected online airport screening simulations used for training purposes and has released an android-based application so that trainees can practice X-ray screening on mobile devices. Another online video from the company Vidisco called "xray security—see inside" features a sequence of still images of objects in visible light contrasted with X-ray images of the objects that expose hidden security threats. Objects include a Winnie the Pooh balloon filled with a bomb, a box of Godiva truffles repurposed as an "IED box" filled with nails, and explosives, a detonator, and a "not so innocent" baby doll turned into a bomb.[88] Finally, a security website describes "how to read an airport security X-ray image,"[89] and explains how the color-coding of X-ray images enables TSA agents to differentiate solid, biological, plastic, and alloy materials and notes the importance of outlines and contours in identifying objects and being able to distinguish a bottle of cologne from a gun.[90] Collectively, the public circulation of X-ray belt simulations not only reveals the kinds of image sequences that airport screeners read day in and day out, but also suggests a heightened levels of awareness about the material composition and form of ordinary objects. The online circulation of these simulations publicizes ways of seeing at the checkpoint so that travelers know how their objects are examined before they fly. It also proliferates suspicions by suggesting that banned items may be embedded in benign things such as a child's balloon, a box of chocolate, or bottle of cologne.

Given the sheer volume of objects X-rayed it is not surprising that forbidden items pass through the checkpoint unnoticed. No matter how diligent and well-trained the TSA staff, the labor of searching for something is hard work, and as mentioned earlier, the eyes tire when faced with a never-ending display of things to examine. When passing through many checkpoints myself I have observed how X-ray belt monitors are examined, and I have seen 2 to 3 screeners cloistered around them at times and one person falling asleep at others, a testament perhaps to the condition of high alert banality that characterizes this visual form. The examination of X-ray sequences is different from basic visual perception: it requires airport screeners to always assume that the most benign object could contain the most serious threat—for instance, that a lipstick could be a knife, a mobile phone could be a gun, a baby's toy could be a bomb. Compounding such issues is the screener's knowledge that TIPS images may be arbitrarily inserted in the sequence or undercover Red Team operations may be underway, as discussed earlier. In the context of such conditions, the screener's look is shaped by skepticism and paranoia; the goal is to resolve the ontological uncertainty of objects passing through the checkpoint and to mitigate risks that they may present.

While simulations enable TSA trainees to virtually experience an X-ray belt sequence at a checkpoint and identify bags with forbidden items, this imagery is instructive in other ways as well. Since 9/11 airport checkpoint X-ray machines have imaged billions of travelers' belongings, generating the most massive object-oriented visual economy the world has possibly seen. The endless X-raying of travelers' bodies and their belongings at the checkpoint resonates with what Jonathan Beller has called the "cinematic mode of production." As Beller suggests,

> Cinema refers not only to what one sees on the screen or even to the institutions and apparatuses which generate film but to the totality of relations which generates the myriad appearances of the world . . . Cinema means the production of instrumental images through the organization of animated materials. These materials include everything from actors, to landscapes, to populations, to widgets, to fighter planes, to electrons. Cinema is a material practice of global scope, the movement of capital in, through, as image.[91]

Though the airport X-ray is not cinematic in the classical sense, Beller's provocative account of cinema as a global material practice in which capital moves in and through the image invites analysis of the X-ray belt's relationship to issues of accumulation, ownership, and value. The conveyor belt, a late nineteenth century technology invented to carry coal and ore to support industrial processes, has been repurposed at the checkpoint and conjoined with X-ray machines and human labor to record and inspect traveler's carry-on items. This assemblage produces a spectral slideshow of twenty-first century consumerism, an immense visual inventory of the things people think they need to have with them during air travel, including currency, passports, identification cards, eyeglasses, umbrellas, snacks, pills, diapers, tampons, baby strollers, makeup, cigarettes, laptops, ipods, mobile phones, shoes, water, documents, magazines, jewelry, and so on. What appear on X-ray monitors are the faint traces of objects at once being protected as consumer possessions and scrutinized as potentially dangerous. TSA screeners use X-rays to re-inspect consumer goods, which have already been inspected on production assembly lines, to clear them for re-circulation into the air and across borders. As part of their efforts to keep the skies safe, screeners reassert the primacy of capitalism and consumerism at the site of air travel. Vertical mediation at the checkpoint ensures that travelers can continue to move with objects of value through the world.

The TSA uses the unique visuality of the X-ray to uncover hidden threats within these objects of value. Akira Lippit suggests that the X-ray provides a visual registration of the invisible, explaining, "X-rays record only the shadows of a secret, its trace, the place where it hides. Not so much an exposure as a disclosure, the X-ray reveals secret visibility as a mode of secret visuality, showing what nonetheless remains invisible, without operation or accident."[92] In the case of airport screening, the X-ray may disclose that lurking within capital accumulation are disastrous threats to its future. Each X-rayed object becomes a reminder that the capacity to see, consume, and move might not last.

FIGURE 2.6 Zappos ran an advertising campaign using the bin space at TSA checkpoints. Photo by Scott Beale/Laughing Squid.

Source: www.flickr.com/photos/laughingsquid/3834440737/—public domain, via Wikimedia Commons

When consumer goods pass through the X-ray belt they are not just objects to be looked at, they often become subject to close sensing as well. The state not only reserves the right to touch what it sees, but also uses its visual capital to "digitally dissect" and manipulate the materiality of objects as part of the process of trying to reduce or eliminate threats to its own future. Put another way, the X-ray sequence is symptomatic of the state's decreasing ability to control and regulate the flow of matter in general, whether weapons, drugs, currency, consumer goods, and/or natural resources in the context of globalization.[93]

Consumerism at the X-ray belt is also signaled in a more explicit way—by the TSA's decision to sell advertising space on plastic bins used on the X-ray belt. In 2006 the TSA approved a year-long experiment that allowed Security Point Media to sell ad space on the bottoms of 14,000 plastic bins at 14 US airports.[94] In exchange for ad space, advertisers agreed to provide new bins, carts, and tables for checkpoints on a regular basis. During the first phase of the experiment the TSA received $435,000 worth of new checkpoint equipment.[95] Ad space was purchased by companies such as Rolodex, Zappos.com, Sony, and Sylvania (see Figure 2.6).[96] Described as "premium space for a premium audience," marketing experts speculated that each ad could be seen by several hundred thousand people per day.[97] As a result the ads sold for $250,000 to 500,000 per year at large airports.[98]

Security Point Media sought to exploit unique checkpoint characteristics, claiming that since people have a heightened sense of awareness at a checkpoint, "they are more open to messages."[99] The head of pharmaceutical company, UrgentRX, explained that using ads in plastic bins allowed his company to refine their direct marketing, explaining, "For us, a targeted consumer in the Northeast who is on the go is who we seek and there is no one better than somebody going through LaGuardia Airport."[100] The initiative recast the airport security checkpoint as a lucrative advertising space with a "captive" and valuable audience. Security Media Point claims its SecureTray System "improve(s) efficiencies in the security screening process while delivering high impact advertising opportunity."[101] The company indicates all travelers are targets, insisting "Everyone goes through security!" and promises the grey bin ads "reach a concentration of affluent and influential decision-makers" in 36 major markets, hailing 1 million people per day.[102] Marketing has long used this targeting discourse to identify and reach audiences and to produce subjects. As Caren Kaplan points out, targeting originates in a military context, but is transposed onto an array of consumer contexts during the twentieth century so that consuming subjects and targets become one and the same.[103]

As these bin advertisements exploit "captive audiences" at the checkpoint, they not only pitch particular products, they also make explicit one of the X-ray belt's functions—to facilitate the global circulation of consumer goods. This too is a dimension of vertical mediation as the site of air travel is organized to reassert the primacy of US global capitalism. Just as body scans allow "freedom of movement," the X-ray belt facilitates the "free flow" of commodities. Embedding ads in bins works to normalize the airport security checkpoint, treating it like any other brand-able space in a consumer society. Colorful distractions in plastic bins appear in the same moment the state uses body scanners and X-ray machines to extract travelers' biometric and consumer data. In this way, the checkpoint also becomes a site of flexible accumulation—it can be used both to advertise products and to collect big data. Furthermore, revenue from the ads is used to subsidize the purchase of TSA checkpoint equipment, outsourcing federal security costs to the private sector. Despite marketers' desire to use the airport checkpoint to target a mobile, influential, and affluent elite, the "captive audience" who encounters the bin ads most frequently are the low-paid TSA screeners who work the X-ray belt day and night. In doing so, they work not only for the state but also for advertisers.

Beyond selling the surface of plastic bins, other forms of privatization occur at the airport checkpoint as well. Key questions about intellectual property emerge in relation to X-ray belt imagery. Technologies at the checkpoint have the potential to produce an enormous visual archive containing a new kind of intellectual property—*X-ray images of travelers' belongings before they entered (or were banned from) the air.* Who owns these big data? Travelers or the state? Where does this checkpoint coverage go after it has been viewed? What kind of value does it have, and how might it be used in the future? Just as the analysis of checkpoint labor and close sensing reveals that airport security has become a site for reasserting power hierarchies organized around class and racial differences, the analysis of the X-ray belt brings forces of consumerism and privatization into relief. Securing the air not only involves sorting and removing banned objects, but also requires organizing the checkpoint so that it advances the free flow of capitalism. After 9/11 the US uses the checkpoint to reassert its economic power at the site of air travel.

Although X-ray belts and body scanners have the potential to accumulate valuable data sets, the TSA provides vague and contradictory information about what happens to these data after use. TSA officers claim checkpoint images are discarded after they are viewed.[104] Yet administration officials also admit that machines are required "to have the capability to retain and export imagines [sic] *only* for testing, training and evaluation purposes."[105] The capabilities to store and send images are not activated on airport machines and only select personnel can activate these functions. The agency also reports there are stiff penalties for TSA staff who use mobile phones to take photos of and/or share any checkpoint scans.[106] In an effort to address concerns about privacy, EPIC submitted FOIA requests to the TSA requesting information about the technical capacities and uses of body scan machines with some results, but the TSA has continued to restrict access to information about checkpoint imagery due to concerns about system subversion.

Given the TSA's reluctance to openly provide details about the storage and/or circulation of these image data, speculation might be in order. It would not be surprising to learn that the TSA stored and archived checkpoint image data, particularly in the wake of Edward Snowden's revelation about the NSA's mass surveillance programs. Whether such data could be turned into digital capital is another question. TSA representatives publicly admit using this image data for training purposes, and hence body scans and X-rays have a value beyond the instance of screening. It is obvious that body scans or X-rays have potential value to law enforcement and national security agencies, but this massive data set—particularly the X-rays of personal belongings—contains a gold mine of information about consumer behavior that is of immense value to product manufacturers, advertising firms, food suppliers, cosmetics companies, and the airlines. Like consumer mailing lists, purchasing histories, or browser meta-data, checkpoint image data will likely become intellectual property sold to generate revenue for the state or its contractors.[107] Body scans and X-rays can be tagged with personal information, which make them even more valuable. After being X-rayed at checkpoints, travelers' possessions can take on a second life of commodification as indicators of consumer choices, states of mind, tastes, or other personal information. Data revealing that a traveler carried particular pills, magazines, or devices, for instance, may be valuable information, if not now, in the future.

Thus, in addition to selling space on grey bin bottoms to subsidize the security apparatus, the state could sell travelers' biometric and consumer data. The need for public understandings of such conditions prompted Simone Browne to characterize airports as sites for "critical biometric consciousness raising."[108] As it stands, travelers' compliance with TSA protocol sustains this system. Their movement through checkpoints and subjection to body scans and X-rays positions them as infrastructural dimensions of airport security. Beyond paying airfares for seats and services on commercial airplanes and extra fees for security, travelers submit to and give up different images of their bodies and belongings each time they fly. Travelers have learned to vertically mediate themselves—to self-screen and prepare their bodies and belongings to enter the air.

Just as the TSA sells ad space on plastic bins and collects biometric and consumer data, the X-ray belt is used to confiscate millions of prohibited and illegal objects at the checkpoint. The TSA refers to these objects as "voluntarily abandoned property" and describes confiscated objects as "excess government property" that is donated to state surplus agencies. These agencies can auction, sell, donate, or dispose this property.[109] Some of these objects accrue value as TSA-seized property. In the years immediately after 9/11, from 2002 to 2005, the TSA confiscated 18 million objects.[110] This number dwindled as passengers internalized the protocols. By 2013 travelers "voluntarily abandoned" 750,000 items.[111] Scissors have been donated to local schools. Intercepted mace cans have been used by law enforcers in training. And state agencies have sold TSA-seized objects online on E-bay. When I searched E-bay in early 2006, I found 138 entries for TSA-seized knives, scissors, nail clippers, corkscrews, wrenches, and pliers. One person describes an "NTSA lot of 8 pounds of scissors," indicating "most are made in China, Japan and Korea," reminding us of the broader global economy from which they emerge. Another describes a "crappy bag of old scissors" as "airport seizure property," suggesting its history of confiscation gives it added value. By 2016, eBay had institutionalized such TSA seizures as part of its marketing and dedicated a special page to "Airport Confiscation: Collectibles," featuring knives for sale in bulk with brands ranging from "Dewalt" to "Leatherman" to "Victorinox."[112] The X-ray belt produces secondary markets for sharp objects confiscated at the checkpoint, and state agencies and entrepreneurs use the Internet to put them back into circulation.[113]

While confiscated knives and tools can be auctioned off and re-sold, liquids cannot. In 2006 the TSA announced a policy banning liquids and gels on all flights to and from the US. This policy was based on an alleged terrorist plot to embed bombs in ordinary objects that would be carried on planes to the US leaving from the UK. This meant that passengers not only had to leave their blades behind, but their bottled water, toothpaste, lotion, eye drops, and cough syrup as well. During August and September 2006, after this policy was implemented, checkpoint trash bins toppled over with containers full of liquids as perturbed passengers reluctantly complied with the abruptly implemented rules. Enormous volumes of shampoo, toothpaste, lotion, soda pop, face cream, hair gel, and other fluids had to be picked up and disposed of by local waste contractors.[114] In October 2006 the TSA carry-on regulations had changed yet again and sandwich-sized Ziploc bags filled with 3 oz. containers of liquids and gels were allowed. Bottled water could be taken on board as long as it was purchased beyond the checkpoint. At Los Angeles International airport in October 2006, TSA staff ordered travelers to throw their $1.00 bottles of water in the trash, indicating they could purchase others for $3.50 beyond the checkpoint. There is a price to pay for a secure sip of water in mid-air. The cost of security in the air is embedded in the exchange value of commodities. Ziploc bags have become part of this economy as well. From 2006 to 2013 the annual revenue of Ziploc's manufacturer, S.C. Johnson, increased from $7.5 billion to $11.75 billion.[115]

Airport screening and the X-ray belt cost travelers in multiple ways. Consumers pay additional fees to commercial airlines for checked baggage, taxes to subsidize the TSA, and are forced to absorb the costs of re-distributing and disposing of TSA confiscated items. After "voluntarily abandoning" their possessions, they can either purchase more expensive replacements beyond the checkpoint or assume a loss. Since 9/11, airports have become fully commercialized spaces. Whatever is seized by the TSA creates an opportunity for a commercial transaction, whether just beyond the checkpoint or upon the traveler's arrival at his/her destination. As already mentioned, travelers also must surrender their biometric and consumer data as they pass through the checkpoint in order to fly, giving up valuable personal information in exchange for aeromobility. Thus, the X-ray belt is part of a broader economy organized to reassert the primacy of capitalist circulation at the site of air travel—if an object is not allowed in the air it can be auctioned off or sold online. The TSA authorizes cities that host airports to dispose of or sell confiscated materials. At the same time, however, the costs of object confiscation, distribution, and disposal are displaced onto travelers who not only are forced to give up certain items and information, but also to pay higher airfares to fly and taxes for their security.

Checkpoint labor, close sensing, and the X-ray belt were all attempts to reassert US vertical hegemony. By screening traveler's possessions, facilitating the flow of already purchased goods, and experimenting with new forms of privatization, the X-ray belt exposed the primacy and persistence of capitalist projects in the context of the war on terror. The 9/11 attacks not only targeted symbols of US global capitalism—the twin towers of the World Trade Center—they also adversely affected the US economy, tanking everything from the stock market to commercial airline revenues.[116] The airport checkpoint became a site for restoring global movement and commerce through the air, which had been so violently and spectacularly disrupted. As checkpoint labor, technologies, and images were combined to sort which commodities could enter the air and which were seized for recirculation or disposal, they participated in practices of vertical mediation. That is, they shaped and transformed materialities of the vertical field to support and extend US strategic agendas. Thus, beyond reinscribing racialized, socio-economic hierarchies, airport screening became a site for venerating capitalist modes of extraction and circulation, whether having passengers give up their biometric data, using plastic bins to sell new ad spaces, or trading confiscated belongings online. Just as the US media and military entities organized televisual formations to reclaim the airwaves, as discussed in Chapter 1, so too have they have used airport checkpoints to "secure the air." In this chapter, I have approached the checkpoint as a site of coverage and practices of vertical mediation where labor, technologies, and images are organized to reassert US hegemony. These socio-technical relations and visualizations at the checkpoint exemplify shifts in biopower in the context of a changing world political order. TSA procedures have produced problematic working conditions for federal employees who are breaking their backs while trying to keep knives out of the air. Their protocols have generated a new regime of close sensing in which looking can become continuous with touching, handling, and manipulation. And, finally, these checkpoint practices have revealed changes in the visual representation and perception of material objects where what may ultimately be seen is the state's struggle to control capital accumulation and circulation. At the airport checkpoint, security involves everything from screeners' back muscles to secret agents' breach scenarios, from trace detection devices to X-rayed pocketknives, from blue latex gloves to CIA torture flights. Much more than a "non-place," as Marc Auge famously described it two decades ago, the airport has become a vital place where security, technology, and capital collide and spur the US social body to recognize its terrorizing interiority.[117]

Combined, checkpoint labor, close sensing, and the X-ray belt are organized to adjudicate which bodies and objects are allowed into the air. Such vertical mediation is biopolitical. The process of sorting who and what can enter the air reproduces and projects racialized, socio-economic hierarchies along a vertical axis of time/space and power. The checkpoint not only determines who populates airplanes, but also operationalizes socio-economic and geopolitical power hierarchies through the vertical field. While social hierarchies have produced the vertical as a space of exclusion for decades, since 9/11 airport screening practices have intensified and reinforced regimes of stratification organized around ethnic/racial, religious, and national differences. Such practices have become most explicit in US travel bans.

In 2017 the US government attempted to implement one of the most aggressive acts of airport security yet. Newly elected President Donald Trump issued a blanket travel ban on people coming into the US from nine Muslim-majority countries. Since most arrive by air this in effect was a flight ban as well. Controversial Executive Order 13769, hastily implemented on January 27, 2017, days after Donald Trump's inauguration, banned US entry for 90 days by citizens of Iraq, Syria, Iran, Libya, Somalia, Sudan, and Yemen, including those already carrying visas. Trump's travel ban met widespread opposition as protesters occupied US airports and demonstrated around the world. US federal judges and district courts in multiple states, including New York and Massachusetts, temporarily blocked part of the order and partially repealed the ban, claiming it discriminates against people on the basis of their religion and therefore violates the First Amendment of the US Constitution. A revised version of the travel ban, Executive Order 13780, was enacted on March 16, 2017, reducing the number of banned countries to six, and allowing visa requests from those who have "close family" members in the US.[118]

In addition to the highly controversial travel ban, Trump's Department of Homeland Security on March 21, 2017 ordered nine airlines to cease carriage of consumer electronics such as laptops, ipads, tablets, and cameras in passenger cabins of flights traveling into the US. These airlines were from eight Muslim-majority countries.[119] Based on US intelligence that suggested ISIS was developing a bomb designed to be hidden in laptop batteries, this order required commercial airlines to insist that passengers place large electronics in checked bags rather than carrying them on board the flight, affecting about 50 flights per day flying into the US.[120] Travelers from these countries strongly objected to the laptop ban. Among other things, it prohibited them from working on laptops during long flights. In this way, the electronics ban controls what airline passengers from other countries do with their hands and their time during flight. It intervenes directly in the aeromobilities of travelers from nine Arab, African, or Muslim-majority countries. Such brazen airport security measures could only be introduced in the context of the widespread normalization of enhanced airport security since 9/11.

As I have suggested throughout this chapter, checkpoint coverage not only points to the ongoing significance of manual labor in an era of digitized security and surveillance. It also reveals how deeply invested US forces are in reinforcing racial and socio-economic power hierarchies at the site of commercial air travel. Such power hierarchies are reasserted not only through racialization of terror and the racial profiling of "suspects" at the checkpoint. They are also manifest in the creation of a disenfranchised class of airport screeners deployed to "the frontlines" of the war on terror to secure the air for a more affluent elite. Though this class of workers may perform important labor for the state, efforts to "diversify" this work force have occurred along with low pay, challenging working conditions, and limited opportunities for advancement. Efforts to control the materiality of air travel are performed by a security underclass tasked with keeping commercial airplanes flying. The checkpoint has been used to promote post-civil rights conditions by producing the appearance of integration. There may be an ethnically diverse team of TSA screeners scanning your body, searching your bags and facilitating "free" movement, but checkpoint labor conditions have sustained structural inequalities organized around gender and race and, in doing so, have further disenfranchised the working class.

Notes

1 Barbara Benham, "Global Airport Security," *Travel and Leisure*, May 4, 2009, accessed August 16, 2017, www.travelandleisure.com/articles/global-airport-security

2 Saulo Cwerner, Sven Kesselring, and John Urry, Eds. *Aeromobilities* (London and New York, Routledge, 2009). Also see, Peter Adey, *Aerial Life: Spaces, Mobilities, Affects* (West Sussex, UK: Wiley-Blackwell, 2010). Rejecting the "divisional artifice between the earth and the sky," Peter Adey suggests "aeriality" is not only about what is in the air, but consists of complex assemblages that enable and constitute "aeromobilities."

3 Kim Zetter, "TSA Leaks Sensitive Airport Screening Manual," *Wired*, December 7, 2009, accessed August 16, 2017, www.wired.com/2009/12/tsa-leak/

4 See Jasbir Puar, *Terrorist Assemblages: Homonationalism in Queer Times* (Durham, NC and London: Duke University Press, 2007); and Ronak Kapadia, *Insurgent Aesthetics of the Forever War* (Durham, NC: Duke University Press), forthcoming.

5 Simone Browne, *Dark Matters: On the Surveillance of Blackness* (Durham, NC and London: Duke University Press, 2015).

6 Didier Bigo, "Globalized (in)Security: the Field and the Ban-opticon," in *Illiberal Practices of Liberal Regimes: The (In)Security Games*, Ed. Didier Bigo et al. (Paris: L'Harmattan, 2006), 35. www.people.fas.harvard.edu/~ces/conferences/muslims/Bigo.pdf, p. 35.

7 As TSA Academy instructor, Bill Morgan, told his class of trainees, "You're at war. Did you know that? You're at war . . . You guys are frontline troops. Because they will continue to attack aviation because it works." Rachel Gillett, "What It's Really Like to Work as a TSA Officer," *Business Insider*, October 12, 2016, accessed August 16, 2017, www.businessinsider.com/tsa-officer-job-work-career-2016-10/#learning-the-ropes-4

8 There are definitely acoustic dimensions to checkpoint operations, but the screening technologies installed since 9/11 are largely organized around sight.

9 United States Congress House of Representatives, Aviation Security (Focusing on Training and Retention of Screeners): Hearing Before the Subcommittee on Aviation of the Committee on Transportation and Infrastructure, March 16, 2000. (Washington, DC: Government Printing Office, 2000).

10 Discussed in Gale Dillingham, Director of Infrastructure, U.S. General Accounting Office (GAO) Report, Aviation Security:_Long_Standing Problems_Impair_Airport _Screeners' Performance: GAO/RECE-00-75, June 2000, p. 37.

11 Ibid, 37.

12 Ibid, 8.

13 Ibid, 3.

14 Sara Keuhaulani Goo, "Airport Screeners' Hiring Under Scrutiny," *The Washington Post*, Sept. 12, 2003, www.washingtonpost.com/archive/business/2003/09/12/airport-screeners-hiring-under-scrutiny/3164c26e-6982-4e17-8cae-9192a5626045/?utm_term=.e82df41679d4

15 G. Leff, "Tourism Suppression Agency," *POSWID*, March 2, 2005.

16 Joe Sharkey, "Airport Hurdles and the Nonflying Nuns," *The New York Times*, March 2, 2004, www.nytimes.com/2004/03/02/business/business-travel-on-the-road-airport-hurdles-and-the-nonflying-nuns.html?pagewanted=all&src=pm

17 Comment from Francine submitted on March 7, 2008 in response to "Why We Do What We Do: When Security Officers Find Illegal Items at the Checkpoint,"

Transportation Security Administration website, March 4, 2008, www.tsa.gov/ blog/2008/03/04/why-we-do-what-we-do-when-security-officers-find-illegal-items-checkpoint

18 James Joyner, "Bad Attitude Punishable? Banned Items in Luggage Bring TSA Fines," *Outside the Beltway*, February 20, 2004, accessed August 16, 2017, www. outsidethebeltway.com/archives/2004/02/bad_attitude_punishable/

19 Kevin Reece, "This Is Not Right," *KOMO TV News,* Des Moines, IA, May 31, 2005, www.komotv.com/news/story.asp?ID=37150

20 See for example Project on Government Oversight/POGO, "Survey of Airport Screeners Shows Problems at TSA," January 20, 2006, accessed August 16, 2017, http://pogoblog.typepad.com/pogo/2006/01/survey_of_airpo.html; and M. Arsenault, "What Screeners Central Is Doing FOIA," *Screeners Central*, 2005.

21 Chris Strohm, "Lawmakers Seek Investigation of TSA Labor Abuses," *Government Executive*, October 4, 2005, accessed August 16, 2017, www.govexec.com/story_page.cfm?articleid=32482&dcn=todaysnews

22 Thomas Frank, "Demands of the Job Strain Airport Screeners, Airport Security," *USA Today*, February 23, 2005, www.usatoday.com/travel/news/2005-02-23-tsa-strained_x.htm

23 Thomas Frank, "Airport Screeners' Strains, Sprains Highest," *USA Today*, January 10, 2005, www.usatoday.com/news/nation/2006-01-10-TSA-injuries_x.htm

24 Frank, "Demands of the Job;" Stephen Barr, "In Unusual Request TSA Seeks $10 million to Address High Turnover," *Washington Post*, February 10, 2006.

25 Jill M. Seagraves, "Transportation Security Administration Occupational Safety and Health Program Overview," PowerPoint presentation, June 10, 2013, accessed August 16, 2017, www.nationalacademies.org/hmd/~/media/129059B30DD8433 B8D7E8A280B8E55DF.ashx

26 United States Congress House of Representatives Committee on Government Reform, *Knives, Box Cutters, and Bleach: A Review of Passenger Screener Training, Testing and Supervision*. Hearing November 20, 2003 (Washington, DC: Government Printing Office, 2003).

27 Ibid.

28 Ibid.

29 Rapiscan, "Advanced Technologies/TIP and TIP Net." Printed copy in author's possession.

30 "Airport Insecurity," *Seattle Times Special Report*, July 11, 2004, http://seattletimes. nwsource.com/news/nation-world/airportinsecurity/breaches/

31 Andy Campbell, "TSA Fails 95 Percent Of Airport Security Tests Conducted by Homeland Security: Report," *Huffington Post*, June 1, 2015, accessed August 16, 2017, www.huffingtonpost.com/2015/06/01/tsa-fails-95-percent-tests-homeland-security_n_7485558.html; Eric Bradner and Rene Marsh, "Acting TSA Director Reassigned After Screeners Failed Tests to Detect Explosives, Weapons," *CNN.com*, June 2, 2015, www.cnn.com/2015/06/01/politics/tsa-failed-undercover-airport-screening-tests/index.html

32 B.R., "Screeners at Minneapolis Airport are Reported to Have a 94% Failure Rate," *The Economist*, July 5, 2017, www.economist.com/blogs/gulliver/2017/07/checking-checkers; Andrew Blake, "TSA Failed to Detect 95 Percent of Prohibited Items at Minneapolis Airport: Report," *The Washington Times*, July 6, 2017, www.washington times.com/news/2017/jul/6/tsa-failed-detect-95-percent-prohibited-items-minn/

33 Rebecca Maksel, "Airport Security: 'Disappointing and Troubling,'" *Air & Space*, November 4, 2015, www.airspacemag.com/daily-planet/airport-security-how-safe-are-we-180957079/?no-ist

34 Scott Perry and John Katko, "Misconduct at TSA Threatens the Security of the Flying Public," House Homeland Security Committee Majority Staff Report,

July 2016, https://homeland.house.gov/wp-content/uploads/2016/07/TSA-Misconduct-Report.pdf

35 Kyle Iboshi, "Hundreds of TSA Workers Failed Drug and Alcohol Tests at Airports Across U.S.," *13 News Now* (Norfolk, VA), April 5, 2017, www.13newsnow.com/news/investigations/hundreds-of-tsa-workers-failed-drug-alcohol-tests-at-airports-across-us/429029436; Tré Goins-Phillips, "Hundreds of TSA Workers at Airports Across the US Failed Drug, Alcohol Tests," *The Blaze*, April 7, 2017, accessed August 16, 2017, www.theblaze.com/news/2017/04/07/hundreds-of-tsa-workers-at-airports-across-the-us-failed-drug-alcohol-tests/

36 46,041 in 2006 to 42,525 in 2016. "Statement by J. David Cox, Sr., National President of the American Federation of Government Employees, AFL-CIO Before the Subcommittee on Transportation Security and the House Committee on Homeland Security on Long Lines, Short Patience: Local Perspectives," American Federation of Government Employees, AFL-CIO, May 26, 2016, http://docs.house.gov/meetings/HM/HM07/20160526/104997/HHRG-114-HM07-Wstate-CoxJ-20160526.pdf

37 Hugo Martin, "Treating TSA Agents Better Might Reduce Airports' Long Lines," *Los Angeles Times*, August 15, 2016, www.latimes.com/business/la-fi-tsa-turnover-20160815-snap-story.html

38 Jad Mouawad, "Catching a Flight? Budget Hours, Not Minutes, for Security," *New York Times*, May 2, 2016, www.nytimes.com/2016/05/03/business/airport-security-lines.html; Katia Hetter and Michael Pearson, "TSA Security Line Waits Inevitable, DHS Secretary Says," *CNN.com*, May 16, 2016, www.cnn.com/travel/article/tsa-long-lines-us-airports/index.html; J. David Cox, Sr., "Why So Many TSA Workers Are Leaving and How to Stop It," *The Hill*, June 28, 2016, accessed August 16, 2017, http://thehill.com/blogs/pundits-blog/homeland-security/285103-why-so-many-tsa-workers-are-leaving-and-how-to-stop-it

39 Kathryn Vasel, "The TSA is Hiring: Here's What You Need to Know," *CNN.com*, May 20, 2016, http://money.cnn.com/2016/05/20/pf/tsa-jobs-hiring/index.html

40 "TSA Recognized for Diversity," Transport Security Administration, February 3, 2011, accessed August 16, 2017, www.tsa.gov/news/releases/2011/02/03/tsa-recognized-diversity

41 Michael S. Schmidt and Eric Lichtblau, "Racial Profiling at Airport, U.S. Officers Say," *New York Times*, August 11, 2012, www.nytimes.com/2012/08/12/us/racial-profiling-at-boston-airport-officials-say.html; Michael S. Schmidt and Eric Lichtblau, "TSA Officers Allege Racial Profiling at Logan," *The Boston Globe*, August 11, 2012, www.bostonglobe.com/metro/2012/08/11/tsa-officers-allege-racial-profiling-logan/oj8AHKCddiUpnTmWgf0mxK/story.html

42 John S. Pistole, "TSA Behavior Detection and Analysis Program," Transport Security Administration, November 14, 2013, accessed August 16, 2017, www.tsa.gov/news/testimony/2013/11/14/tsa-behavior-detection-and-analysis-program

43 "Testimony of Andrew Rhoades, Assistant Federal Security Director at the Office of Security Operations, Transport Security Administration Before the House Oversight and Government Reform Committee Concerning Examining Management Practices and Misconduct at TSA," April 27, 2016, https://oversight.house.gov/wp-content/uploads/2016/04/Rhoades-TSA-Statement-4-27-TSA-Workforce-I.pdf; Ron Nixon, "Minnesota T.S.A. Manager Says He Was Told to Target Somali-Americans," *New York Times*, April 27, 2016, www.nytimes.com/2016/04/28/us/politics/minnesota-tsa-manager-says-he-was-told-to-target-somali-americans.html; Paul McEnroe and Allison Sherry, "Angry Local Somalis Allege Racial Profiling, Harrassment at Airports," *Star Tribune*, March 1, 2015, www.startribune.com/angry-local-somalis-allege-racial-profiling-harassment-at-airports/294527011/; Rene Marsh, "TSA Official Says He Was Instructed to Racially Profile

Somali-Americans," *CNN.com*, April 27, 2016, www.cnn.com/2016/04/27/politics/transportation-security-administration-racial-profiling/index.html

44 "Bad Trip: Debunking the TSA's 'Behavior Detection' Program," ACLU, February 2017, www.aclu.org/report/bad-trip-debunking-tsas-behavior-detection-program?redirect=bad-trip

45 Ella Shohat and Robert Stam, *Unthinking Eurocentrism*.

46 Ronak Kapadia, *Insurgent Aesthetics*; Inderpal Grewal, *Saving the Security State*; Eric Tang, *Unsettled*; Simone Browne, *Dark Matters*.

47 Naomi Klein, The Shock Doctrine: The Rise of Disaster Capitalism (New York: Picador, 2007).

48 "Mission." Transportation Security Association website, undated, www.tsa.gov/about/tsa-mission

49 Herman Gray, "In Search of the Black Fantastic: Politics and Popular Culture in the Post Civil-Rights Era (Review)," *American Studies* 50, no. 3/4 (2009): 151–152, https://muse.jhu.edu/article/453578

50 As Stuart Hall writes, "By inferential racism I mean those apparently naturalised representations of events and situations relating to race, whether 'factual' or 'fictional', which have racist premises and propositions inscribed in them as a set of unquestioned assumptions. These enable racist statements to be formulated without ever bringing into awareness the racist predicates on which the statements are grounded." Stuart Hall, "The Whites of Their Eyes: Racist Ideologies and the Media," in *The Media Reader*, Ed. Manuel Alvarado and John O. Thompson (London: British Film Institute, 1990), 13.

51 Lisa Cartwright, *Screening the Body: Tracing Medicine's Visual Culture* (Minneapolis, MN: University of Minnesota Press, 1995). Cathy Hannabach explores the tight relationship between medical imaging and militarism, pointing to work by Cartwright and others that reveals the same imaging technologies used to map, target, and bomb during the Gulf War were also incorporated in medical imaging systems. Cathy Hannabach's *Blood Cultures: Medicine, Media, and Militarisms* (New York: Palgrave Macmillan, 2015), 57.

52 Marks invokes the haptic to critique post-Enlightenment rationality and its privileging of distant and detached modes of observation. Laura U. Marks, *Touch: Sensuous Theory and Multisensory Media* (Minneapolis, MN: University of Minnesota Press, 2002), 2. Also see See Margaret Morse, *Virtualities: Television, Media Art and Cyberculture* (Bloomington, IN: Indiana University Press, 1998).

53 Marks, xiii.

54 Rapiscan, "Advanced Technologies/Target."

55 Paul Virilio, *War and Cinema: The Logistics of Perception* (London: Verso, 1989), 3.

56 S.K. Goo, "Airport Pat-Down Protocol Changed," *Washington Post*, December 23, 2004.

57 Associated Press, "Women Complain About Airport Patdowns," *MSNBC*, November 30, 2004, www.msnbc.msn.com/id/6617853/

58 Toby Beauchamp, "Artful Concealment and Strategic Visibility: Transgender Bodies and U.S. State Surveillance After 9/11," *Surveillance & Society* 6, no. 4 (2009): 356–366, available at: https://ojs.library.queensu.ca/index.php/surveillance-and-society/article/view/3267

59 Jack Jenkins, "Anti-Muslim Profiling At Airports Goes Beyond the TSA," *Think Progress*, January 20, 2016, accessed August 16, 2017, https://thinkprogress.org/anti-muslim-profiling-at-airports-goes-beyond-the-tsa-4e4a6265610d#.i6fuaytmh. The Boston Marathon bombing on April 15, 2013, perpetrated by Tamerlan and Dzhokkar Tsarnaev, killed three and injured several hundred. The San Bernardino shooting on December 2, 2014 by Syed Farook and Tashfeen killed 14 people and 22 injured during a training event and Christmas part at the Inland Regional Center.

60 Ibid.

61 Frances Kai-Hwa Wang, "Brooklyn Men Allege Discrimination, File $9 Million Lawsuit After American Airlines Encounter," *NBC News*, January 21, 2016, www.nbcnews.com/news/asian-america/brooklyn-men-allege-discrimination-file-9-million-lawsuit-after-american-n501476

62 Kelly Yamanouchi, "Group Files Complaint Against Delta, Alleging Racial Profiling," *The Atlanta Journal Constitution*, August 4, 2016, accessed August 16, 2017, www.myajc.com/business/group-files-complaint-against-delta-alleging-racial-profiling/tkIXSBVshHyZDm2cZtiXBK/

63 Michael T. Luongo, "Traveling While Muslim Complicates Air Travel," *New York Times*, November 7, 2016, www.nytimes.com/2016/11/08/business/traveling-while-muslim-complicates-air-travel.html

64 Joe Sharkey, "With Hair Pat-Downs, Complaints of Racial Bias," *New York Times*, August 15, 2011, www.nytimes.com/2011/08/16/business/natural-hair-pat-downs-warrant-a-rethinking.html?_r=0

65 "Civil Rights Complaint on Behalf of Malaika Singleton Against the TSA," ACLU, January 12, 2015, www.aclunc.org/our-work/legal-docket/civil-rights-complaint-behalf-malaika-singleton-against-tsa. As an ACLU attorney stated, "The humiliating experience of countless black women who are routinely targeted for hair pat-downs because their hair is 'different' is not only wrong, but also a great misuse of TSA agents' time and resources." Julia Craven, TSA Says It Will Stop Touching So Many Black Women's Hair," *Huffington Post*, April 3, 2015, accessed August 16, 2017, www.huffingtonpost.com/2015/04/03/tsa-hair-pat-downs_n_6996790.html

66 Browne, *Dark Matters*, 138.

67 Ibid, 132. After pop music star Solange Knowles had a TSA afro pat-down, Knowles described it as a "Discrim-FRO-nation." Katia Hetter, "Beyonce's Sister Claims 'Discrim-FRO-nation,'" *CNN.com*, November 15, 2012, www.cnn.com/2012/11/15/travel/solange-knowles-hair-search/

68 Joe Sharkey, "Airport Screeners Could Get X-Rated X-Ray Views," *The New York Times*, May 24, 2005. Bart Elias, "Changes in Airport Passenger Screening Technologies and Procedures: Frequently Asked Questions," Congressional Research Service, January 26, 2011, www.fas.org/sgp/crs/homesec/R41502.pdf

69 By 2008 Congress allocated $250 million for advanced checkpoint technologies. Elias, "Changes in Airport Passenger Screening."

70 Electronic Privacy Information Center (EPIC), "Spotlight on Surveillance: Transportation Agency's Plan to X-Ray Travelers Should be Stripped of Funding," June 2005, www.epic.org/privacy/surveillance/spotlight/0605/

71 Leslie Miller, "Airport Screeners May Get X-Ray Vision," *Associated Press*, June 25, 2003, http://campaignfortruth.com/Eclub/210703/CTM-airportxray.htm

72 John W. Sedat to John P. Holdren, "Letter of Concern," April 6, 2010, www.ucsf.edu/sites/default/files/legacy_files/concern.pdf; Jennifer O'Brien, "UCSF Scientists Speak Out Against Airport Full-Body Scans," University of California, San Francisco News Center, November 4, 2010, accessed August 16, 2017, www.ucsf.edu/news/2010/11/5810/ucsf-scientists-speak-out-against-airport-full-body-scans; John L. McCrohan and Karen R. Shelton Waters, "Response to University of California—San Francisco Regarding Their Letter of Concern, October 12, 2010," U.S. Food and Drug Administration, October 12, 2010, accessed August 16, 2017, www.fda.gov/radiation-emittingproducts/radiationemittingproductsandprocedures/securitysystems/ucm231857.htm; Julie Accardo and M. Ahmad Chaudhry, "Radiation Exposure and Privacy Concerns Surrounding Full-Body Scanners in Airports," *Journal of Radiation Research and Applied Sciences* 7, no. 2 (2014): 198–200, www.sciencedirect.com/science/article/pii/S1687850714000168

73 Louise Amoore and Alexandra Hall, "Taking People Apart: Digitised Dissection and the Body at the Border," *Environment and Planning D: Society and Space* 27, no. 3 (2009), 452. They emphasize "the conjoined nature of the practices of taking apart and making visible." 452.

74 Ibid, 457.

75 The TSA planned to bring the level of AIT installations to 1800 by FY 2014, costing a total of $1.17 billion. Bart Elias, "Airport Body Scanners: The Role of Advanced Imaging Technology in Airline Passenger Screening," Congressional Research Service, September 20, 2012, www.fas.org/sgp/crs/homesec/R42750.pdf

76 Carol Kuruvilla, "TSA Has Completely Removed Revealing X-Ray Scanners from America's Airports: Rep," *New York Daily News*, May 31, 2013, www.nydailynews.com/news/national/tsa-completely-removed-full-body-scanners-rep-article-1.1360143

77 Kelly Hoggan, "TSA's Use of Technology to Support a Layered Approach to Security," Transportation Security Administration, June 19, 2012, accessed August 17, 2017, www.tsa.gov/news/testimony/2012/06/19/tsas-use-technology-support-layered-approach-security

78 "TSA Takes Next Steps to Further Enhance Passenger Privacy," Transportation Security Administration, July 20, 2011, accessed August 17, 2017, www.tsa.gov/news/releases/2011/07/20/tsa-takes-next-steps-further-enhance-passenger-privacy

79 Robert J. Hawkins, "Oceanside Man Ejected from Airport for Refusing Security Check," *The San Diego Union-Tribune*, November 14, 2010, www.sandiegouniontribune.com/news/sdut-tsa-ejects-oceanside-man-airport-refusing-security-2010nov14-htmlstory.html; "CNN: John Tyner to TSA security 'Don't 'touch my junk,'" YouTube video, 2:05, posted by "CNN," November 17, 2010, www.youtube.com/watch?v=Laxmx4cE3aE

80 "CNN: John Tyner"; "CNN Official Interview: John Tyner speaks about 'Don't touch my junk' incident," YouTube video, 4:49, posted by "CNN," November 17, 2010, www.youtube.com/watch?v=80jG5T-c3cw

81 See for example Richard Norton-Taylor, "MPs Dismiss Torture Flight Denial," *The Guardian*, December 2, 2005, http://politics.guardian.co.uk/foreignaffairs/story/0,11538,1655980,00.html; Amy Goodman, "U.S. Operating Secret 'Torture Flights,'" *Democracy Now*, November 7, 2004, www.democracynow.org/article.pl?sid=04/11/17/1525208; and Michael Hirsch, Mark Hosenball, and John Barry, "Aboard Air CIA," *Newsweek*, February 28, 2005. Also see Trevor Paglen and A.C. Thompson, *Torture Taxi: On the Trail of the CIA's Rendition Flights* (Brooklyn, NY: Melville House, 2006).

82 Rachel Hall, *The Transparent Traveler: The Performance and Culture of Airport Security* (Durham, NC and London: Duke University Press, 2015).

83 Douglas Hester, "Right to Record Checkpoints Despite Long-Established Legality," *Photography is Not a Crime*, July 23, 3015, accessed August 17, 2017, http://photographyisnotacrime.com/2015/07/23/tsa-continues-to-deny-citizens-the-right-to-record-checkpoints-despite-long-established-legality/ Printed copy in author's possession.

84 Hester, "Right to Record Checkpoints."

85 The initial link has been removed; *Wired* did a similar project here: Alex Davies, "Can You Spot the Contraband in These Airport Baggage X-Rays?," *Wired*, December 22, 2015, accessed August 17, 2017, www.wired.com/2015/12/can-you-spot-the-contraband-in-these-airport-baggage-x-rays/

86 Alex Davies, "Can You Spot the Contraband In These Airport Baggage X-Rays?" *Wired*, December 22, 2015, www.wired.com/2015/12/can-you-spot-the-contraband-in-these-airport-baggage-x-rays/

87 "X-ray images reveal just how eagle-eyed security staff have to be," YouTube video, 0:58, posted by "L News16," December 23, 2015, www.youtube.com/watch?v=4quGx4kWpek; the same images appear as photo illustrations in this article: Caroline Mcguire, "Would YOU Be Able to Locate These Banned Items in Airport Hand Luggage? X-Ray Images Reveal Just How Eagle-Eyed Security Staff Have to Be," *Daily Mail*, December 22, 2015, accessed August 17, 2017, www.dailymail.co.uk/travel/travel_news/article-3370591/Would-able-locate-banned-items-airport-hand-luggage-X-ray-images-reveal-just-eagle-eyed-security-staff-be.html

88 "x ray security—see inside," YouTube video, 4:24, posted by "Vidisco X-ray," December 18, 2013, www.youtube.com/watch?v=gzqiwoxSO_M&t=11s

89 "How to Read an Airport Security X-Ray Image," *Snälla Bolaget*, accessed August 17, 2017, http://snallabolaget.com/?page_id=666

90 Ibid.

91 Jonathan L. Beller, "Kino-World: Notes on the Cinematic Mode of Production," in *Visual Culture Reader 2.0*, Ed. N. Mirzoeff (London and New York: Routledge, 2002), 67.

92 Akira Mizuta Lippit, *Atomic Light (Shadow Optics)* (Minneapolis, MN: University of Minnesota Press, 2005), 32.

93 For an interesting take on this issue see Moisés Naím, *Illicit: How Smugglers, Traffickers and Copycats Are Hijacking the Global Economy* (New York: Doubleday, 2005).

94 Lisa Lerer, "What's Next in Airport Security? Advertising," *Forbes*, January 10, 2007, www.forbes.com/2007/01/10/securitypoint-rolodex-advertising-tech-security_cx_ll_0110tsa.html

95 Thomas Frank, "TSA Allows Ads in Bins Across U.S.," *ABC News*, accessed August 17, 2017, http://abcnews.go.com/Travel/story?id=6175777&page=1

96 For further information on the Zappos campaign see: https://laughingsquid.com/wp-content/uploads/zappos-airport-security-bin-faq.pdf

97 Ibid.

98 Thomas Frank, "Coming to an Airport Checkpoint Near You: Ads in the Security Bins," *USA Today*, January 10, 2007, https://usatoday30.usatoday.com/travel/news/2007-01-09-tsa-ads_x.htm

99 Ibid.

100 Ed Sealover, "Is That My Company's Ad in an TSA Airport Collection Bin?," *Denver Business Journal*, October 28, 2013, www.bizjournals.com/denver/news/2013/10/25/is-that-my-companys-ad-in-a-tsa.html

101 "Overview: Moving People. Making Connections.," *SecurityPoint Media*, accessed August 17, 2017, http://securitypointmedia.com/about/overview/

102 "SecureTray System: Everyone Goes Through Security!," *SecurityPoint Media*, accessed August 17, 2017, http://securitypointmedia.com/advertising/securetray/; see video on "Overview: Moving People" page (see above).

103 Caren Kaplan, "Precision Targets"; Also see, Rey Chow, *The Age of the World Target* and Mary Ebeling, *Healthcare and Big Data*.

104 Joshua Norman, "Naked Body Scan Images Never Saved, TSA Says," *CBS News*, November 16, 2010, www.cbsnews.com/news/naked-body-scan-images-never-saved-tsa-says/

105 Gale D. Rossides to Bennie G. Thompson, untitled correspondence, February 24, 2010, https://epic.org/privacy/airtravel/backscatter/TSA_Reply_House.pdf

106 Declan McCullagh, "Feds Admit to Storing Checkpoint Body Scan Images," *CNET*, August 4, 2010, accessed August 17, 2017, www.cnet.com/news/feds-admit-storing-checkpoint-body-scan-images/

107 John Cheney-Lippold, *We Are Data*; Mary Ebeling, *Heathcare and Big Data*.

108 Browne, *Dark Matters*, 140.

109 Blogger Bob, "What Happens to Your Prohibited Items?," Transportation Security Administration, September 21, 2009, accessed August 17, 2017, www.tsa.gov/blog/2009/09/21/what-happens-your-prohibited-items?page=2

110 Monica Novotny, "TSA on E-Bay: Items That Didn't Make It On-Board Now Sold Online," *MSNBC*, April 28, 2005, www.msnbc.msn.com/id/7670500/

111 Mike M. Ahlers and Rene Marsh, "Need a Tribal Spear or a Horse Whip? Try TSA Resale," *CNN.com*, March 14, 2013, www.cnn.com/2013/03/13/travel/tsa-surrendered-items/index.html

112 Some have used these raw materials to create art. See: "Airport Confiscations," eBay, accessed August 17, 2017, www.ebay.com/bhp/airport-confiscation#; See also: "TSA Lot," eBay, accessed August 17, 2017, www.ebay.com/bhp/tsa-lot; the site of air travel is used to reassert and reinforce dominant forms of power ranging from racism to consumerism.

113 Kimberly Chun, "Michele Pred: Turning Confiscated Items Into Art," *SFGATE*, September 8, 2011, www.sfgate.com/art/article/Michele-Pred-Turning-confiscated-items-into-art-2310356.php

114 Stephanie Chen, "From Carry-On to eBay: The Journey of Airport Security Booty," *CNN.com*, September 21, 2009, www.cnn.com/2009/TRAVEL/09/21/tsa.contraband.sale/index.html

115 "S.C. Johnson & Son," *Wikipedia*, accessed August 17, 2017, https://en.wikipedia.org/wiki/S._C._Johnson_%26_Son

116 International Air Transport Association, "The Impact of September 11, 2011 on Aviation," undated, www.iata.org/pressroom/Documents/impact-9-11-aviation.pdf

117 Marc Auge, Non-Places: Introduction to an Anthropology of Supermodernity (London: Verso, 1995).

118 Sudan, Somalia, Iran, Yemen, Syria and Libya; Tom McCarthy and Oliver Laughland, "Travel Ban Goes into Effect Despite Courts Saying Security Issues Unfounded," *The Guardian*, June 29, 2017, www.theguardian.com/us-news/2017/jun/29/trump-travel-ban-us-airports-security-concerns-unfounded

119 Egypt, Turkey, Saudi Arabia, UAE, Qatar, Jordan, Kuwait, Morocco, and Saudi Arabia; Jon Ostrower, Charles Riley, and Mark Thompson, "U.S. and U.K. Ban Laptops and Other Devices on Flights From Middle East," *CNN.com*, March 21, 2017, http://money.cnn.com/2017/03/21/news/airline-electronics-ban-middle-east-africa/index.html?iid=EL; Ron Nixon, Adam Goldman, and Eric Schmitt, "Devices Banned on Flights From 10 Countries Over ISIS Fears," *New York Times*, March 21, 2017, www.nytimes.com/2017/03/21/us/politics/tsa-ban-electronics-laptops-cabin.html

120 Nixon, Goldman, and Schmitt, "Devices Banned."

3

MONITORING

Geospatial Imagery and the Wars in Afghanistan and Iraq

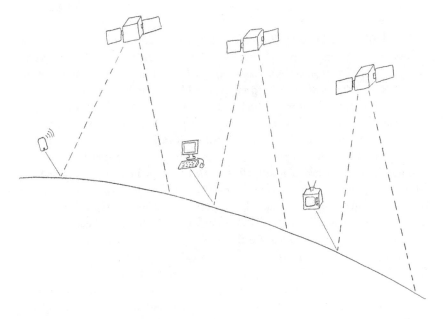

FIGURE 3.1 "Monitoring." Concept sketch by Lisa Parks.

Source: The author

As televisual formations and airport security protocols were mobilized in the wake of 9/11 to reassert US control over the vertical field, remote-sensing satellites enabled the US military and corporations to monitor sites on the earth's surface and operationalize strategic agendas. Immediately before and after the 9/11 attacks, the National Reconnaissance Office (NRO) launched three new satellites from California's Vandenberg Air Force base, sending up a Lacrosse radar imaging satellite on August 17, 2001, a signal detection satellite on September 9, and a K-11 satellite known as USA-116 on October 5.[1] In addition, two new commercial remote-sensing satellites—Ikonos owned by SpaceImaging, which later became GeoEye, and QuickBird owned by Digital Globe—were launched in 1999 and 2001 respectively. These state and commercial satellite projects, planned long before the 9/11 attacks, have bolstered US control of vertical space in the context of the war on terror. To support the US invasion of Iraq in March 2003, the NRO reportedly had six spy satellites flying over the country each hour.[2] Between 2001 and 2016, the NRO launched an estimated 31 more satellites into orbit[3] and has several more waiting in the wings, and US private remote-sensing companies have launched six more earth-imaging satellites.[4]

Aerial reconnaissance long precedes the historical conjuncture of the war on terror and the age of the satellite, extending back centuries, as Caren Kaplan powerfully shows in *Aerial Aftermaths*, and includes more recent events like the Cuban Missile Crisis of 1962.[5] However, the US military's use of vertical views and orbital platforms has intensified since 9/11 as geospatial images have been mobilized to fight a war imagined as global and perpetual—an "everywhere war," as Derek Gregory has called it, and a "forever war" as Dexter Filkins describes it.[6] The contemporary use of geospatial images by US state and corporate entities is part of a broader struggle for vertical hegemony that also includes efforts to commandeer the airwaves, regulate aeromobilities through new regimes of airport security, and target and destroy sites and people on the earth's surface using unmanned aerial vehicles (UAVs) or drones. Such aero-orbital maneuvers are interwoven with what Eyal Weizman calls "the politics of verticality," which involves, among other things, the assertion of control over the airspace above a territory as part of an effort to regulate and control what happens on the ground beneath it.[7] Though Weizman's concept emerges from a detailed analysis of Israel's attempts to "control the air" over Palestine, as we shall see in Chapter 4, similar strategies have informed practices of targeted killing and broader struggles for US vertical domination since 9/11.[8]

What further distinguishes the current historical conjuncture of the war on terror are the shifting institutional and socio-technical contexts of aerial and satellite imagery. Since 2001 the restructuring of government agencies, the emergence of new remote-sensing companies, and the proliferation of digital technologies have increased consumer and military access to high-resolution aerial and satellite images. Now referred to by state officials and scientific experts as the *geospatial industry*, this sector includes a host of federal agencies and commercial firms that participate, often collaboratively, in the production, distribution, and interpretation of aerial and satellite imagery. Historically, the NRO and the National Imagery and Mapping Agency (NIMA) led strategic US aerial and satellite reconnaissance and image intelligence activities. In 2003 a federal bill authorized NIMA to change its name to the National Geospatial-Intelligence Agency (NGA). The NGA, whose motto is "Know the Earth . . . Show the Way. . . . Understand the World" employs 16,000 people, most of whom work in one of the largest federal buildings in Washington, DC.[9] The NRO describes itself as "the nation's eyes and ears in space," and employs 3,000 personnel.[10] In 2013 the NRO's annual budget was $10.3 billion while the NGA's was $4.9 billion.[11] Combined, the two budgets exceed that of the Central Intelligence Agency.

Alongside these federal agencies are two commercial remote-sensing satellite operators, DigitalGlobe and GeoEye. These companies surfaced in 1992 and began to compete on the international market in 1994 after President Clinton issued a Presidential Directive that privatized the US remote-sensing sector, which the government had controlled since 1960.[12] DigitalGlobe and GeoEye became major players in the geospatial sector, selling high-resolution satellite imagery on the international market and enjoying a steady flow of major US government contracts. The companies merged in 2012. That year DigitalGlobe's revenue was $421.4 million, up 24% from 2011.[13] And in 2011 GeoEye brought in $356.4 million, an 8% increase from 2010.[14] Most of their revenue comes from US government contracts. In 2010 the NGA awarded both companies 10-year contracts to develop the "Enhanced View" program, which amounted to a combined total of $7.35 billion with all options exercised.[15] Information giant, Google, whose revenue hit a record $50 billion in 2012, began emerging as another key player in the geospatial sector when the company purchased the digital mapping company, Keyhole, Inc. in 2004.[16] Keyhole's 3-D interactive mapping interface became the basis for Google Earth, which by 2011 had more than 1 billion downloads.[17] Keyhole had been backed by the CIA private venture firm Intel-Q and was named after the Keyhole reconnaissance satellite program. Google expanded its assets in the geospatial sector by acquiring SkyBox Imaging (now called Terra Bella), for $500 million in 2014.

The restructuring of government aerial and satellite reconnaissance, the growth of commercial remote sensing, and the increasing availability and use of geospatial images via Google Earth form the backdrop of issues to be explored in this chapter. The close collaboration of federal agencies such as the NRO and NGA with corporations such as DigitalGlobe, GeoEye, and Google makes it increasingly challenging to differentiate state, military, and civilian activities in relation to geospatial images as well as the actions that they are used to mobilize and rationalize. Companies such as DigitalGlobe and Google wield a growing amount of political and economic clout as their products support the US Defense

Department in various strategic initiatives designed to support US planetary dominion. By 2016 DigitalGlobe's gross earnings were $725 million and Google's were nearly $89.5 billion.[18] Though these private firms are not typically thought of as media companies, they have become integral to the "military-industrial-media-entertainment network."[19] Caren Kaplan traces the military histories of satellite-based geo-location systems such as GPS and GIS, and explores how systems designed to support "surgical strikes" in the Persian Gulf War have become part of a broader consumer culture that transposes subjects with targets and "habituates citizen/consumers to a continual state of war understood as virtual engagement."[20] As products of the "military-industrial-media-entertainment network," geospatial images collapse consumer and military divides, and as such constitute an important space for analyzing shifting relations of power and verticality after 9/11. The geospatial image is implicated in the restructuring of media coverage as it has been used to assemble and articulate strategic US agendas.

This chapter explores how geospatial images have been used to reassert US vertical hegemony in the context of the war on terror. Approaching these images as part of militarized media culture, I consider what is at stake when major state and military decisions—such as whether, where, and how to fight war—pivot around the capacity to detect and display light and heat patterns on the earth's surface. Geospatial images are not benign abstractions; they are used to catalyze geopolitical agendas, rationalize military interventions, and develop postwar futures. Like the televisual formations analyzed in Chapter 1, geospatial images are implicated in relations of power, vision, and verticality. As the co-editors of *Observant States* suggest, in such images "the logic of geopolitical reason is . . . inseparable from its visual representation."[21] At the same time, however, Laura Kurgan has suggested that the unique vantage point of the overhead view might enable ways of thinking about earthly matters from oblique political angles.[22] In other words, even though a geospatial image emerges from the military-industrial complex, its uses and interpretations are not always aligned with strategic state or military agendas.

To explore these issues further, this chapter examines a series of geospatial images as vertical mediations of the US wars in Afghanistan and Iraq. Such vertical mediations mark not only the technical process of transforming material phenomena into framed images, but also the multitude of imprints, traces, or residues left in the air, on the ground, and in the water by acts of war. As Sarah Kember and Joanna Zylinska explain, mediation is more than representation: it "can be seen as another term for 'life'—for being-in and emerging-with the world."[23] Approaching the geospatial image as a *vertical mediation* involves exploring how the stretch of space between the earth's surface and aero-orbital platforms becomes part of vital processes, life worlds, and ways of life. It involves explicating the kinds of capacities and forces the geospatial image is used to demonstrate, enact, or mobilize, while remaining attentive to its limits and constraints and the unpredictable reversals of power it may be implicated within as well. In short, it involves treating the geospatial image not as a static frame of image data, but as part of biopolitical processes, as part of processes of ". . . becoming, of bringing-forth and creation."[24]

I argue in this chapter that geospatial images have been used not only to *document* or *represent* conditions on earth, but also to stage, enact, and bring about material transformations on the earth's surface. In an effort to approach geospatial images in such a way, the chapter opens with a discussion of US Secretary of State Colin Powell's use of satellite images on the eve of the 2003 US invasion of Iraq. In this globally televised presentation, Powell demonstrated how to read satellite images like a state. This moment prompted public critique and reflection about the documentary status of the satellite image and led to growing awareness of the ways geospatial image data can be spun. In an effort to delve deeper into the materiality of geospatial images and suggest potentials for alternate readings of them, I then explore the *microphysics of geospatial imagery*—the sociotechnical and power-laden processes by which electromagnetic radiation traveling through the atmosphere is detected and turned into imagery. Drawing upon research in the areas of object-oriented ontologies and new materialisms, I consider the *surplus matter of satellite images*—the content of overhead views that becomes a backdrop for various graphic inscriptions, whether circles, arrows, or squares. I suggest that critical attention to this backgrounded content and the object it features can be used to read satellite images from different perspectives. Finally, I demonstrate what is at stake when state, military, and corporate entities are able to use satellite images to advance strategic agendas without public deliberation. Focusing on processes of mediascaping, natural resource speculation, monitoring of reconstruction projects, and predictive analytics, I show how geospatial images participate in practices of vertical mediation. The vertical mediation of Afghanistan and Iraq in the context of the war on terror has involved a process of transforming the territories of sovereign nation-states into geospatial data that becomes the intellectual property of the US government or corporations so that it can be stored, shared, acted upon, and/or traded in the global digital economy. This has become yet another way the US forces have worked to reassert vertical power after 9/11.

Reading Satellite Images Like a State

In the months after 9/11, the US government purchased exclusive rights to all US commercial satellite images of Afghanistan so that its military coalition had sole access to them.[25] Between 2001 and 2003, the satellite images of Afghanistan that circulated in news media were carefully selected and integrated into Defense Department press conferences, often to demonstrate the Taliban or Al Qaeda targets struck by coalition forces. Given the tight control around US satellite images during the early stages of the war in Afghanistan, it was quite surprising when on February 5, 2003 then Secretary of State, Colin Powell, delivered a live television presentation to the UN Security Council making a case for war against Iraq that was based largely based upon them.

Armed with a flashy audiovisual PowerPoint presentation entitled "Iraq: Failing to Disarm," Powell insisted that Saddam Hussein was in material breach of UN resolution 1441, a unanimous vote by the council to disarm Iraq of weapons of mass destruction. Powell claimed to present "undeniable proof" that Hussein was developing biological, chemical, and nuclear weapons, expanding Iraq's ballistic missiles capabilities, fostering links to global terrorists, and refusing to cooperate with UN weapons inspectors. Throughout the presentation, all eyes drifted between Secretary Powell and large projection screens placed on either side of the room where he adduced his evidence, which included transcriptions of barely audible telephone exchanges between senior officers of Iraq's Republican Guard and declassified satellite images of alleged weapons facilities. My analysis of Powell's presentation demonstrates what it means to read satellite images like a state—to fuse satellite images with strategic state and military objectives.

After presenting three audio recordings of senior members of the Iraqi Republican Guard allegedly obstructing UN weapons inspection, Powell delivered a

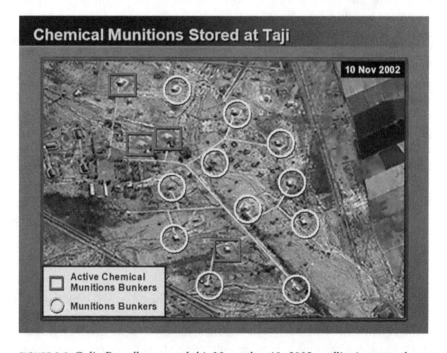

FIGURE 3.2 Colin Powell presented this November 10, 2002 satellite image to the UN Security Council, alleging it revealed chemical munitions being stored at a facility in Taji, Iraq.

Source: https://georgewbush-whitehouse.archives.gov/news/releases/2003/02/20030205-1.html—public domain

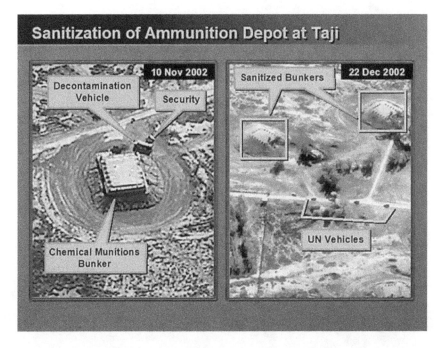

FIGURE 3.3 Colin Powell presented this December 22, 2002 satellite image to the UN Security Council, alleging it revealed the "Sanitization of Ammunition Depot at Taji."

Source: https://georgewbush-whitehouse.archives.gov/news/releases/2003/02/20030205-1.html—public domain

sequence of eleven satellite images to further make the case. The first, a November 10, 2002 view of the "Chemical Munitions Stored at Taji," was imprinted with eleven yellow circles and four red squares (see Figure 3.2). Powell explains that the circles and squares specify the locations of "munitions bunkers" and "active chemical munitions bunkers" and queries, "How do I know that? How can I say that? Let me give you a closer look." He then offers a frame that compares the satellite view of the same facility on November 10, 2002 to one acquired on December 22, 2002, which is labeled "Sanitization of Ammunition Depot at Taji." The first view features one chemical bunker inscribed with yellow arrows indicating the location of a decontamination vehicle and a security post. In the second, yellow arrows point out two "sanitized bunkers" and several UN vehicles apparently en route to the site (see Figure 3.3). Powell suggests that when looked at together, the satellite images reveal the chemical bunker was "cleaned up" and the decontamination vehicle was removed by the time UN inspectors visited the facility on December 22, 2002. Yet, given the different angles of the images and scales of objects depicted, it is altogether unclear whether the satellite images represent the same bunker and hence whether they

Pre-Inspection Al Fatah Missile Removal Al-Musayyib Rocket Test Facility

10 Nov 2002

Airframes

Missile Storage Canisters

Warhead Canisters

Missile Storage Canisters in Cargo Truck

FIGURE 3.4 Colin Powell presented this November 10, 2002 satellite image to the UN Security Council, alleging it demonstrated missile removal at the Al-Musayyib rocket test facility before a UN weapons inspection visit.

Source: https://georgewbush-whitehouse.archives.gov/news/releases/2003/02/20030205-1.html—public domain

even merit such a comparison. Commenting on Powell's presentation, London-based satellite image expert Bhupendra Jasani indicated it is difficult to accurately identify bases, weapons, and vehicles in these images, admitting, "When I look at it I can't be sure what I'm seeing."[26] Image data itself does not mean anything. It requires a rendering, a frame, and an interpretation.

Powell continued with three more satellite images representing further Iraqi "housecleaning." Each of them, according to Powell, serves as evidence that Iraq dodged the UN weapons inspection process when it resumed in November 2002. The first, entitled "Pre-Inspection Al Fatah Missile Removal Al-Musayyib Rocket Test Facility," dated November 10, 2002, relies on yellow arrows and text to indicate the presence of cargo trucks moving missiles away from the site (see Figure 3.4). In the second image, "Pre-Inspection material Removal Amiriyam Serum and Vaccine Institute," dated November 25, 2002, Powell points to a truck caravan that appeared two days before inspectors arrived (see Figure 3.5). And in the final image, "Pre-Inspection Materiel Removal, Ibn al Haytham," dated November 25, 2002, cargo trucks and a truck-mounted crane were allegedly there to move missiles away from the area just before an inspection (see Figure 3.6). Unlike the first series of images, Powell provided no comparative views of these facilities and left his audience only with his verbal assurance that "Days after this activity, the vehicles and the equipment that I've just highlighted disappear and the site returns to patterns of normalcy." Not only were viewers asked to place blind trust in Powell's word, they were also forced to accept his inconsistent and arbitrary use of satellite images as a form of irrefutable evidence. Why is it, for instance, that some satellite images have full dates and others only specify month and year? Why is it that Powell offers contrasting views of some sites and not others? Which satellites acquired the data used to generate these images? How is it that a handful of US satellite images can supersede an entire UN weapons inspection process taking place on the ground? What is at stake, in other words, is the question of visual literacy—that is, we are asked to view and accept satellite images as visual evidence of Iraq's weapons of mass destruction but there are no conventions or standards among state officials, or members of the public, for using and interpreting geospatial images in a global political forum. Because of this lack of standards and limited public knowledge about

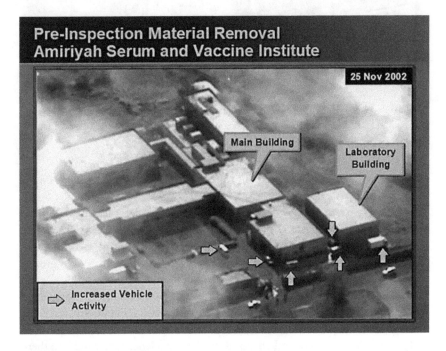

FIGURE 3.5 Colin Powell presented this November 25, 2002 satellite image to the UN Security Council, claiming a truck caravan moved material away from the Amiriyam Serum and Vaccine Institute two days before weapons inspectors arrived.

Source: https://georgewbush-whitehouse.archives.gov/news/releases/2003/02/20030205-1.html—public domain

FIGURE 3.6 Colin Powell presented this November 25, 2002 satellite image to the UN Security Council, indicating cargo trucks and a truck-mounted crane were there to move missiles away from Ibn al Haytham before a UN weapons inspection.

Source: https://georgewbush-whitehouse.archives.gov/news/releases/2003/02/20030205-1.html—public domain

geospatial imagery, Powell was able to use these media to advance the case for war against Iraq.

The final two satellite images Powell presents were used to allege that chemical weapons were transported from Al-Musayyib in May 2002. The entire facility is shown as literally "covered up" with freshly graded earth in a comparative image dated July 2002. Since the latter view is presented from such a greater distance and a much different angle it is virtually impossible, especially for the "lay reader," to determine whether it is actually the same facility. Again we are expected to accept Powell's interpretation of the image: "The topsoil has been removed. The Iraqis literally removed the crust of the earth from large portions of this site in order to conceal chemical weapons evidence that would be there from years of chemical weapons activity."

What was striking about this presentation was Powell's stately use of close analysis. The Secretary of State did precisely the kind of thing that media scholars do—select media content, think about its structure and context, re-view it, decode it, and formulate a thesis about its meaning and significance that can be defended. What is unique about the close analysis of satellite images, however, is that given limited public literacy, the traces of interpretation are typically inscribed upon them, and these traces signify more than the image data itself. Powell makes this clear in his presentation, when he identifies the two arrows as "sure signs" that bunkers are storing chemical munitions, not the bunkers themselves. Discussing another satellite image, he explains, "What makes this picture significant is that we have a human source who has corroborated that movement of chemical weapons occurred at this site at that time. So it's not just the photo and it's not an individual seeing the photo. It's the photo and then the knowledge of an individual being brought together to make the case." Simply put, if these images were not imprinted with red squares and yellow circles and arrows, or anchored by informants on the ground, Powell and his viewers would likely be at a complete loss. As interpretation is encoded into the satellite image, its ontological status becomes that of an image that has been "already read" or perhaps more appropriately in this case, "already spun." Powell's comment also suggests that a "human source" in the vicinity can enhance the evidentiary value of the satellite image by "corroborating" what the satellite reveals, which further complicates the alleged neutrality, transparency, or objectivity often associated with orbital vision.

Because of the abstraction of raw satellite image data, Powell invokes the necessity of "expert analysis." "Sometimes these images are hard for the average person to interpret, hard for me." Powell explains. "It takes experts with years and years of experience poring for hours and hours over light tables" to interpret these images. But his attempts to articulate these images with experts' credibility were ultimately unsuccessful. In the days after his presentation, the press, former intelligence officers, and citizens raised legitimate questions such as "How do we know those are decontamination vehicles?" "How do we know based on these images what is inside those buildings?" "How do we know cargo trucks were moving materials away to be hidden from weapons instructors?" The Independent Media Center in Urbana-Champaign even posted a parody of Powell's satellite photos in which a graduated zoom from the orbital view to a close up shows the back door of a children's school bus filled with the words "decontamination vehicle" on its backside.[27]

For many, the circulation of satellite images and the "expert" interpretations imprinted upon them ultimately aroused further concerns about US motives and positioned the Bush administration as much of a potential threat to global security as Iraq, particularly since the US went to such extreme lengths to rationalize its case for military intervention, refused to listen to members of the UN Security Council, and decided to act unilaterally. The credibility of Powell's presentation was further compromised when Britain's Channel 4 reported that much of its content had been based on a British dossier entitled "Iraq—Its Infrastructure of Concealment, Deception and Intimidation,"[28] plagiarized from an essay by graduate student Ibrahim al-Marashi who had published much of the information in *Middle East Review of International Affairs* months earlier in September 2002. Despite these disturbing discoveries, media critic Normon Solomon has argued Powell remained in a media bubble, insulated from direct challenges and thus seemingly beyond reproach.[29] Yet a decade later Powell indicated that he regreted making this presentation and characterized it as a "great intelligence failure."[30] In hindsight, what is perhaps most troublesome about Powell's (mis)use of US satellite images is that it compromised the credibility of any future use of them by the US in a global forum. Prior to 2003, the US State Department had released satellite images to expose atrocities in other conflict zones. In 1995, Secretary of State Madeline Albright took six weeks to declassify and share crucial satellite evidence of mass graves in the UN-protected safe haven of Srebrenica, Bosnia.[31] At that time, US officials attributed the delayed circulation of the satellite images to infoglut. Data mining, filtering, and pattern recognition software were not yet powerful enough to rapidly sort through huge amounts of satellite image data. Powell's 2003 presentation marked a reversal by circulating satellite images preemptively rather than retrospectively. This shift was consistent with the broader operative logic of the war on terror, which Brian Massumi has conceptualized as one of preemption. As Massumi explains, "The most effective way to fight an unspecified threat is to actively contribute to *producing* it." Preemption involves going "on the offensive to make the enemy emerge from its state of potential and take actual shape. The exercise of . . . power is *incitatory*. It contributes to the actual emergence of the threat."[32] Powell's use of satellite images was designed to just that—this coverage was used not only to monitor weapons, but also to produce the threat of terror in Iraq. After 9/11, practices of vertical mediation—from remote sensing to PSYOPS leafleting from airport screening to targeted killing—were mobilized in US efforts to "make the enemy emerge from its state of potential." US forces used the vertical field to simultaneously produce and mitigate the threat of terror.

While Powell's presentation demonstrated the state's strategic investment in the satellite image, it also revealed that such coverage could be used to expose strategies of power. The satellite images that Powell presented became sites of public scrutiny and critical analysis as well. Mark Dorrian, for instance, argues that Powell's presentation used graphic overlays as "a kind of overwriting" that privileged the interpretations of imagery specialists and buried "the evidential object (the photographic document), covering it over, and almost effacing it with a supplementary graphic and textual discourse."[33] Laura Kurgan characterizes Powell's presentation as exemplifying the "opacity of transparency," explaining that his satellite images "were interpretations presented as facts and in a way that prevented anyone else from examining the uninterpreted data."[34] And Fraser Macdonald, Rachel Hughes, and Klaus Dodds suggest that what emerged from Powell's display was "a set of visual instructions—protocols for looking." It was, they argue, "an attempt to instruct the audience in a particular way of seeing."[35]

As Powell directed viewers to recognize the color coded circles, squares and arrows layered upon these satellite images, he was quite literally asking viewers to *see and read satellite images like a state*. In his book *Seeing Like a State*, James Scott argues that modern states make phenomena legible to assert their social and territorial control. To make things legible, states work in various ways to simplify reality and fit it into their own administrative categories, often discarding local or complex knowledges. Scott characterizes the production of state legibility and power in the following way:

> Certain forms of knowledge and control require a narrowing of vision. The great advantage of such tunnel vision is that it brings into sharp focus certain limited aspects of an otherwise far more complex and un- wieldy reality. This very simplification, in turn, makes the phenomenon at the center of the field of vision more legible and hence more suceptible to careful measurement and calculation. Combined with similar observa- tions, an overall, aggregate, synoptic view of a selective reality is achieved, making possible a high degree of schematic knowledge, control, and manipulation.[36]

Phenomena, Scott further explains, do not even have to actually be seen to be made legible by the state; they simply need to be "read" by examining documents or maps held by the state.[37] This is precisely why interdisciplinary analysis of vertical power is necessary: it works against the tunnel vision of the state and attempts to brings out complexities wherever the state tries to circumscribe or suppress them. By approaching Powell's satellite images as vertical mediations, we begin to see a more multivalent power structure at work.

Though Scott was writing about the rise of modern state in the late eighteenth century, his ideas resonate poignantly with twenty-first-century US efforts to render threats legible in the context of the war on terror. Powell not only used satellite images to produce threats premptively, but also simplified and rendered legible Iraq's alleged weapons of mass destruction at a time of growing concern about US national security and terror attacks around the world. In his presentation, Powell read satellite images like a state: he advanced a "synoptic view" that left no room for alternate readings. The satellite images in Powell's presentation were not offered as sites of discussion or deliberation; rather, they were used to showcase the orbital platforms, image intelligence, and "expert" interpretions that are uniquely able to give the state authority and make its vertical power known. Reading satellite images like a state also involved the power to modulate the classification and declassfication of image intelligence in ways that aligned with broader strategic agendas. Powell read satellite images in a way that reinforced American exceptionalism during the war on terror, which involved using the 9/11 attacks to legitimate any kind of lawful or unlawful action (from surveillance to torture to targeted killings), arbitrarily expanding the territorial scope of the war on terror, and acting pre-emptively and unilaterally to mitigate threats and manage risks.[38]

Despite the fact that members of the intelligence community and global publics objected to Powell's presentation, by March 2003 the US proceeded with a full-fledged "shock and awe" campaign in Iraq, using the air, airwaves, and orbit in a most calculated manner to orchestrate the violent termination of Saddam Hussein's regime. By the time Powell delivered this presentation to the UN Security Council, US military troops had already commandeered Iraqi airspace and airwaves and were conducting PSY-OPS using airplane broadcasting and leafleting, as discussed in Chapter 1. US satellite monitoring of WMDs in Iraq looked relatively innocent when compared to the full-fledged aerial assaults the US waged in the skies above Iraq in the months and years after Powell's presentation. These vertical practices, which ranged from US satellite surveillance to aerial bombardment to telecommunications commandeering— became known in US military parlance as "full spectrum dominance."[39]

Powell's presentation functioned as a key moment in US efforts to assert vertical power and hegemony after 9/11. Never before had a US leader presented such a carefully packaged series of satellite images (and other intelligence) in a global media forum.[40] In the process of making the case for war against Iraq, Powell's presentation integrated satellite images in ways that resonated with CNN coverage after 9/11. While CNN used satellite images to demonstrate that the US could monitor the Taliban from above, Powell deployed them to showcase US monitoring of Hussein's alleged weapons of mass destruction. In both cases, vertical views emphasized US capacity to use orbital platforms and the electromagnetic spectrum to track, document, and/or spin "enemy" activities. In this case, *reading satellite images like a state* involved using vertical views to support preemptive destruction of Hussein's alleged WMDs in the name of "preserving" Iraqi air and territory, including oil resources underground.

The Microphysics of Geospatial Images

The struggle over the meanings and uses of geospatial images requires greater critical attention to their discursive contexts and material specificities. Geospatial images are generated by processing data gathered by aircraft or satellites. Though aerial and satellite images involve different technologies, organizations, and companies, when they circulate in mass media culture they are often used interchangeably and without source information. US State or Defense Department officials who release these images as declassified intelligence usually offer little, if any, detail about the satellite, aircraft or sensing instruments that acquired the image-data. Captions or taglines in the press often reiterate officials' statements or press releases and provide little information about the provenance of the image and sometimes exclude the date of its acquisition. Furthermore, as Powell's presentation implied, it is challenging for most viewers to distinguish a satellite image from an aerial image since both look down on the earth's surface from slightly oblique angles and rely on similar sensing instruments and imaging software. Compounding this confusion is the fact that government agencies, military units, the press, and private companies refer to aerial and satellite images in different ways. When the US State or Defense Department uses aerial or satellite images they are called *reconnaissance* images, and historically have also been referred to as PHOTOINT, IMAGEINT, and, more recently, GEOINT. When geographers or earth scientists use these images they are *remote sensing* or *geospatial images*. Those who want to convey that a satellite or an aircraft acquired the image-data might refer to them as *satellite images* or *aerial images*, or, more vaguely, as *overhead images*. The integration of aerial and satellite imaging, interactive mapping software, graphic design, and computer networking within the NGA and Google Earth has resulted in a shift away from platform-specific terminology (satellite reconnaissance) and toward the more integrative concept of *geospatial imagery or intelligence* or GEOINT.

This section is focused on geospatial imagery gathered by contemporary remote-sensing satellites. These satellites are equipped with instruments that can detect visible light and other frequencies of electromagnetic radiation reflected off of or emanating from objects or surfaces on earth. As Jody Berland suggests, remote sensing augments human perception by making phenomena visible that would not otherwise be perceived.[41] A geospatial image in the visible light register reveals surfaces and objects on the ground as well as the sunlight or artificial light reflecting off of them, which is what makes them visible. A geospatial image in the infrared register shows surfaces and objects on the ground via the infrared or thermal radiation that they emanate. Infrared radiation has longer wavelengths than visible light and is imperceptible to the naked eye. Infrared geospatial images can show the relative temperature of objects and surfaces on or below the earth's surface, and are also used to increase in-the-dark visibility because they reveal the contours of surfaces and objects based on their thermal radiation rather than their reflection of visible light. As a result, infrared images are often used to track and target heat-bearing objects such as energy plants, communication transmitters, moving vehicles, weapons, or human bodies, as will be discussed further in Chapter 4.

As remote-sensing satellites move through low earth orbits, they pass over and scan particular areas of the earth's surface, turning those areas into swaths or scene footprints. Commercial satellites such as Ikonos, QuickBird, and the KH-11 and KH-12 spy satellites, all used in the wars in Afghanistan and Iraq, carry multi-spectral sensors that detect radiation across various parts of the electromagnetic spectrum, from visible light to infrared to radio waves. Multispectral sensing is geared toward the production of efficient and information-rich geospatial imagery, since data across multiple frequencies of the spectrum can be simultaneously collected during one satellite pass. For instance, multispectral sensors on QuickBird collect data in the blue, green, red, and near infrared bands, which can be used to generate images with resolutions ranging from 60 centimeters to 2.4 meters.[42] Quickbird has a storage capacity of 128 Gigabits, which is equivalent to approximately 57 single area images. A single image represents an area of 18 × 18 km and Quickbird can revisit a site every 1–3.5 days. Quickbird's replacement satellites, WorldView-1 and -2, were financed in part by the National Geospatial Intelligence Agency and launched in 2007 and 2009, respectively. Worldview-1 can gather 750,000 square kilometers of 0.5-meter resolution imagery per day.[43] Another commercial satellite, GeoEye-1, funded by the NGA and Google, was launched in 2008 and can acquire images with 16-inch ground resolution.[44] In 2014 the US Department of Commerce approved DigitalGlobe's license to sell imagery of even higher resolution. The company successfully launched Worldview-3, which acquires 0.31-meter resolution imagery, and moved its Worldview-1 satellite into another orbit so that its constellation could "monitor changes on earth at various times during the day."[45] This higher resolution and "temporal diversity," DigitalGlobe promised, would "help our customers see the earth more clearly."[46]

Since 9/11 the NRO has increasingly relied on commercial satellite imagery from operators such as SpaceImaging and DigitalGlobe. Because commercial remote-sensing satellites are not subject to the strict classification rules of NRO satellites, their imagery can be shared more readily with coalition partners.[47] As in other spheres of government and military affairs, services in the geospatial sector once carried out by state agencies are being outsourced to commercial entities. As one news report in the weeks after 9/11 put it, "the appetite for satellite information has become ravenous . . . the US government is gobbling up unclassified satellite imagery. . . ."[48] Commercial remote-sensing operators have been able to composite data from multiple satellites and produce comprehensive coverage of a country or region often more quickly than the NRO. Since the war on terror involves so many battlefronts and coalition partners, being able to rapidly share unclassified commercial geospatial images with allies has become not just a matter of convenience, but of national security.

Given this, the NRO and NGA have recently publicized their growing reliance on commercial GEOINT. In 2015 the NGA released a "Commercial GEOINT Strategy" that emphasized the agency's "commitment to harnessing unclassified sources of GEOINT as the foundation for global awareness and persistence." The report further explained that the "NGA requires a seamless integration of all GEOINT, regardless of source or classification, to enable anticipatory analysis and to create online, living knowledge that reduces the time between questions and answers. . . ."[49] In 2016 the NRO—which collects satellite imagery—and the NGA—which processes and interprets that imagery— announced a collaboration called "Commercial GEOINT Activity," designed to "help their organizations exploit commercial satellite imagery," by, as one expert put it, "leveraging everything that commercial industry has and minimizing stovepipes."[50]

While Colin Powell may have read satellite images like a state, such NRO and NGA "leveraging" reveals that state-run war is being replaced by commercially run war. Commercial satellite operators are outpacing state agencies in terms of technical innovation, revenue generation, and regulatory workarounds. Such corporate advances pose challenges to state sovereignty. As Inderpal Grewal argues, US sovereignty has largely been devolved from the state to private corporations and citizens, who perform work that the state previously did, including military actions.[51] Within the context of such conditions, the capacity to understand the material production of satellite imagery and alternate modes of engaging with it become all the more vital.

Once a satellite gathers data, it is temporarily stored, encrypted, and transmitted back to earth where it is archived in databases. To generate a satellite image, a user must extract data from the database and calibrate it using radiance and geolocation software so that it can be rendered as a grid or raster made up of pixels. For each pixel in the image there are multiple channels of information that can be activated, depending on how many frequencies of the spectrum data was collected in. These channels or registers can be turned on or off during image processing to support what the user seeks to view, convey, or highlight in the image. These images can appear in black and white or color and can be used comparatively or composited or "mosaicked" together. When declassified geospatial images are publicly released and discussed by US officials, they often appear in black and white and are inscribed with various graphics that are designed to guide interpretation.[52] Graphic inscriptions render geospatial images intelligible as they circulate in mass media culture, and articulate these images with particular geopolitical agendas.

The geospatial image is one of the most technologized kinds of image, since its production is based on so many layers of machine automation—remote sensing, data encryption, signal transmission, data storage, and image processing. As a rendering of detected electromagnetic radiation, the geospatial image is a computational image: its view has been scanned by electronic sensors rather than seen through a looking glass. While it is somewhat in vogue in media studies to celebrate the machinic aspects of computational images,[53] there is a tendency to overlook the myriad forms of human labor that support their production. To think of the geospatial image as purely machinic or computational, I would argue, ignores its complex materialisms—the scattering of materials, labor, energy, affect, and discourse that undergirds its production, circulation, and signification. Despite the computational status of the geospatial image, humans participate in the design and manufacture of satellites and sensing instruments and extract natural resources to make them. They monitor interfaces in earth stations to track these objects from afar and determine which parts of the earth they scan. They navigate software menus and make decisions in the process of rendering and interpreting image data. They use geospatial images to advance scientific arguments, make business speculations, and carry out military assaults. And humans and non-humans across the planet are profoundly impacted by such uses. Since the geospatial image is as reliant upon humans as it is upon machines, it makes more sense to approach it as part of a techno-social formation, actor network, or human–machine assemblage than it does to posit it as an autonomous technical form. The geospatial image is made not only by remotely controlled aerial and orbital machines; it is arguably the product of janitors who ensured the clean room was "clean," communications specialists who track satellites, and mechanics who fueled rockets before take-off. The geospaptial image is also produced through algorithms that are created by human laborers, even if their labor has been turned into code.[54]

Part of a techno-social formation, the geospatial image is, like other images, imbricated within what Michel Foucault calls the "microphysics of power"—the strategies, tactics, techniques, and concrete functionings of power.[55] The transformation of electromagnetic radiation into data, image, and discourse brings it within the realm of power and enables it to affect and become part of—to mediate, in a most vital way—human and non-human relations, territories, and actions on and beyond the earth. As Foucault insists, power can move "through progressively finer channels, gaining access to individuals themselves, to their bodies, their gestures and all their daily actions."[56] Like multispectral satellite coverage, power is mobilized across multiple "bandwidths" and generates higher "resolutions." It sets out to make everything and everybody visible. Though the geospatial image can be understood as participating in the quest for what Foucault calls "power through transparency" or "subjection by illumination," its unique qualities—namely, its capacity to detect the presence of human *and non-human phenomena* such as radiation, landscapes, vegetation, animals, and objects—compels a recognition of its potential to activate imaginings of difference, estrangement, and Otherness.[57] Satellite coverage, as discussed in the last section, can be used strategically to expose or illuminate some matters while overlooking or covering up others.

The aesthetic qualities of geospatial imagery at once make us to strain to see the human significance in its abstraction and demand object-oriented modes of engagement as it always renders phenomena that are non-human. To embolden the analysis of power and geospatial imagery, we might turn to recent formulations by Jane Bennett and Graham Harman, who develop critical theories and philosophies to account for the presence and dynamism of non-human entities, objects, and matter. Bennett sets out "to highlight what is typically cast in the shadow: the material agency or effectivity of nonhuman or not-quite-human things."[58] In the process of elaborating a theory of "vibrant matter," she argues:

> . . . the image of dead or thoroughly instrumentalized matter feeds human hubris and our earth-destroying fantasies of conquest and consumption. It does so by preventing us from detecting (seeing, hearing, smelling, tasting, feeling) a fuller range of nonhuman powers circulating around and within

human bodies. These material powers, which can aid or destroy, enrich or disable, ennoble or degrade us, in any case call for our attentiveness or even "respect". . . .[59]

Significantly, she asks:

How would political responses to public problems change were we to take seriously the vitality of (nonhuman) bodies? By 'vitality' I mean the capacity of things –edibles, commodities, storms, metals—not only to impede or block the will and designs of humans but also to act as quasi agents or forces with trajectories, propensities, or tendencies of their own.[60]

Seeing satellite images like a state—that is, approaching them only as views or documents of human ("terrorist") activities—negates the agential capacities of multiple kinds of materials and objects in the visual field. This tendency reinforces a humanist verticality that is premised upon social hierarchies and fantasies of control inherited from centuries of imperialism and conquest.

Emergent philosophies focused upon objects suggest that the geospatial image could be read and used differently. Graham Harman insists we must account for objects "that are neither physical nor even real," explaining, "Along with diamonds, rope, and neutrons, objects may include armies, monsters, square circles, and leagues of real and fictitious nations. All such objects must be accounted for by ontology, not merely denounced or reduced to despicable nullities."[61] For Harman, "Objects are units that both display and conceal a multitude of traits."[62] Emphasizing the idea that the ontology of objects exceeds the visible he sets out to describe "how objects relate to their own visible and invisible qualities, to each other, and to our own minds—all in a single metaphysics."[63] Beyond this, Harman embraces the complexity of objects and suggests they have realities that are distinct from human subjects or consciousness. He writes, "Objects need not be natural, simple, or indestructible. Instead, objects will be defined only by their autonomous reality. They must be autonomous in two separate directions: emerging as something over and above their pieces, while also partly withholding themselves from relations with other entities."[64] Ultimately, Harman offers a philosophy that refuses reductionism, and insists ". . . the world in itself is made of realities withdrawing from all conscious access."[65]

Taking the ideas of Bennett and Harman into consideration would entail not only treating satellites and their images as vibrant matter or complex objects, but also recognizing that objects have visible and invisible qualities, the capacity to become something beyond themselves, and to have relations to other objects. Satellite images, for instance, always mediate a multitude of objects, non-human bodies, and vital things—air, trees, buildings, vehicles, lands, plants, rock, snow, insects, minerals, roads, etc. Such objects are often latent or dormant in the visual field, perceptible but unintelligible, present but not seen, locatable but without a position in a story or discourse. I call this the *surplus matter of geospatial imagery*—the earthly stuff that is detected by sensors and turned into imagery yet appears as background or peripheral and hence is not immediately registered as significant or of interest. The geospatial image becomes part of the microphysics of power not only by mediating sites and objects of interest but also by *overlooking*—myriad other material forms—both in the sense of passing over and in the sense of abstracting and minimizing their presence and/or significance. Approaching such an image as *coverage* involves recognizing and rendering intelligible buried or suppressed forms. Coverage is not simply a view that passes over; it is the excavation—the critical mapping—necessitated by a socio-technical system that can "overview" and, hence, "overlook." The geospatial image's broad inventory of surplus objects and phenomena beckons the viewer to recognize the complex materialisms that constitute this view. The surplus matter of the geospatial image complicates, destabilizes, and obstructs its strategic/militaristic deployment. Put another way, lurking within every geospatial image's registry of spectral radiation is a story to be plumbed about vibrant matter.

Strategic US uses of geospatial images can be complicated by the traits of objects included in or inferred by the views. For instance, in the weeks after 9/11, US news media circulated several DigitalGlobe satellite images allegedly revealing "enemy hideouts" in the Darunta Lake region of Afghanistan, discussed in Chapter 1.[66] Like those in Powell's presentation, these images use squares and arrows to identify particular sites as significant, while flattening the stature of the mountains nearby. As geological objects with massive scale, solidity, and vertical depth, these mountains are challenging to navigate on the ground or from the air, and there have been countless stories about US troops' inability to physically maneuver through such treacherous terrain in Afghanistan, which became a rationale for drone warfare. Excavating and raising questions about the surplus matter in such images—in this case, the mountains—can complicate the ways in which graphics are used to overdetermine geospatial images as targets, and bring Other matter, whether visible or inferred, to the surface. The geological composition and topography of mountainous terrain poses challenges to satellite imaging. Topographic effects can cause a difference in radiance values between inclined and horizontal surfaces.[67] Satellite images of mountain areas, especially, require "geometric or ortho-rectification . . . to overcome the distortions related to the sensor (e.g., jitter, view angle effects), satellite (e.g., attitude deviations from nominal), and Earth (e.g., rotation, curvature, relief)."[68] Recognizing such factors not only acknowledges the challenges that mountains pose to geospatial imaging, but also registers the potential of these objects to obstruct or complicate strategies of precision targeting.

To delineate another object-oriented geospatial analysis, we can turn to satellite images of bombed communication infrastructure sites in Afghanistan and Iraq. Declassified images released by the US Defense Department show before and after scenes of targeted sites (see Figure 3.7), and, in so doing, infer the

FIGURE 3.7 This satellite image demonstrates that the US Defense Department bombed an Iraqi television station in March 2003, but it also serves as a reminder the US cannot destroy the electromagnetic spectrum.

Source: https://commons.wikimedia.org/wiki/File%3AUS_Navy_030327-D-0000X-001_A_pre-strike_and_post-strike_photo_of_a_Television_and_Communications_Facility_in_Iraq_shown_in_a_press_conference_with_embedded_media_in_the_media_center_in_Qatar.jpg—public domain, via Wikimedia Commons

presence of invisible objects—frequencies of the electromagnetic spectrum that carry military and civilian communication to and from such sites via vertical domains.[69] Like mountains, such frequencies can be used to complicate or thwart US military actions, hence the forceful annihilation of the facilities that carry these frequencies. The US attacks on communication infrastructure sites may have disrupted access to and use of the airwaves by Iraqi and Taliban military units from these sites, but these attacks could not destroy the spectrum itself. The radio frequency bands of the spectrum have extensive and elusive properties and, as such, pose challenges for US vertical hegemony. Frequencies can be used, intercepted, jammed, and/or commandeered, as discussed in Chapter 1, but the phenomenon of radiation or dynamically moving wavelengths cannot simply be contained. The persistence of the spectrum contests vertical domination by creating a space of radiographic potential. In an era in which the US military audaciously claims to have the power to see, know, and destroy everything, it is worth adopting a diffractive position in relation to such geospatial images, and using them (perhaps paradoxically) to acknowledge that some things cannot simply be seen and destroyed.

In making this point, I do not mean at all to diminish the horrific and systematic military violence that US troops have perpetrated on people and things in Afghanistan and Iraq during the past decades. Rather, I am seeking to formulate a post-humanist critique of geospatial images that acknowledges the humans and non-humans that are constitutive of and connected to these views and their uses, and to highlight the wide array of organic and inorganic objects, materialities, or phenomena that are part of any war theater and thus are potentially impacted by geospatial imaging and aerial assaults. Even though the US has been able to visualize and attack sites throughout Afghanistan and Iraq from above, insurgents in both countries have used ground tactics to challenge US vertical hegemony, reinforcing the reality that it technologized power is not total. Developing critical dispositions and literacies in relation to geospatial images seems all the more urgent given their ongoing use in military campaigns, their integration within everyday media culture, and the billions of US taxpayer dollars spent on generating them. And while I want to explore different ways of critically engaging with geospatial images, I also want to consider how the commercialization of geospatial imaging and its integration within media culture is articulated with broader hegemonic efforts to control the vertical field and materially reorder life in Afghanistan and Iraq.

From Shutter Control to Google Earth

In 2000 the US Departments of Commerce, State, Defense, and Interior and members of the Intelligence community signed an inter-agency memorandum called the Shutter Control Rule. The rule authorizes the US Government to shut down US commercial remote-sensing operators whenever national security concerns dictate, such as in time of armed conflict. This capability is deemed of great importance to military operations as it ensures that high-resolution imagery depicting US military maneuvers, facilities. and personnel locations will not be made available to the general public by US satellite operators.[70] Commercial remote-sensing operators, journalists, and humanitarian organizations objected to the rule for various reasons. Satellite operators asserted that the conditions for implementation were vague, that there were no clear guidelines as to when shutter control may be invoked, and that the rules could damage the business of the remote-sensing industry.[71] Journalists argued that shutter control violated the First Amendment of the US Constitution.[72] Early on Barbara Cochran, president of Radio Television News Directors Association, called the rule "unconstitutional, a violation of the First Amendment right of the press to publish or broadcast without government interference. . . ."[73] She went on to argue that with the use of satellite images, "stories can be more accurate and truthful and can give the public access to geographic areas that are politically inaccessible or too expensive to get to."[74] Claims were made that government exercise of shutter control "constitutes prior restraint of publication of the image" in that it was a government action that would prevent important communication from reaching the public.[75] Finally, humanitarian organizations that use satellite images in relief efforts objected to the shutter control rule on the grounds that it would slow down the process of getting aid to those who need it.[76]

Given the various objections and the threat of constitutional litigation, the US government has been reticent to officially exercise shutter control. In October 2001, however, as the US military prepared to attack the Taliban in Afghanistan, the National Geospatial Intelligence Agency entered into a contract with Space Imaging Corporation (SIC, which later became GeoEye) that allowed the agency exclusive access to all of SIC's Ikonos satellite imagery of Afghanistan. The US government paid $2 million per month for three months of exclusive access to the imagery.[77] By purchasing exclusive rights of access to Ikonos images for a short term, the US government transformed shutter control into a financial transaction, and denied news agencies grounds to sue the federal government for violating the first amendment (prior restraint). This act of "checkbook shutter control" blocked news agencies and humanitarian organizations from accessing the only available high-resolution US commercial satellite images of Afghanistan during the first three months of the war, whether to conduct independent investigations of war casualties, or to provide assistance to displaced persons and refugees throughout the region.[78]

After January 2002 when the exclusive licenses expired, Space Imaging made Ikonos satellite images of Afghanistan commercially available. In a matter of years, Afghanistan and Iraq went from being strictly regulated visual domains to ones open for anyone in the world to see as Google Earth, which emerged in 2005, circulated geospatial images of these war-torn countries as part of a new form of commercial media culture. As geospatial images have become more widely available through the Internet, strategic practices historically associated with intelligence agencies such as the NRO and NGA have been normalized as part of everyday civilian life, creating a culture of open-source geointelligence (GEOINT) on demand. In this sense, Google Earth not only serves as another media site for circulating geospatial imagery; it is also a material enactment and manifestation of a set of technological, economic, and political relations between federal intelligence agencies and the commercial geospatial sector. Though its composited interface is made of geospatial image data gathered and licensed by state and commercial satellite and aircraft operators around the world, its digital architecture—that is, the capacity to arrange and display the world in this way—is the intellectual property of Google and the result of a history of coordinated federal and corporate financial, technological, and political transactions.

The Google Earth interface turns this model of GEOINT on demand into a privatized consumer media experience that is accessible as a download on computers and smart phones. The interface is made of composited, publicly and privately sourced aerial and satellite imagery that is periodically updated. Datasets turned into graphic displays known as "layers" can be formatted as kmz or kml files and dropped into Google Earth so they can be superimposed on the geo-spatial interface. Not only is geospatial imagery in Google Earth highly processed and composited, it is covered up with icons, shading, and text as layers are activated. This results in a version of geospatial imagery that is so heavily inscribed with graphics that the initial image data recedes and becomes little more than a background for the inscription of iconography. Like Colin Powell's presentation, the Google Earth interface attempts to regulate how one reads geospatial images and offers a specific way of reading them. Like CNN and Fox News coverage, discussed in Chapter 1, Google Earth presents the cartographic and vertical perspectives in ways that celebrate US state and corporate power, articulating geospatial views as worldviews. Such vertical mediations work to normalize US digitization and corporatized ownership of overhead views of all the world's sovereign territories.

As Google Earth assembles and asserts US vertical hegemony in this way, it reduces the potential for public geospatial image literacy by instrumentalizing the image. When the Digital Globe layer is activated, color-coded square lines and DG brand icons appear in the visual field (see Figure 3.8). The color-coded square lines, called "scene footprints," function as traces of a satellite's pass over a specific part of the earth. When composited, they form a historical record of satellite image data acquisitions during a certain time period, as well as reveal a slice of Digital Globe's inventory. The Google Earth interfaces of Afghanistan and Iraq provide Digital Globe satellite coverage from 2002–2010. Clicking on a DG icon opens a frame with data about the image including the acquisition

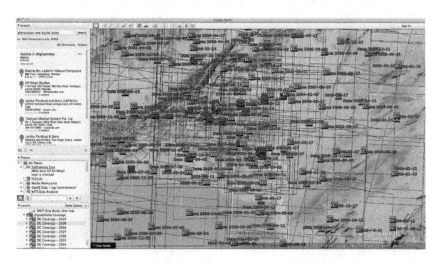

FIGURE 3.8 When the Digital Globe layer is activated in Google Earth, color-coded square lines known as "scene footprints" and Digital Globe icons appear in the visual field.

Source: Google Earth. Screen capture used under the Fair Use Doctrine

date, cloud cover, and an environmental quality rating. If the user clicks on "preview," she/he enters a meta-browser featuring the single satellite image captioned with information about how to purchase it or others from Digital Globe.

The US exercised "checkbook shutter control" to restrict access to satellite imagery of Afghanistan for three months in 2001, but military use of commercial satellite imagery intensified so much after 9/11 that by 2005 Google, Digital Globe, and GeoEye (previously, Space Imaging Corporation) created an international business that turned the territories of Afghanistan and Iraq (as well as those of other countries) into digital real estate—intellectual property produced, owned, and distributed by US corporations. Just as the leveling of communication infrastructure provided opportunities for US contractors to restructure and rebuild Afghan and Iraqi broadcast and telecom systems, as discussed in Chapter 1, Google Earth's vertical mediation of Afghanistan and Iraq was designed to boost the business potentials and profits of US companies as the geospatial image has been used both to stage the eradication of Taliban and Hussein systems and as a platform upon which to imagine, design, and map new ones. In this way, the geospatial image is implicated not in the benevolent production of overhead views, but in the material restructuring or vertical mediation of nation-states. As described in the examples below, aero-orbital platforms are not only technologies of monitoring, but of inscription. This coverage is articulated with processes that involve the material restructuring or "rewriting" of conditions on, around and beneath the earth's surface.

Mediascaping

Google Earth has been used, for instance, to map Iraq's newly privatized media sector. A layer called "Iraq Media Mapping" released by the Open Source Center visualizes a plethora of new commercial television and radio networks that sprouted up in Iraq after the fall of Saddam Hussein's regime and during the US occupation (see Figure 3.9). The interactive layer specifies the names of TV and radio stations, the locations of their headquarters and transmitters, and potential audience size, and uses color-coded shading to indicate the stations' coverage zones. While the layer provides a useful overview of the media industry within Iraq, many of the key stakeholders of Iraq's media system exist beyond the country's borders. Several of the new Iraqi TV networks were developed through US Defense Department contracts or are owned by wealthy Iraqis in exile. Al Iraqiya, for instance, an Iraqi news and entertainment TV network, was founded as Iraqi Media Network in 2003 and developed by US defense contractor Science Applications International Corporation for an initial no-bid contract of $82.3 million, which was supplemented by hundreds of millions of dollars.[79] Another TV network, Al Sharqiya, was launched in 2004 and is owned by Iraqi media tycoon Saad Al-Bazzaz who lives between London and Dubai.[80] And TV

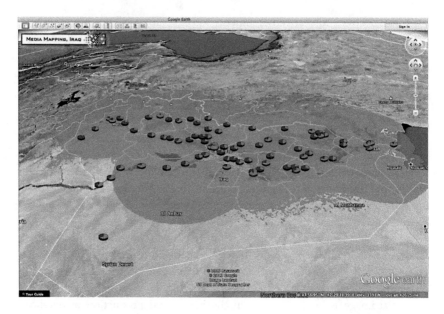

FIGURE 3.9 The Media Mapping Iraq layer in Google Earth demonstrates the mediascaping of Iraq after the 2003 war.

Source: Open Source Data Center. Screen capture used under the Fair Use Doctrine

channel, Al Baghdadiya, which emerged in 2005, is owned by Cairo-based Iraqi businessman, Awn Al Khashlouk. These US-supported networks emerged after US military airplane broadcasting and leafleting programs traversed Iraqi skies in 2003, delivering PSY-OPS messages and inaugurating the overhaul of the Iraqi broadcast system. These new commercial networks replaced the media system controlled by Saddam Hussein and emerged to provide national and local services and compete with other Arab-language networks such as Al Jazeera. This Google Earth interface remediates Iraq as multiple layers of media privatization: it inscribes the footprints of new private broadcast networks' upon commercial geospatial imagery that is accessible through a digital platform owned by Google. In this carefully mediascaped environment, geospatial images are used not only to map media privatization, but also to enact it. US vertical hegemony produces conditions in which Iraqis in Iraq have minimal ownership or control over their airwaves or geospatial images of their sovereign territory.

Similar projects exist in relation to Afghanistan. For instance, InterNews posted a geospatial interface called "Media Landscape in Afghanistan," based on 2010 data gathered by Altai Consulting in a USAID-funded project (see Figure 3.10).[81] The interface provides information about population size, literacy rates, and electrical access as well as preferred medium use across all districts of Afghanistan and across urban, suburban, and rural areas within a given district. The visualization revealed that while many had access to radio and television, very few had access to the Internet. Though this interface provides useful demographic information about media use in Afghanistan, it is important to raise the question of who its presumed audience is. Given the focus on medium access across various districts and population sizes, the interface functions as much as an invitation to foreign media developers and investors as it does as a resource for Afghani civilians, for it enables interested parties to identify and exploit market opportunities. The geospatial interface presents a baseline of Afghanistan's media infrastructure and, given limited conditions, calls forth further media prospecting and privatization—or what I call mediascaping. Contemporary mediascaping involves the use of geospatial images, digital platforms, and other resources (including military force) to organize, visualize, and implement the privatization of media sectors.

Rather than read these geospatial interfaces as simple tales of "media development," I argue that this coverage showcases US efforts to use orbit-to-ground platforms to meddle in sovereign countries' airspace and airwaves—to map, monitor, and shape Afghani and Iraqi ownership and control over media systems in the name of fighting terrorism. In this way, such geospatial campaigns can be understood as part of what Matt Sienkiewicz calls "the other air force," a "soft psy" approach to US media intervention that involves the "melding of market-oriented 'soft power' strategies with more rigid and content-oriented ideas typified my military 'psyops.'"[82] The mediascaping of Iraq and Afghanistan

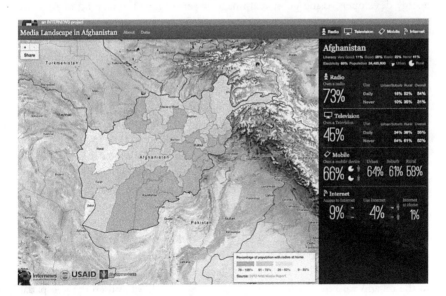

FIGURE 3.10 Internews' Media Landscape in Afghanistan interface provides information about the use of media technologies that also can be used to support mediascaping by foreigners.

Source: http://data.internews.org/af-media/—screen capture used under the Fair Use Doctrine

via geospatial interfaces is fully continuous with the "psyops" practices of airplane broadcasting and leafleting discussed in Chapter 1. These geospatial interfaces make US vertical strategies intelligible, providing overviews of the calculated and coercive "liberalization" of others' airwaves and territories.

Resource Speculation

In addition to mapping the commercial restructuring of Iraq's broadcast sector, US geospatial imagery has also been used to identify other forms of material value near sites that have been bombed or destroyed. The US Geological Survey has used DigitalGlobe satellite images and geographic information systems (GIS) more refined than Google Earth, such as ArcGIS, to scout natural resources in Afghanistan and Iraq and share this information with interested parties and investors.[83] Geospatial images have been used to pinpoint Afghanistan's coal, oil, and natural gas, mineral, and hydrologic assets, and function as treasure maps or invitations for foreign corporate development and extraction.[84] As the USGS explains, geospatial data sets are "vital to short-term and long-range planning regarding management of these resources, as well as for identifying potential new resources that may attract foreign investment and create employment opportunities for Afghans."[85] The organization even offers geospatial "information packages" as well as an interactive "Afghanistan Oil and Natural Gas Viewer" for potential energy developers, using geospatial images to encourage the tapping of Afghani resources under ground.[86] Here the geospatial image becomes part of extractive geo-economic strategies that resemble colonial-era practices. What differs, however, is the way in which the widespread availability of such images through the web and Google Earth has the effect of normalizing these views as ethical.

When US agencies use geospatial imagery to spot and exploit valuable resources beneath the earth's surface, they participate in vertical mediation. A US strategy in the war on terror has been to control the flow of resources so that terrorist organizations are unable to use them. Thus, satellite coverage is used not only to locate materials of value, but also to organize and monitor the processes of extraction. Such processes are vertical and topographical: they rely on satellites to transform terrain, infrastructure, and lifeworlds on and beneath the earth's surface. Whether reorganizing Afghan and Iraqi broadcast spectrum or identifying natural resources, when satellite coverage identifies material of value, it becomes highly coveted and protected as a site of wealth in its own right. Thus, in addition to restructuring the earth's surface, geospatial imagery cultivates economic development at many levels, from intellectual property of the image data itself to the oil and gas reserves that such data locates. The US has used the geospatial image as a technology of privatization and globalization in efforts to divert resource wealth into the pockets of allies and away from terrorist organizations.

Such vertical mediation practices have taken shape in relation to Afghanistan's mineral deposits as well. In 2014 NBC news reported "Afghanistan Sits on

$1 Trillion in Minerals," and presented a list of rare earth and other elements found there by US researchers. Combining aerial surveys and past data from the Soviet Union,[87] researchers located geological reserves throughout the country and reportedly found 60 million tons of copper, 2.2 billion tons of iron ore, 1.4 million tons of rare earth elements such as lanthanum, cerium, and neodymium, and aluminum, gold, silver, zinc, and lithium as well.[88] US researchers began conducting magnetic gravity and hyperspectral aerial surveys in 2006 and mapped 70% of the country's territory in two months. One article describes these surveys as "treasure maps," which "let the mining companies know what minerals are there, how much is there, and where they are, all to attract bids on the rights to the deposits."[89] Like maps, geospatial images become sites of prospecting and valuation as foreign companies compete for rights to extract and sell these materials. Such images are also used by the USGS to train Afghani geologists how to use remote sensing to "sustainably develop" their natural resources. Whether the USGS and foreign companies have the right to remotely sense, map, and develop Afghanistan's natural resources is never questioned or deliberated. Some reports, however, emphasize that foreign surveying and development of natural resources in Afghanistan is challenging because of security risks and energy infrastructure issues.[90]

Though cartographic prospecting of natural resources in Afghanistan has taken place for centuries, since 9/11 the US military and USGS and have used geospatial imagery to remediate and lay claim to the country's vertical domains (air, airwaves, and geology) as a counterterrorism strategy. Just as the media mapping layer of Iraq enacts media privatization, geospatial imagery of natural resources in Afghanistan invites excavation by foreign entities willing to contend with security risks and energy infrastructure challenges in the country. Geospatial images not only serve as "treasure maps" by mediating the geological layers beneath the earth's surface and making sites of value visible and available to developers, but also function as vertical mediations by bringing forth material transformations above and beneath the earth's surface.[91] Natural resource development alters the air above, geological layers and aquaducts beneath, and economies upon the earth's surface.

Monitoring Reconstruction

At the same time that geospatial systems are being used for mediascaping and resource prospecting, organizations such as USAID have adopted Google Earth to track and verify the flow and use of reconstruction funding, which is sometimes parachuted into remote regions. Given the corrupt handling of US reconstruction funds in Afghanistan (billions are siphoned out of Afghanistan each year), USAID grantee Mercy Corps sends Afghani partners to contentious or remote regions with GPS cameras to photograph people performing work leading to the fulfillment of US contracts. The photos are uploaded into a "Google Earth-style program" so that Mercy Corps "can track projects and their participants."[92] The system, reportedly, allows Mercy Corps to "extend its reach" and work in areas where "it's too insecure to work, or too remote."[93] This program was created in response to the "cash exodus" of nearly $1 billion per year intended for Afghanistan, but often ending up in the Gulf region.[94] Here, Google Earth and geospatial imagery are used to remotely monitor financial flows and reconstruction processes—to ensure that projects on the ground conform to externally developed plans and visions.

While Mercy Corps uses these technologies to ensure proper use of funds and project completion at the local level, satellite images have also exposed problematic reconstruction projects. For instance, in 2015 the Special Inspector General of Afghanistan Reconstruction (SIGAR), John F. Sopko, released a report entitled "$36 million Command and Control Center at Camp Leatherneck, Afghanistan: Unwanted, Unneeded, and Unused," describing the construction of a 64,000 square foot military headquarters building that was never used.[95] In its coverage, *The Washington Post* published a series of Digital Globe satellite images released by the Special Inspector General for Afghanistan Reconstruction (SIGAR) in May 2015 showing the development and abandonment of this command and control building between 2011 and 2015. The satellite images reveal the construction of a massive white building at Camp Leatherneck between April 2011 and January 2014. As *The Washington Post* noted, such images "would not typically be released while the U.S. military was using the base, but concerns appear to have waned now that the military drawdown there is complete."[96] Just as geospatial images can be used to monitor aid implementation in remote areas, they can be used to expose the US Defense Department's miscommunication and mismanagement of reconstruction funds.

While geospatial imagery operationalizes practices of vertical mediation to control material conditions such as financial flows and reconstruction projects, coverage can also expose the limits, challenges, or impossibilities of such projects. The monitoring of postwar reconstruction projects in Afghanistan by US organizations continues to be a challenge due to conditions in what the SIGAR describes as "high risk areas." These activities range from Taliban attacks to staffing issues in various ministries, from corruption to poor contract management. Between 2002 and 2016, the US spent $113 billion on Afghanistan reconstruction projects. In 2017 the SIGAR requested an additional $54.9 million to continue the projects, while recognizing that challenges in monitoring the use of these funds persist.[97] In his Congressional request for a new budget allocation, the SIGAR stated, ". . . the risk of fraud, waste, and abuse of reconstruction funds in Afghanistan is growing, even as the ability to exercise effective oversight is increasingly constrained."[98] Within this context, geospatial imagery and GPS are perceived as essential tools of remote governance and management, and their presence works to rationalize and secure funding allocations, as grantors anticipate funds can be tracked. As the SIGAR indicates, his organization "has expanded its use of remote monitoring and geospatial imaging" by working with the National Geospatial Intelligence Agency and, like Mercy Corps, uses "third-party monitors to go where SIGAR employees cannot . . . checking Global Positioning System data against satellite photos."[99] Such practices turn the tracking of aid and monitoring of reconstruction in Afghanistan into vertical mediations that regulate where money flows and whether projects are completed.

Predictive Analytics

In addition to supporting media sector restructuring, natural resource speculation, and reconstruction initiatives, geospatial images have been used to track insurgents' movements in Afghanistan and Iraq and formulate predictive analytics designed to mitigate improvised explosive device (IED) attacks. In 2009 the Open Source Data Center released a detailed report (including a Google Earth layer) about insurgent incidents that occurred in Afghanistan and the FATA region of Pakistan between 2004 and 2008, offering a "hot spot" analysis designed to "provide valuable information for those responsible for operations in the region."[100] The Google Earth layer enables users to view the data in different ways, according to incident density, deaths, wounded, kidnappings, and perpetrators. Using data from the National Counterterrorism Center's Worldwide Incidents Tracking System, the report mapped a total of 4,129 incidents and projected their locations onto a Landsat image. During the four-year period, 64% of the incidents were allegedly committed by the Taliban, 42% were caused by IEDs, and 36% were armed attacks. Like weather forecasters using geospatial imagery to predict the intensity of a storm, Open Source Data Center analysts assess past data to predict the location of future insurgent attacks coding high-probability areas in sienna and low-probability areas in yellow. As Mark Andrejevic suggests, the tendency of such projects "is to portray predictive analytics as a crystal ball whose view of the future becomes clearer with every new piece of data about the present—as if at the very point when we can capture the entirety of the present in a database, the future will simultaneously be pinned down."[101] In this context, coverage is mobilized in an attempt control the future, and vertical mediation becomes as much an intervention in time as in space. US agencies' use of geospatial images to monitor past IED attacks and predict future ones is implicated in what I have called *diachronic omniscience*—the strategic use of satellite images to claim the capacity to see from above and through time.[102]

While geospatial interfaces have been used in efforts to predict IED attacks, they have also been used to visualize violence against journalists in Afghanistan. In 2011 an organization called Nai Supporting Open Media in Afghanistan released a geospatial interface documenting violence against journalists in Afghanistan based on data from 2001–2011, and the visualization was updated in 2017 (see Figure 3.11). When first released the map registered a total of 266 incidents, and this figure jumped to 722 by December 2017.[103] This geospatial

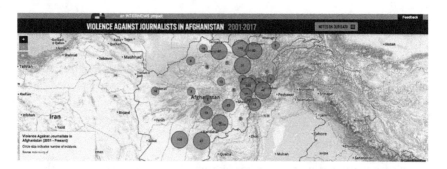

FIGURE 3.11   This geospatial interface, built with open source software called TileMill, maps the location and frequency of incidents in which journalists were threatened, beaten, or killed in Afghanistan from 2001–2017.

Source: http://data.nai.org.af/—screen capture used under the Fair Use Doctrine

interface, built with open source software called TileMill, uses red shaded circles scaled from small to large to mark the location and frequency of incidents in which journalists were threatened, beaten, or killed in Afghanistan. This attack data layer can be combined with other layers, including the number of journalists and media outlets, security incidents each year, and a safety index.[104] The interface also provides access to information about each incident, including date, incident type, and gender and affiliate organization of the journalist attacked. Most of the journalists attacked are male and targeted organizations include ToloTV, Al Jazeera, Ariana News, the BBC, as well as many others, including freelancers. This geospatial interface reveals an ongoing struggle over Afghani airwaves and suggests that foreign-supported media organizations in Afghanistan using the airwaves for reporting or in efforts to "liberalize" and "privatize" national media have become targets. The violent attacks on journalists and the geospatial interface that visualizes them both communicate fierce opposition to foreign use of Afghani airwaves and media space.

While this geospatial interface, like the IED heat map discussed above, can function as part of a regime of predictive analytics and be used to inform journalists where reporting is most risky or dangerous, it can have other effects as well. For instance, it can be used to steer journalists and their organizations away from particular areas or issues that demand investigation, or limit journalists' insurance coverage when venturing into certain regions, which is part of a broader set of labor conditions in the news reporting industry.[105] It can also be used to rationalize and intensify further militarization and policing throughout Afghanistan. Despite the fact that Nai has been collecting and sharing this data for years, conditions for journalists have not improved. In October 2016 Nai pressured the Afghani government to address the issue after documenting nearly 370 incidents of violence against journalists in 2016 alone and indicating that 300 journalists and media workers also left their jobs that year.[106] Such conditions serve as a stark reminder that a geospatial interface that tracks violence is different from deterring violence on the ground.

Other organizations have used geospatial images to map attacks by the Islamic State in Iraq. An online platform called *War on the Rocks* features two "heat maps" developed in partnership with the National Consortium for the Study of Terrorism and Responses to Terrorism (START) and using data from the Global Terrorism Database.[107] The first shows attacks in Baghdad from 2009–2013 attributed to ISIS/ISIL using bright red circles that are "weighted by incident casualties."[108] The circles are inscribed upon a map of urban districts that is color-coded by religious majority. The second visualization, "ISIS/ISIL Attacks, 2009–2013," represents attacks on a regional geospatial image and varies using red to yellow dots, with red indicating the highest level of fatalities and injuries resulting from a given incident. While ISIS has perpetrated many acts of violence in Iraq and elsewhere, these images demonstrate a symbolic and discursive continuity with the satellite images Colin Powell presented to the UN Security Council in 2003, in that they are designed to publicly build a case for US military action based on a visual rhetoric of geospatial inscription—that is, geospatial images become backdrops for graphically communicated arguments for military intervention. In the context of the war on terror, the geospatial image has been used to align and synchronize foreign policy, military strategy, and public sentiment.

By 2016 the US war against ISIS/ISIL was in full force in Iraq and elsewhere. One article described "how big data is joining the fight against ISIS," and detailed the US military's use of geospatial interfaces to "detect and defeat IEDs" in Iraq. One such system, known as BOOM, or "Blast Origin Overpressure Modeler," enables troops to ascertain how large the explosion of a detected IED will be and generates a Google Earth layer with concentric circles specifying the anticipated areas of fragmentation and overpressure from a given device.[109] Across the border, in northern Syria, Kurdish troops (Y.P.G.) fighting ISIS use Google Earth on their Samsung tablets to coordinate US airstrikes against ISIS. The Kurds reportedly use yellow dots to indicate where they are stationed and red dots to identify buildings occupied by ISIS fighters, and US airstrikes on ISIS are orchestrated accordingly.[110] Both BOOM and the Kurds' use of Google Earth involve attempts to visualize and control the aeromobility of objects, whether by tracking the debris clouds of IEDs or guiding airstrikes to targets.

Geospatial imagery can be integrated with photographs, full motion video sensors, location-based applications, and open source information, including social media data.[111] Such integration extends the content, form, and reach of coverage, and modifies its communicative capacities and discursive modalities. This convergence can turn the Google Earth interface into a system of pattern recognition and social control as opposed to one of virtual navigation and discovery. The mapping and identification of "hot spots" via Google Earth may appear to occur virtually and remotely, but it has material affects. Such visualizations can alter the geopolitical status of particular locations in the world, impact who can move freely in and through those locales, shape what resources are available, and determine the degree to which sites and peoples in the vicinity are monitored. Predictive analytics, then, are not only temporal, they are territorial and have embodied affects—their very production has the potential to materially transform conditions and/or regulate movements in particular locations.

Vertical mediation occurs when the US uses orbital platforms to monitor sites from above while materially transforming them on the ground below. US military and commercial organizations have used aero-orbital platforms to turn the world's territories into digital intellectual property that can be used both to perpetrate military assaults and remodel others' sovereign territories. This vertical mediation of Afghanistan and Iraq has involved the use of geospatial imagery to visualize and enact the privatization of mediascapes, the prospecting and speculation of natural resources, the monitoring of reconstruction, and policing of local communities. Such processes, facilitated by geospatial imaging, have become integral to digital capitalism—that is, to the development of "an economywide network that can support an ever-growing intracorporate and intercorporate business practices."[112]

The vertical mediation of Afghanistan and Iraq is continuous with political economic practices that preceded the 9/11 attacks. In his analysis of the demise of the World Trade Center, Vincent Mosco reminds us that this structure could only be built ". . . because the state condemned the existing properties, appropriated the land, paid for construction, [and] provided tax subsidies higher than anywhere else in the city. . . ."[113] Similarly, the transformation of Afghan and Iraq national territories into networked digital intellectual property appropriates particular sites, resources, and lifeworlds in order to make them available to additional extractive and development processes, while evacuating the power of the state and extending neoliberalism. Mosco poignantly states that within neoliberalism, "a retreat from the state . . . means a retreat from the collective management of expanding networks at the national and international levels."[114] In this sense, the kinds of capital exchanges that were once located at ground zero have been satellitized—shifted to commercial satellites that image and administer political economic and geopolitical relations elsewhere.

Given these enactments and inscriptions of power, the geospatial image can be understood as a signature site for studying vertical mediation and the war on terror. In this chapter I have approached the geospatial image, on the one hand, as a site for a critical and diffractive object-oriented analysis designed to complicate strategic looking, and, on the other hand, as a site that makes hegemonic use of the vertical field intelligible and exposes efforts to remediate the landscapes and lifeworlds of untold and unnamed Others. Much more than remote views, these vertical mediations are implicated in the material restructuring of life on earth. They are part of broader regimes of targeting, striking, and eradicating, which leave holes and eliminate people such that new governments, social orders, and built environments must be imagined, developed, and put in place. At the same time, by detecting human and non-human, organic and inorganic, earthly and circumterrestrial objects and phenomena, geospatial images reveal that war always exceeds the frame, as Rey Chow and Judith Butler powerfully remind us, and is inscribed as traces, residues, layers, chemical compounds in the air, the earth's crust and water, as well as in the flesh and minds of bodies.[115] Geospatial images help us to think about the ways war remediates life itself.

It is crucial that hegemonic uses of geospatial images and their institutional underbellies be excavated in the process of critically engaging with them. At the same time, the fact that state and military organizations use geospatial images strategically does not mean we have to inherit and idly adopt those ways of looking at and using them. In fact, one might argue that the increased circulation of geospatial images has created a crucial turning point in visual culture in which we have to struggle to maintain the right to interpet itself, especially given that so many geospatial images come into circulation as always already read—that is, with dense layerings of graphics, icons, and arrows inscribed in the view, which regulate acts of interpretation and sense-making. True GEOINT—geospatial intelligence—is not housed in the NRO or the NGA, but would involve fostering geospatial imaging literacies among citizens so they could engage with such images on different terms and from multiple vantage points and begin to question and fracture the now normalized process of waging war and conducting foreign policy by sensing radiation emanating from the surface of the earth.

What I am ultimately suggesting is a need to further situate the geospatial image within critical dialogues on media and democracy and media conglomeration. The geospatial image is not only helping to shape perceptions and worldviews; it is also being used to remodel life on earth as part of the war on terror. Given the high stakes of geospatial imaging, it is vital that scholars from an array of disciplines interrogate the effects of its development and continuing use. For instance, to what extent are Iraqi or Afghani citizens able to access and use Google Earth's "free" platform to support their agendas and interests? What policies and regulations have been applied to DigitalGlobe and Google Earth as they turn the planet into a proprietary geospatial archive and digital platform? Why are there so few humanitarian geospatial projects like Satellite Sentinel and so many militaristic ones?

Founded by activist John Prendergast and Hollywood actor George Clooney in 2010, the Satellite Sentinel Project set out to become "the first sustained public effort to systematically monitor and report on potential hotspots and threats to human security in near real-time," using DigitalGlobe satellite imagery, data analysis, and ground reports.[116] Though the project lasted only five years, it collected evidence of atrocities in South Sudan in an effort to hold perpetrators accountable and delivered a series of incisive geospatial analyses of the Sudanese civil war as well as a final report in 2015 on armed actors and natural resource theft in the Congo.[117] In other words, those involved in the project read satellite images in ways that differed from the state. As James Scott reminds us, "We must keep in mind not only the power of state simplifications to transform the world but also the capacity of the society to modify, subvert, block, and even overturn the categories imposed upon it."[118] In the context of geospatial images, the struggle over interpretation—including the refusal to read satellite images like a state—becomes a vital dimension of challenging strategies of vertical domination. Satellite Sentinel used geospatial images to question militarized aggression and vertical power hierarchies rather than trying to reinforce or naturalize them. Its initiatives used aero-orbital platforms to monitor and critique militarized violence against civilians, rather than idly accept it. Because of this, Satellite Sentinel provides a vital model for engaging with the vicissitudes of vertical power and violence discussed in the next chapter, which explores the US drone wars in Pakistan and the Horn of Africa region.

Notes

1   "Yugoslavia, Afghanistan, Iraq: The Satellite Wars," *Space Today*, accessed August 21, 2013, www.spacetoday.org/Satellites/YugoWarSats.html#afghanistan
2   Ibid.
3   "List of NRO Launches," *Wikipedia*, accessed October 3, 2016, https://en.wikipedia.org/wiki/List_of_NRO_launches
4   Matt Flannery, DigitalGlobe, Edelman Corporate and Public Affairs e-mail message with Vicky Zeamer, November 3, 2016.
5   Caren Kaplan, *Aerial Aftermaths* (Durham, NC: Duke University Press, 2017).
6   Derek Gregory, "The everywhere war," *The Geographical Journal* 177, no. 3 (2011): 238–250. Dexter Filkins, *Discipline and Punish: The Birth of the Prison* (New York: Vintage, 2009).
7   Eyal Weizman, "Control in the Air," *Open Democracy*, May 2, 2002, accessed September 20, 2013, www.opendemocracy.net/ecology-politicsverticality/article_810.jsp
8   Lisa Hajjar, "Lawfare and Targeted Killing: Developments in the Israeli and US Contexts," *Jadaliyya*, January 15, 2012, accessed May 15, 2013, www.jadaliyya.com/pages/index/4049/lawfare-and-targeted-killing_developments-in-the-I
9   "The Advent of the National Geospatial Intelligence Agency," Office of the NGA Historian, 2011, accessed November 1, 2013, www1.nga.mil/About/Documents/04a_History.pdf
10 "The Nation's Eyes and Ears in Space," National Reconnaissance Office, accessed July 22, 2017, www.nro.gov/about/nro/NRO_Fact_Sheet.pdf
11 Wilson Andrews and Todd Lindeman, "The Black Budget," *The Washington Post*, August 29, 2013, accessed September 10, 2013, www.washingtonpost.com/wp-srv/special/national/black-budget/
12 Ann M. Florini and Yahya A. Dehqazada, "No More Secrets?: Policy Implications of Commercial Remote Sensing Satellites," *Carnegie Endowment for International Peace*, July 1, 1999, accessed July 22, 2017, http://carnegieendowment.org/1999/07/01/no-more-secrets-policy-implications-of-commercial-remote-sensing-satellites-pub-150.
13 DigitalGlobe, "DigitalGlobe Reports Fourth Quarter and Full Year 2012 Results," DigitalGlobe press release, 2013, accessed November 1, 2013, http://media.digitalglobe.com/press-releases/digitalglobe-reports-fourth-quarter-and-full-year--nyse-dgi-990509
14 GeoEye, "GeoEye Reports Fourth Quarter and Fiscal Year 2011 Earnings Results," *PR Newswire*, March 12, 2012, accessed November 1, 2013, www.prnewswire.com/

news-releases/geoeye-reports-fourth-quarter-and-fiscal-year-2011-earnings-results-142380305.html

15 David Hubler, "GeoEye, DigitalGlobe Gain $7.3b in NGA Contracts," *Washington Technology*, August 10, 2010, accessed August 21, 2013, https://washington technology.com/articles/2010/08/10/geoeye-digitalglobe-nga-contracts.aspx

16 Google, "Google, Inc. Announces Fourth Quarter and Fiscal Year 2012 Results," Google website, 2013, accessed November 1, 2013, http://investor.google.com/earnings/2012/Q4_google_earnings.html

17 Matthew Shaer, "Google Earth Passes 1 Billion Download Mark," *Christian Science Monitor*, October 6, 2011, accessed September 10, 2013, www.csmonitor.com/Technology/Horizons/2011/1006/Google-Earth-passes-1-billion-download-mark

18 DigitalGlobe, "2016 Annual Report," DigitalGlobe Investor Relations website, accessed July 22, 2017, http://investor.digitalglobe.com/phoenix.zhtml?c=70788&p=irol-reportsannual; "Google's Revenue Worldwide from 2002 to 2016," Statista.com, 2017, www.statista.com/statistics/266206/googles-annual-global-revenue/

19 James Der Derian, *Virtuous War: Mapping the Military-Industrial-Media-Entertainment Network* (New York: Basic Books, 2001).

20 Caren Kaplan, "Precision Targets: GPS and the Militarization of Consumer Identity," *American Quarterly* 58, no. 3 (2006): 705.

21 Fraser MacDonald, Rachel Hughes, and Klaus Dodds, *Observant States: Geopolitics and Visual Culture* (London and New York: I.B. Tauris, 2010), 7–8.

22 Laura Kurgan, *Close Up at a Distance: Mapping, Technology, and Politics* (New York: Zone Books, 2013).

23 Sarah Kember and Joanna Zylinska, *Life after New Media: Mediation as a Vital Process*, 1st ed. (Cambridge, MA: The MIT Press, 2012), 23.

24 Ibid, 22.

25 Duncan Campbell, "US Buys Up All Satellite War Images," *The Guardian*, October 17, 2001, accessed July 22, 2017, www.theguardian.com/world/2001/oct/17/physicalsciences.afghanistan

26 Will Knight, "US intelligence on Iraq 'compelling,' but limited, *New Scientist*, February 6, 2003, www.newscientist.com/article/dn3365-us-intelligence-on-iraq-compelling-but-limited/

27 Website removed. Printed version in author's possession.

28 Michael White and Brian Whitaker, "US war dossier a sham, say experts," *The Guardian*, February 7, 2003, www.theguardian.com/politics/2003/feb/07/uk.internationaleducationnews

29 Normon Solomon, "Colin Powell Is Flawless—Inside a Media Bubble," FAIR website, February 6, 2003, https://fair.org/media-beat-column/colin-powell-is-flawless-8212-inside-a-media-bubble/

30 Jason M. Breslow, "Colin Powell: U.N. Speech 'Was a Great Intelligence Failure,'" *PBS Frontline*, May 17, 2016, accessed July 22, 2017, www.pbs.org/wgbh/frontline/article/colin-powell-u-n-speech-was-a-great-intelligence-failure/

31 Lisa Parks, "Satellite Witnessing: Views and Coverage of the War in Bosnia," in *Cultures in Orbit* (London and Durham, NC: Duke University Press, 2005): 77–108.

32 Brian Massumi, "Potential Politics and the Primacy of Preemption," *Theory & Event* 10, no. 2 (2007), section 16 (not paginated), http://muse.jhu.edu/journals/theory_and_event/v010/10.2massumi.html

33 Mark Dorrian, "Transcoded Indexicality," *Log*, Spring/Summer (2008): 111. Dorrian argues that the situation ultimately "bear[s] witness to the contemporary tendency of the evidential object to disappear from view, to subside beneath its interpretation" such that interpretation is "delivered up as evidence" (114).

34 Kurgan, *Close Up at a Distance*, 25–26.

35 MacDonald, Hughes, and Dodds, *Observant States*, 9, 10.

36 James C. Scott, *Seeing Like a State: How Certain Schemes to Improve the Human Condition Have Failed* (New Haven, CT: Yale University Press, 1998), 11.

37 Ibid, 46; ". . . state simplifications . . . are always far more static and schematic that the actual social phenomena they presume to typify."

38 As Donald Pease explains, "American exceptionalism is the name of the much-coveted form of nationality that provided U.S. citizens with a representative form of self-recognition across the history of the cold war. As a discourse, American exceptionalism includes a complex assemblage of theological and secular assumptions out of which Americans have developed the lasting belief in America as the fulfillment of the national ideal to which other nations aspire." Donald E. Pease, *The New American Exceptionalism* (Minneapolis, MN and London: University of Minnesota Press, 2009), 7.

39 Stephen Graham, *Cities Under Siege: The New Military Urbanism* (London: Verso, 2011), 156.

40 In the previous decade US officials had publicly presented satellite images in connection with the Srebrenica massacre in Bosnia in 1995, the US attack on Afghanistan in 1998, and strike on the Al-Shifa pharmaceutical factory in Sudan in 1998, but these were short press conferences.

41 Jody Berland, *North of Empire: Essays on the Cultural Technologies of Space* (London and Durham, NC: Duke University Press Books, 2009).

42 "Quickbird," *Wikipedia*, accessed July 21, 2014, http://en.wikipedia.org/wiki/QuickBird

43 "Worldview-1," *Wikipedia*, accessed November 1, 2013, http://en.wikipedia.org/wiki/WorldView-1

44 "GeoEye-1," *Wikipedia*, accessed July 21, 2014, http://en.wikipedia.org/wiki/GeoEye-1

45 DigitalGlobe, "U.S. Department of Commerce Relaxes Resolution Restrictions DigitalGlobe Extends Lead in Image Quality," *MarketWired*, June 11, 2014, accessed July 22, 2017, www.marketwired.com/press-release/us-department-commerce-relaxes-resolution-restrictions-digitalglobe-extends-lead-image-nyse-dgi-1919482.htm

46 DigitalGlobe, "Regulatory Change Will Help Our Customers See the Earth More Clearly!" *DigitalGlobe*, accessed July 22, 2017, http://blog.digitalglobe.com/news/resolutionrestrictionslifted/

47 Eric Lipton, "3-D Maps From Commercial Satellites Guide G.I.'s in Iraq's Deadliest Urban Mazes," *The New York Times*, November 26, 2004: 24. Also, see Marcus Wesigerber, "DigitalGlobe: Lift US Restrictions on Commercial Satellite Imagery," *DefenseNews*, October 23, 2013; "U.S. Satellite Resolution Restrictions—LIFTED!" DigitalGlobe press release, June 11, 2014, http://blog.digitalglobe.com/news/resolution restrictionslifted/

48 Ann Schrader, "Colorado Plays Role in Orbital Espionage," *The Denver Post*, September 30, 2001: A01.

49 National Geospatial Agency, "Commercial GEOINT Strategy," October 2015, www.nga.mil/MediaRoom/. . ./2015/NGA_Commercial_GEOINT_Strategy.pdf, p. 2

50 Mike Gruss, "Improving What the IC Sees," *SpaceNews*, August 15, 2016, accessed July 22, 2017, www.spacenewsmag.com/feature/improving-what-the-ic-sees/; see also Robert P. Otto, "Commercial Space-Based Geoint," Intelligence, Surveillance and Reconnaissance Office, United States Air Force, accessed July 22, 2017, www.defenseinnovationmarketplace.mil/resources/Commercial_GEOINT_Vision.pdf

51 Inderpal Grewal, *Saving the Security State: Exceptional Citizens in Twenty-First-Century America* (London and Durham, NC: Duke University Press, 2017).

52   Lisa Parks, "Satellite Witnessing."

53   Friedrich Kittler, *Gramophone, Film, Typewriter*, trans. Geoffrey Winthrop-Young and Michael Wutz, First Ed. (Stanford, CA: Stanford University Press, 1999); Friedrich Kittler, *Optical Media*, trans. Anthony Enns, First Ed. (Cambridge, UK and Malden, MA: Polity, 2009); Wolfgang Ernst, *Digital Memory and the Archive*, Ed. Jussi Parikka (Minneapolis, MN: University Of Minnesota Press, 2012).

54   John Cheney-Lippold, *We Are Data: Algorithms and the Making of Our Digital Selves* (New York: New York University Press, 2017).

55   Michel Foucault, *Discipline & Punish: The Birth of the Prison*, trans. Alan Sheridan (New York: Vintage Books, 1995), 26.

56   Michel Foucault, *Power/Knowledge* (New York: Vintage, 1980), 152.

57   Ibid, 153; 154.

58   Jane Bennett, *Vibrant Matter: A Political Ecology of Things* (Durham, NC: Duke University Press Books, 2010).

59   Ibid, ix.

60   Ibid, viii.

61   Graham Harman, *The Quadruple Object*, reprint ed. (Winchester, UK and Washington, DC: Zero Books, 2011), 5.

62   Ibid, 7.

63   Ibid.

64   Ibid, 18.

65   Ibid, 38.

66   "Afghanistan—Darunta Camp Complex,"*Globalsecurity.org*, page last modified September 7, 2011, accessed August 25, 2013, www.globalsecurity.org/military/world/afghanistan/darunta.htm

67   T.D. Frank, "Mapping Dominant Vegetation Communities in the Colorado Rocky Mountain Front Range with Landsat Thematic Mapper and Digital Terrain Data," *Photogrammetric Engineering and Remote Sensing* 54 (1988): 1727–1734.

68   Hammad Gilani, "GUEST POST: Challenges—Geometric Correction of Optical High Resolution Satellite Imaging," *EarthEnable*, February 2, 2015, accessed July 22, 2017, https://earthenable.wordpress.com/2015/02/03/guest-post-challenges-geometric-correction-of-optical-high-resolution-satellite-imaging/

69   "Eyes on Saddam U.S. Overhead Imagery of Iraq," *National Security Archive Electronic Briefing Book No. 88*, Ed. Jeffrey T. Richelson, April 30, 2003, accessed July 21, 2014, www2.gwu.edu/~nsarchiv/NSAEBB/NSAEBB88/; "Afghanistan—October 23, 2001," *Globalsecurity.org*, accessed July 21, 2014, www.globalsecurity.org/intell/library/imint/kabul_radcom-station-nw-post.htm

70   Raphael Prober, "Shutter Control: Confronting Tomorrow's Technology with Yesterday's Regulations," *Journal of Law and Politics* 19 (2003). Also see James Keeley and Robert Huebert, Eds., *Commercial Satellite Imagery and United Nations Peacekeeping: A View From Above* (Farnham, UK: Ashgate, 2004).

71   For a broad discussion of the implications of shutter control see: Ann M. Florini and Yahya Dehqanzada, "Commercial Satellite Imagery Comes of Age," *Issues in Science and Technology* 16, no. 1 (1999), www.issues.org/16.1/florini.htm

72   Cheryl Arvidson, "Journalists Denounce Government 'Shutter Control' Idea for Satellite Images," *The Freedom Forum Online*, March 17, 2000, accessed April 6, 2011, www.freedomforum.org/templates/document.asp?documentID=11944

73   Barbara Cochran, "Fighting the Feds Over Shutter Control," *Communicator*, December 1999, accessed July 3, 2008, www.rtdna.org/pages/media_items/fighting-the-feds-over-shutter-control210.php, 113–115.

74   Ibid, 113.

75   Ibid, 113–115.

76 Humanitarian organizations such as Refugees International and Human Rights Watch have relied upon satellite images to identify groups of displaced persons, deliver aid, and monitor human rights violations in conflict zones. Jessica Altschul, "Commercial Satellite Imagery Poses a Challenge to Pentagon Planners," *Global security.org*, February. 28, 2002, accessed April 6, 2011, www.globalsecurity. org/org/news/2002/020228-eye.htm

77 Joan Johnson-Freese, *Space as a Strategic Asset* (New York: Columbia University Press, 2007), 112.

78 Katherine Shrader, "Curbs on Satellite Photos May be Needed," *San Francisco Chronicle*, May 8, 2007, accessed July 3, 2008; David Corn, "Their Spy in the Sky," *The Nation*, November 8, 2001, accessed July 4, 2008, www.thenation.com/doc/ 20011126/corn; Duncan Campbell, "US Buys Up All Satellite War Images," *The Guardian*, October 17, 2001, accessed April 6, 2011, www.guardian.co.uk/world/ 2001/oct/17/physicalsciences.afghanistan

79 C.S. Goldstein, "A Strategic Failure: American Information Control Policy in Occupied Iraq," *Military Review*, April 2008, accessed July 20, 2014, www.army. mil/professionalWriting/volumes/volume6/april_2008/4_08_1_pf.html; Bruce B. Auster, "Broadcast Blues," *U.S. News and World Report*, January 26, 2004, accessed July 20, 2014, www.corpwatch.org/article.php?id=7884

80 Tim Arango, "Iraq Revokes Licenses of Al Jazeera and 9 Other TV Channels," *The New York Times*, April 28, 2013, accessed January 15, 2014, www.nytimes. com/2013/04/29/world/middleeast/iraq-suspends-al-jazeera-and-other-tv-channels. html?_r=0

81 "Media Landscape in Afghanistan: Visualizing Media Access," *Internews*, accessed July 22, 2017, http://data.internews.org/af-media/about/

82 Matt Sienkiewicz, *The Other Air Force: U.S. Efforts to Reshape Middle Eastern Media Since 9/11*, reprint ed. (New Brunswick, NJ: Rutgers University Press, 2016), 2–3.

83 "USGS Iraq Project: USGS Activities in Support of Economic Development and Stabilization in the Natural Resource Sectors of Iraq," U.S. Geological Survey, accessed September 5, 2013, http://iraq.cr.usgs.gov/; "USGS Projects in Afghanistan: a brief history," U.S. Geological Survey, accessed September 5, 2013, http:// afghanistan.cr.usgs.gov/background

84 Peter G. Chirico, "Natural Resource Assessments in Afghanistan Supported by High Resolution Digital Elevation Modeling and Multi-spectral Image Analysis," (presented at Civil Commercial Imagery Evaluation Workshop, Laurel, MD, March 14–16, 2006), accessed September 5, 2013, http://calval.cr.usgs.gov/JACIE_files/ JACIE06/Files/213Chiri.pdf

85 "USGS Projects in Afghanistan.*"*

86 "USGS Afghanistan Oil and Natural Gas Viewer," U.S. Geological Survey, accessed September 5, 2013, http://afghanistan.cr.usgs.gov/flexviewer/

87 Jeff Doebrich and Ronald Wahl, compilers, "Open-File Report 2006–1038: Geologic and Mineral Resource Map of Afghanistan," U.S. Geological Survey, last modified April 2, 2013, accessed July 22, 2017, http://pubs.usgs.gov/of/2006/1038/

88 Charles Choi, "Rare Earth: Afghanistan Sits on $1 Trillion in Minerals," *NBC News—Science*, September 4, 2014, accessed July 22, 2017, www.nbcnews.com/ science/science-news/rare-earth-afghanistan-sits-1-trillion-minerals-n196861

89 Charles Choi, "$1 Trillion Trove of Rare Minerals Revealed Under Afghanistan," *Live Science*, September 4, 2014, accessed July 22, 2017, www.livescience.com/ 47682-rare-earth-minerals-found-under-afghanistan.html

90 Rex Dalton, "Geology: Minegames," *Nature*, October 22, 2007, accessed July 22, 2017, www.nature.com/news/2007/071024/full/449968a.html

91 For further discussion of media and geology see Jussi Parikka, *A Geology of Media*, (Minneapolis, MN: University of Minnesota Press, 2015).

92 Nathan Hodge, "Using Google Earth and GPS to track Afghanistan cash," *Wired*, February 25, 2010, accessed September 4, 2013, www.wired.com/dangerroom/ 2010/02/using-laptops-cameras-and-gps-to-track-afghanistan-cash/

93 Ibid.

94 Andrew Higgins, "Officials Puzzle Over Million of Dollars Leaving Afghanistan by Plane for Dubai," *Washington Post*, February 25, 2010, accessed July 22, 2017, www.washingtonpost.com/wp-dyn/content/article/2010/02/24/AR2010022404 914.html

95 Special Inspector General for Afghanistan Reconstruction, "$36 Million Command and Control Facility at Camp Leatherneck, Afghanistan: Unwanted, Unneeded, and Unussed," *Office of Special Projects*, May 2015, accessed July 22, 2017, www.sigar.mil/ pdf/special%20projects/SIGAR-15-57-SP.pdf

96 Dan Lamothe, "Satellite Photos of Camp Leatherneck in Afghanistan, Before and After U.S. Withdrawal," *Washington Post*, May 20, 2015, accessed July 22, 2017, www.washingtonpost.com/news/checkpoint/wp/2015/05/20/satellite-photos-of-camp-leatherneck-in-afghanistan-before-and-after-u-s-withdrawal/

97 Special Inspector General for Afghanistan Reconstruction, "Statement for Record: Challenges to Effective Oversight of Afghanistan Reconstruction Grow as High-Risk Areas Persist: Statement of John F. Sopko, Special Inspector General for Afghanistan Reconstruction," Committee on Appropriations, Subcommittee on the Department of State, Foreign Operations, and Related Programs U.S. Senate, February 24, 2016, accessed July 22, 2017, www.sigar.mil/pdf/testimony/SIGAR-16-18-TY.pdf

98 Ibid, 2.

99 Ibid.

100 "Afghanistan: Geospatial Analysis Reveals Patterns in Terrorist Incidents 2004–2008," *Open Source Data Center*, April 20, 2009, accessed September 4, 2013, http://fas.org/ irp/dni/osc/afghan-geospat.pdf

101 Marc Andrejevic, *Infoglut: How too Much Information is Changing the Way We Think and Know* (New York: Routledge, 2013): 32.

102 See Lisa Parks, "Satellite Witnessing," pp. 91, 137.

103 "Violence against Journalists in Afghanistan," *developmentSEED*, accessed July 22, 2017, https://developmentseed.org/projects/internews-vj/; "Violence against Journalists in Afghanistan (2001–2006)," *Internews*, accessed July 22, 2017, http://data.nai. org.af/

104 "Violence against Journalists in Afghanistan."

105 See Lindsay Palmer, *Becoming the Story: War Correspondents after 9/11*, (Champaign-Urbana, IL: University of Illinois Press, 2018).

106 Nabilla Ashrafi, "Nai Asks Govt To Probe Cases of Violence Against Journalists," *TOLO News*, October 30, 2016, www.tolonews.com/en/afghanistan/28079-nai-asks-govt-to-probe-cases-of-violence-against-journalists

107 "Information on More than 150,000 Terrorist Attacks," *Global Terrorism Database*, accessed July 22, 2017, www.start.umd.edu/gtd/

108 "Attacks in Baghdad Attributed to ISIS/ISIL, 2009–2013," *War on the Rocks*, http://cdn.warontherocks.com/wp-content/uploads/2014/07/ISIS_ISIL_Baghdad_ Attacks_WOTR.png

109 Patrick Tucker, "How Big Data Is Joining the Fight Against ISIS in Mosul," *The Fiscal Times*, October 21, 2016, accessed July 22, 2017, www.thefiscaltimes.com/ 2016/10/21/How-Big-Data-Joining-Fight-Against-ISIS-Mosul

110 Rukmini Callimachi, "Inside Syria: Kurds Roll Back ISIS, but Alliances Are Strained," *New York Times*, August 10, 2015, accessed July 22, 2017, www.nytimes. com/2015/08/10/world/middleeast/syria-turkey-islamic-state-kurdish-militia-ypg. html?_r=1

111 Peter Buxbaum, "Predictive Analytics for Intel Advantage," *Intelligence Geospatial Forum: The Magazine of the National Intelligence Community*, February 6, 2014, accessed July 22, 2017, www.kmimediagroup.com/gif/424-articles-gif/predictive-analytics-for-intel-advantage

112 Dan Schiller, *Digital Capitalism: Networking the Global Market System* (Cambridge, MA: MIT Press, 1999), 1.

113 Vincent Mosco, *The Digital Sublime: Myth, Power, and Cyberspace* (Cambridge, MA: MIT Press, 2005), 182.

114 Ibid, 182.

115 Rey Chow, *The Age of the World Target: Self-Referentiality in War, Theory, and Comparative Work* (Durham, NC: Duke University Press Books, 2006); Judith Butler, *Frames of War: When Is Life Grievable?*, reprint ed. (London and New York: Verso, 2010).

116 "Our Story," *The Satellite Sentinel Project*, accessed July 22, 2017, www.satsentinel.org/our-story

117 See the project's website: www.satsentinel.org/

118 James Scott, *Seeing Like a State*, 49.

4

TARGETING

Mediating US Drone Wars

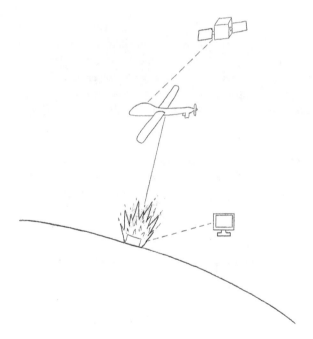

FIGURE 4.1 "Targeting." Concept sketch by Lisa Parks.

Source: The author

As US entities were commandeering airwaves, reorganizing airport security, and expanding geospatial imaging in the years after 9/11, they were also mobilizing drones to fight terrorism on multiple battlefronts. Also known as unmanned aerial vehicles or UAV's, drones have become some of the US military's most strategic assets. Remotely controlled by "pilots" from bases in sites such as Langley, Virginia and Creech Air Force base in Nevada, drones are designed to be relatively invisible in the sky. They can conduct multispectral aerial surveillance and seek and destroy targets with Hellfire missiles or 500-pound bombs. Predator and Reaper drones supporting the US war on terror were developed during the 1990s and first tested during the war in the former Yugoslavia.[1] By 2011 the US Air Force and CIA had more than 7,000 UAVs in service around the world, compared to 50 a decade prior, with their most visible presence in Pakistan, Somalia, Libya, and Yemen. The US Air Force now trains more pilots to fly drones than conventional aircraft, and the US spent $5.78 billion on drone procurements in 2013.[2]

Like other vertical mediations discussed throughout this book, drone operations occur through the air and bring together technologies of flight, telecommunication, and imaging. The US has used drones in Pakistan, Yemen, and Somalia as instruments of surveillance, reconnaissance, intelligence, and targeted killing. Although these operations have been ongoing since 2001, they first made US news headlines in 2009 when investigative reporter Jane Mayer published a detailed *New Yorker* exposé about the CIA's secret drone war in Pakistan.[3] One of the first journalists to publicly question the secret program, Mayer remarked,

> It's easy to understand the appeal of a "push-button" approach to fighting Al Qaeda, but the embrace of the Predator program has occurred with remarkably little public discussion, given that it represents a radically new and geographically unbounded use of state-sanctioned lethal force. And, because of the C.I.A. program's secrecy, there is no visible system of accountability in place, despite the fact that the agency has killed many civilians inside a politically fragile, nuclear-armed country with which the U.S. is not at war.[4]

Though some would question the "appeal of the 'push-button' approach" to counterterrorism, Mayer's powerful report, coupled with Google Earth's accidental release in 2009 of a satellite image showing Predators at a CIA-run airbase in Shamsi, Pakistan, spawned subsequent US news reports and editorials.

The press coverage that followed largely supported the US drone strategy, highlighting the technology's alleged efficiency, cost-effectiveness, and surgical precision. A bold endorsement by the *Wall Street Journal* celebrated the drone program's success in Pakistan and featured a graphic of a Predator with the caption "Combat by Remote Control" and a list of top-priority targets killed by drones since summer 2009, along with their alleged roles.[5] A *Wall Street Journal* editorial a few months later declared that "drones have made war-fighting more humane" and concluded, "When Pakistan's government can exercise sovereignty over all its territory, there will be no need for Predator strikes. In the meantime, unmanned bombs away."[6] *The New York Times* published a feature entitled, "War Evolves with Drones," which included photographs and technical descriptions of drones as well as a forecast about the next generation of the machines designed to be the size of birds and insects, including one modeled after a hummingbird that can fly at 11 miles per hour and perch on a windowsill.[7] Building on the idea that the drone represents an "evolution" in warfare, a subsequent *New York Times* editorial insisted, "There is no question that the drone program has been successful, enabling the United States to disrupt Al Qaeda and its allies in Pakistan's lawless border region"; and then encouraged the Obama administration to be more transparent about its drone program and provide details about the number of civilian casualties.[8] Finally, an *Economist* article called "Flight of the Drones," replete with drone schematics and a chart entitled "Rise of the machines," showing UAV ownership by country (with the US far in the lead owning 56% of the world's drone's with China, Israel, Russia, Britain, France, and Italy owning between 12 and 2%), suggests the drone has augured a "revolution in warfare," and raises questions about its use ranging from its effects on pilots, to the potential for jamming, to the rules of engagement.[9] This broad editorial endorsement of US drone war in the press resonated with US television news networks' (especially, CNN's and Fox News') support for US military attacks on Afghanistan just after 9/11, as discussed in Chapter 1.

While mainstream news media touted the US drone program as a "military success," a "technological evolution," or "revolution in warfare," other organizations were more skeptical. In 2010 the American Civil Liberties Union under the Freedom of Information Act asked the US government to disclose the legal basis for its use of Predator drones to conduct targeted killings overseas with particular concern about US (non-)compliance with international laws related to extrajudicial killings.[10] In 2009 London-based human rights lawyer and head of a legal defense organization called Reprieve, Clive Stafford Smith, filed lawsuits against CIA's former legal chief John Rizzo on behalf of several Pakistani victims who were injured in US drone attacks.[11] And UN special rapporteur Philip Alston publicly called for an end to US drone attacks in Pakistan, indicating they had resulted in "the displacement of clear legal standards with a vaguely defined license to kill, and the creation of a major accountability vacuum." Implicitly questioning the "appeal of a 'bush-putton' approach" alluded to by Mayer, Alston went on to suggest that illegal drone attacks led to a "risk of developing a 'Playstation' mentality to killing."[12] Finally, law professor and former Navy officer, David Glazier, suggested that CIA drone pilots could be tried for war crimes because their armed attacks "clearly fall outside the scope of permissible conduct. . . ." Pointing out the hypocrisy of the US drone attacks, Glazier has stated that they "ought to be reconsidered, particularly as the United States seeks to prosecute members of its adversaries for generally similar conduct."[13]

When I began conducting research on US drone wars in 2011, there was limited public information available about the grounded dimensions of US drone strikes and their affects on civilians in Pakistan, Yemen, and Somalia. Since then, a plethora of insightful academic scholarship has since emerged on drone technology and warfare,[14] but I want to highlight the path-breaking writings of investigative reporters, which catalyzed and enabled much of this scholarship. Reporters such as Jane Mayer, Craig Whitlock, Jeremy Scahill, Glenn Greenwald, Nick Turse, and others presented crucial evidence of US drone wars across multiple regions, described the effects of these operations upon particular people and locales, and questioned the legality and effectiveness of this counterterrorism strategy. Investigative reporters, including those working with The Bureau of Investigative Journalism, led the way in circulating details and information that publics needed to deliberate and assess the viability and ethics of drone warfare, during a time when US government officials remained tight-lipped and committed to strategies of obfuscation.[15]

This chapter explores how US drone wars in Pakistan and the Horn of Africa region participate in vertical mediation. Drawing upon various forms of drone coverage, including drone attack photos, aerial assault videos, drone protest media, drone infrastructure views, infrared images, and drone crash scene photos, I analyze material dimensions of drone warfare that extend from orbit to the ground. The coverage I analyze ranges from photos on the ground to views from above, from infrared to visible light images, from documentary evidence to parodic commentaries, and has emerged from sources as diverse as the US government, YouTube, Pakistani peace activists, and Al Shabaab militants. Collectively, this coverage helps to communicate how drone war has impacted conditions on the ground below and in the sky above, and hence how it participates in vertical mediation.

Vertical mediation in this context refers not only to the capacity of drone sensors to detect phenomena on the earth's surface so it can be rendered as live video feeds at terminal interfaces, but also to the drone's potential to materially alter or affect conditions through the air, spectrum, and/or ground. As I have demonstrated throughout this book, vertical mediation is a process that far exceeds the screen and involves the capacity to register the dynamism of occurrences within, upon or in relation to myriad materials, objects, sites, surfaces, or bodies on earth.[16] As a drone flies through the sky it alters the chemical composition of the air. As it hovers above the earth it can change movements on the ground. As it projects announcements through loudspeakers it can affect thought and behavior. And as it shoots hellfire missiles it can turn homes into holes and the living into the dead. Irreducible to the screen's visual display, the drone's mediating work happens extensively and dynamically through the vertical field—through a vast expanse that extends from the earth's surface, including the geological layers below and built environments upon it, through the domains of the spectrum and the air to the outer limits of orbit. The point here is that drones do not simply float above—they rewrite and re-form life on earth in a most material way. Drone operations shape where people move and how they communicate, which buildings stand and which are destroyed, who shall live and who shall die. The drone is as much a technology of inscription as it is a technology of sensing or representation.

To demonstrate this, I organize the chapter into two main sections. The first focuses on the US drone war in the Federally Administered Tribal Areas (FATA) region of Pakistan and explores how drone attack photos, aerial assault videos, and protest media draw attention to grounded dimensions of drone war and registered peoples' objections and resistance to US vertical power.[17] The chapter's second section shifts focus to the US drone war in the Horn of Africa and explores how drone media help to bring the infrastructural, perceptual, and forensic materialities of drone warfare to the surface. Combined, these two sections demonstrate how war on terror coverage draws attention to and maps a vertical field of biopower, exposes the logics of speculation and uncertainty that underpin drone warfare, and makes legible a new disenfranchised class that I refer to as "the targeted"—people who are the intentional or incidental victims of aerial violence. As in earlier chapters, my central concern is to highlight vertical forms of US power that emerged after 9/11 and to analyze their relation to US struggles for hegemony. While previous chapters focused on US media and military operations in Afghanistan and Iraq, this chapter shifts critical attention to other theaters of the war on terror—Pakistan, Somalia, and Yemen—and demonstrates how the US has appropriated the flexibility and efficiency of drone technology to wage undeclared wars in diverse parts of the world.

War Theater One: Federally Administered Tribal Areas of Pakistan

Since 2001 the CIA has conducted a secret drone war in the Federally Administered Tribal Areas (FATA) of Pakistan, a contentious and difficult to access rural region on the border of Afghanistan that is inhabited by Pashtun tribes, controlled by the Taliban, used by Al Qaeda operatives, and occupied by the Pakistani military. The FATA region is extremely difficult for international journalists to access, and locals have been punished simply for carrying cameras there. As Jane Mayer reported, "The Pakistani government and the military have tried to wall off the tribal areas from journalists."[18] Pakistani journalist, Farhat Taj, claimed the Taliban has been involved in such practices as well, explaining, "immediately after every [drone] attack the Taliban terrorists cordon off the area and no one, including the local villagers, is allowed to come near the targeted place." Taj has loudly challenged the drone casualty counts published in a widely cited New America Foundation report, pointing out that all of the data are based upon second-hand news reports. She suggests, "No reporters of the media organizations referred to by the writers have direct access to or a presence in Waziristan due to bad security," and insists, "There are no media organizations with 'deep reporting capabilities' in this lawless Taliban-controlled area."[19] Because of this she urged researchers "to be critical of the Pakistani news reports about FATA and NWFP" (Northwest Frontier Province).[20] In response to critiques like Taj's, the Bureau of Investigative Journalism has compiled and compared data from an array of sources over time and estimates that since 2004 there have been between 2,511 and 4,020 killed and 1,161 to 1,747 injured by US drone strikes in Pakistan.[21]

Drone Attack Photos

Photographing scenes in the aftermath of such strikes is a risky business. On one occasion the Taliban captured a man who was investigating drone attacks that killed civilians, and held him for 63 days alleging he was a US spy.[22] On another a 16-year-old Pakistani boy, Tariq Aziz, was mysteriously killed by a US drone three days after agreeing to be trained as a drone attack scene photographer.[23] While the Taliban reportedly rigidly controls access to drone attack scenes, the Pakistani Inter-Services Intelligence (ISI) and Minister of Interior have also been involved in monitoring and inspecting these sites to confirm casualties. In addition, a handful of professional journalists have managed to photograph some of them as well. Wire services such as Associated Press, Agence-France Press, Reuters, and Getty Images have distributed drone attack scene photos in international news outlets ranging from the BBC to PakAlert Press, from CNN to Indian Express.

Whether taken by professionals or amateurs, drone attack scene photos often appear online without any or with minimal captions and credits, much like the geospatial images, discussed in Chapter 3, which often circulate without metadata. Some such photos have been re-posted as general "stand in" images to accompany reports or commentaries on the US drone attacks rather than as illustrations or evidence of a particular attack, which is consistent with the general pattern of secrecy and obscurity that has defined this CIA campaign. Within such conditions, the images that do surface and circulate online are all the more charged and loaded with the burden to communicate information about the drone attacks, even if their truth status is somewhat confusing or uncertain.

Drone attack scene photos depict areas on the ground in the aftermath of drone strikes and fit into three general categories: survivors amidst ruins; funerals; and dead or injured bodies. The first category features survivors and/or bystanders standing among and picking through ruins, presumably after a drone strike has occurred. An uncaptioned AFP-Getty photo from February 2011 published on a website called The Raw Story features several men standing next to a building in ruins destroyed in a US drone attack.[24] The roof of the building has been

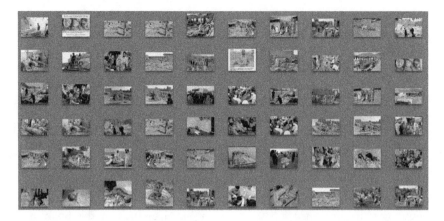

FIGURE 4.2 Ground perspectives of drone strike scenes, funerals, and bodies reveal the ruined life worlds left in the wake of US drone strikes in the FATA region.

Source: AFP-Getty photo; URL removed. Screen capture used under the Fair Use Doctrine

blown away and turned into a pile of rubble, and the re-bar that once held it in place is exposed and bent toward the ground. A photo that appeared in *The Telegraph* on August 11, 2011 reveals a boy standing in front of a mound of cement bricks and strewn debris as he looks toward the camera. Its caption describes the November 19, 2008 scene as the "site of suspected U.S. drone attacks in the Janikhel tribal area in Bannu District of North West Frontier Province in Pakistan."[25]

Another photo from June 2009 shot by Tariq Mahmood appeared on CNN's website with the caption, "Drone strikes are unpopular in the region because of the threat to civilians." The photo features three men and a child picking through a pile of rubble above which two giant wooden crossbeams have fallen. When I looked for further detail about the photo on the Getty images website I found another caption indicating the image had nothing to do with a drone attack and was in fact the site of a Taliban suicide attack in Peshawar. The caption indicated: "Pakistani residents stand amongst the rubble of a classroom after militants blew up a girls' school on the outskirts of Peshawar on June 22, 2009."[26] The inclusion of this photo in CNN's drone strike story exposes the generalized confusion and lack of specificity that underpins much drone war reporting by mainstream media networks. Despite this, these and other photos of rubble function as coverage that visualizes the material effects of drone warfare, foregrounding the thick accumulations, blockages, and grounded messes that are vivid counterparts to the drone's orderly cockpits and aerial viewfinders. The photos of ruins also serve as bold reminders that drone warfare is fundamentally an attempt to control the surface of the earth, to reshape and reform the material world.

The second category of drone attack photos features funeral processions or gatherings to honor the dead. Photography at such events is often forbidden, but there is a vested interest in allowing the world to witness the affects of the US drone attacks and thus sometimes it is permitted. A Reuters photo taken in February 2009, which appeared on the UK's Channel 4 website, features several caskets with white flags implanted in them as a crowd of over one hundred "Pakistani tribesmen" stands in the distance and to "offer funeral prayers for the [27] victims of a missile strike attack in Miranshah." The caption indicates, "A suspected US missile strike destroyed a major Taliban training camp in killing at least 27 people, said to be militants (Reuters)."[27] Phrases of uncertainty such as "suspected US missile strike" and "said to be militants" are characteristic of drone attack reporting, though are applied unevenly as "major Taliban training camp" goes unquestioned. Coverage, as suggested throughout this book, not only reveals, but can also be mobilized in ways that cover up or occlude. A photo that appeared in *The Christian Science Monitor* in June 2011 reveals four caskets propped on platforms in a rural location as about one hundred "Pakistani villagers" "offer funeral prayers for people *reportedly* killed by drone attack in Miranshah. . . ."[28] None of the identities of those killed are revealed and the remains of their bodies are contained in boxes. Since most Muslim funerals occur within 24 hours after death, these photos convey hurried efforts to honor drone victims.

While these images create a dividing line between the living and the dead, they do not distinguish the militant from the civilian and neither do many US drone strikes.[29] On some occasions, funerals and cemeteries themselves have become drone targets. A 2006 photo taken by a Predator and later provided to NBC allegedly shows a group of almost 200 Taliban insurgents gathered for a funeral at a cemetery in Afghanistan. US military officers apparently wanted to attack targets within this group, but claim to have held off because the rules of engagement prohibit attacks on cemeteries.[30] In 2009, however, a US drone attack on a funeral procession in the Makeen district of South Waziristan killed at least 60 people and left many others injured.[31] Funerals and other public gatherings, including weddings, have been singled out for so-called "signature strikes," which target groups of men believed to be associated with terrorists but whose identities are not always known.[32]

The third category of drone attack scene photos foregrounds the damage drones do to the flesh, representing dead or injured bodies. These photos have been shot either at an attack scene, a hospital, or a funeral, and at times are used in a sensationalistic manner, often featuring children. One such image that has circulated on multiple websites comes from the South Asian News Agency (SANA) and shows the faces of three dead children as a triptych. One's head is bandaged, another has part of his skull missing, and a third is charred and covered in dried blood. The photo's caption asks, "Who will avenge the blood of these Pakistanis" and indicates that these "innocent children" were "murdered by American drones" in an attack on Dande Darpa Khel that killed twelve people.[33] Other photos in this category feature survivors wearing bandages, casts, or wearing prosthetics, emphasizing the long-term effects that the drone war has upon Pakistanis. A photo of 19 year-old Sadaullah Wazir is accompanied by a caption that indicates he was 15 when he lost both of his legs and an eye in a drone attack that destroyed his home and killed nine people.[34] And an AFP/Getty photo posted on the Another World is Possible website on August 12, 2011 reveals a wounded Pakistan boy being lifted from rubble by several men. Blood is smeared across his face and his eyes are barely open as men try to save his life.[35]

While these photos document the fatal effects of the US drone attacks, it is important to remember that not all victims' bodies can be found and represented. Some drone attacks are so forceful that human bodies are unrecognizable when survivors arrive on the scene. One man who lost his brother-in-law in a drone attack recounted that the damage was so severe "that they could not even distinguish the bodies from one another—even the bones of the people were completely blown apart. The dead were completely unrecognisable. My brother in law's coffin was tightly sealed and we were not allowed to open it to view anything. We had the coffin with us for 30 minutes before it was taken away for burial."[36] In such cases, the explosive force of drone attacks further compounds the challenge of counting and accounting for casualties, whether "militants" or "civilians." International law stipulates that it is the perpetrator's obligation to properly identify every casualty after an attack, but the regulations for counting civilian casualties have been violated in US drone attacks in Pakistan and elsewhere.[37]

So distressed by the US drone attacks in his homeland, journalist Noor Behram returned to Waziristan in 2008 after living and working abroad for several years, and spent three years trying to photograph as many drone attack sites as possible. In some cases, Behram arrived on scene minutes after an explosion and put his camera aside to dig through debris and search for survivors.[38] By July 2011 Behram had photographed 60 drone attack scenes in Waziristan. Photographs from 27 of these scenes (70 of his 200 photographs) were featured in a London art exhibition at the Beaconsfield gallery, entitled "Gaming in Waziristan," during the summer of 2011.[39] Behram's photos constitute the first publicly known, comprehensive photographic record of drone attack scenes in Waziristan and have become an essential dimension of The Bureau of Investigative Journalism's effort to compile evidence that can be used against the US in legal proceedings related to the drone attacks in Pakistan.[40]

Many of Behram's photos show the faces of dead children in close-up just before burial. One features 8-year-old Noor Syed as her body is laid upon a stretcher before burial. Her lips are covered in bright red lipstick and yellow flowers tucked behind her ears softly frame her cheeks. Her head is wrapped in white cloth and her eyes are slightly open, but rolled back. Another, dated August 21, 2009 features 7-year-old Syed Wali Shah who was killed, along with

9 to 20 other civilians, in an attack on Danda Darpakhel, Miram Shah, in North Waziristan.[41] Yet another shows the face and upper body of a dead 10-year-old boy, Naeem Ullah, who was hit by shrapnel when a double drone strike hit a home and car in Datta Khel on October 18, 2010.[42] Naeem's hand is charred, his arms are burned, and his chest and shoulders are covered with white bandages. By 2017 the Bureau of Investigative Journalism estimated that between 172 and 207 children had been killed in US drone attacks in Pakistan.[43]

By framing ruins, funeral processions, and injured and dead bodies, drone attack scene coverage encourages viewers/users to imagine what it would be like to be on the receiving end of a strike. They have the potential to make the grounded experiences of drone warfare vivid and palpable as they circulate. While this potential exists, it is often impossible for the viewer/user (or news agency) to determine whether the photos of rubble, funerals, and carnage are the actual consequences of US drone strikes. Since the strategy of a covert operation is to keep public knowledge about the operation limited and therefore "uncertain," speculation and conjecture must be mobilized as tactics rather than being seen as liabilities in efforts to glean information about US drone strikes. In the heightened security culture of the war on terror, coverage can activate the potential to obscure or deny as much it can to expose or admit. Coverage can insulate state actors from accountability and provide cover for journalists or activists trying to investigate the actions of such states. When drone attack photos circulate, reliable details about their provenance or the locations, events, and subjects represented are not always present, but this paucity of detail is understandable given that those who take such photos assume great risk by exposing the potential culpability of any number of powerful organizations, whether the CIA, the Taliban, or Pakistan's ISI.

While Behram's drone attack photos are aligned with professional journalistic standards and institutional endorsements, many others are not. This does not prevent them from serving as viable platforms for imagining the grounded dimensions of US drone strikes. Given the potential for image fabrication and manipulation in the digital age, the authenticity of all images is uncertain, particularly as they circulate on the Internet. Recognizing this, Tiziana Terranova insists that such images should not be thought of as records or documents, but as "bioweapons" that can affect or infect thought, behaviour, and feelings in multifarious ways and thus intervene directly within power relations. She writes, "It is no longer a matter of illusion or deception, but of the tactical and strategic deployment of the *power of affection* of images. . .It is no longer a matter of truth and appearance . . . but of images as bioweapons, let loose into the information ecology with a mission to infect."[44] Given this, the critical disposition toward images must extend beyond "truth" assessment or authentication alone and move toward an evaluation of their affective politics so that the question becomes: how and for whom is this image useful, meaningful or disruptive? Rather than: is this real? This is not to say that accuracy is not important; rather, it is to recognize how power relations and image use have shifted in the context of digitization and the war on terror.

Aerial Assault Videos

While drone attack photos convey details about the grounded dimensions of drone war in Pakistan, dozens of US aerial assault videos related to the war on terror appeared on YouTube, Dvids, and Live Leak between 2001 and 2017. Released by the US Defense Department or leaked online, these videos feature attacks on targets in Afghanistan and Iraq (though not in Pakistan) by Apaches, C-130, F-16, and Predator drones. Many of the videos claim to represent "insurgents," "terrorists," or "enemies" on the ground participating in an alleged suspicious behavior in Iraq and Afghanistan. Voiceover communication on some of the videos reveals that this behavior can include such acts as carrying rod-shaped or heat-bearing objects, assembling on a rooftop or on a street, standing or digging in a field or near a roadside, riding motorcycles on desert roads, or participating in activities near a mosque. In contrast to drone attack photos, which are captured in the visible light part of the electromagnetic spectrum, aerial assault videos, like the geospatial images discussed in Chapter 3, can be presented in infrared. In such sequences, targets appear as white or black blotches (depending on image processing selections) that signify moving bodies, or are identified as the buildings or vehicles in which these bodies seek cover.[45] Once the targets are confirmed, those manning the aircraft drop a hellfire bomb or spray machine gunfire on the targets below and they disappear into fiery explosions and clouds of smoke. Like the monitoring of activities in Afghanistan and Iraq via geospatial interfaces, this aerial assault coverage makes processes of vertical mediation intelligible as drones rely on satellites and multi-spectral sensors to identify and strike targets on the ground. However, the vertical strategies of drone operations are designed to be much more forceful and fatal than the geospatial interfaces used to privatize media systems or pinpoint natural resources. US vertical hegemony is achieved and sustained through the multiple strategic options offered and afforded by aero-orbital platforms.[46]

While as of 2017 there are no leaked videos of US drone attacks in Pakistan, those showing UAV attacks in Afghanistan and Iraq are instructive as they demonstrate how strikes look from the perspective of drone sensors. One 16-second video entitled "UAV Hits Taliban Column," which has been viewed 124,521 times, was posted in June 2009 by fellfam09. This video shows the viewfinder slightly panning right and left as walking people, appearing as black dots, are visible. Just as the viewfinder locates and focuses on a target, a missile plunges into the area next to a building, and a small object—likely a dog—can be seen running away from the blast.[47] Another example, designed to showcase the US military's restraint, is entitled "Afghanistan War: Proof of the care taken to not injure civilians: UAV Aborted attack."[48] In this aerial video, which has

5,470 views, US troops decide to abort an attack on targets because there are "friendly individuals with a goat in the vicinity." The decision-making process is audible and we hear a commander direct the remote pilot to wait until the "friendlies" have left the "danger zone" and try again at a later stage.

Sometimes these "death from above" sequences are released in US Defense Department press briefings or appear in cable TV news segments. In these contexts, the material is anchored and framed in relation to the ideological positions and strategies of the US government or the commercial news media. When these videos circulate on the Internet they can be commented upon, downloaded, shared, and/or recirculated. My review of viewer comments posted in response to aerial assault videos reveals that the videos elicit an array of responses and extensive speculation and discussion, but there were two general tendencies. The first approaches these videos' depiction of the killing or death of people on the ground as a source of entertainment and visual pleasure such that these sequences function as a kind of *aerial snuff*. The second tendency is to use the videos to scrutinize US military policies, actions, or violence, so that they function as *aerial exposés* that question the rules of engagement or condemn specific attacks. Box 4.1 contains a sampling of comments on "UAV Hits Taliban Column" to highlight these two tendencies and the contradictory status of the videos, which are used to both celebrate US targeted killings and to scrutinize, critique, and protest them. As these aerial assault videos work to assert US vertical hegemony, staging US dominance from above, they elicit affective responses ranging from bravado to regret, gratification to shame, strength to precariousness.

This coverage—the aerial assault videos and the comments posted along with them—suggests that US military drones participate in what Judith Butler calls the "differential distribution of precariousness." As Butler suggests, "War is precisely an effort to minimize precariousness for some and to maximize it for others."[49] Here precariousness is registered along an axis of invisibility–visibility where US troops are invisible (even if audible) as weaponized aircraft hover above people who appear as moving dots of black or white (body heat), signaling the presence of "the targeted." The levels of precariousness in these sequences are contingent upon differential access to aerial and terrestrial space, telecommunication, artillery, positions, and vantage points. Apprehending precariousness according to Butler requires a shift beyond "us and them" and "victim/perpetrator" paradigms such that these "frames of war" reveal precariousness *for all involved*. That is to say, precariousness is part of life for everyone, even for remote pilots situated thousands of miles away. It is registered in their heavy breathing and in the tension and anxiety in their voices, which are audible on some of the videos' soundtracks. Precariousness also emerges in what we do not see framed such as the bad dreams, nightmarish visions, and unassimilable experiences of veterans' futures. Like other examples of

BOX 4.1

Sample Comments on "UAV Hits Taliban Column" video posted on YouTube.

> I watch video like this when I'm having a bad day or am depressed. It perks me right up! Watching the bearded bad guys getting sent to Allah like this is a tonic!
>
> Sodnal

> 2 problems with UAV's . . .
>
> 1) is that youll NEVER know whos in the blast radius – nothing to say shrapnel wont kill a kid who happened to be nearby and
> 2) this is a "war" where the average insurgent wouldnt say no to bringing his kids along for the ride.
>
> UAV's exist only as a political tool of war – "hey look no Allied forces have been killed for ages cuz we use loadsa UAV's and Apaches instead!" – everyones happy. . . so long as nobody hears about the "collateral" in the media.
>
> dannyday58218195

> @Drcrazy93 pause the clip @0:01 the all black figure is a woman (last in line). Woman wear all black vails!! There all walking in single file and stay close to the buildings. @0:06 seconds what looks like a smaller figure (child?) break the line and go off to the left where 2 figures one being possibly the child's mother quickly pull him back inline then BANG! he may of seen the dog and wanted to stroke it? Fuck knows really why they were killed but they didn't look threatening to me.
>
> robtang10304

> Snuff film.
>
> guyboy625

> need some popcorn. I can watch this stuff all day. Have fun in your fucking paradise u low-life pieces of shit. I hope the dog was ok.
>
> gl797

> @haskapaska They are truly regettable, i am unhappy about them and i wish they would never happen. Attacks on civilians, commited by whoever are a disgrace and i condemn BOTH sides for doing them.

> But my point is that these airstrikes, while they may lead to civilian deaths, are never purposefully targetted at civillians with the intention of killing them. On the other hand we have the taliban who will quite happily murder scores of their own people just to kill one or two NATO vis a vis the IED!

These are sample comments that were posted in relation to a video called "UAV Hits Taliban Column" which was posted on YouTube.

Source: YouTube. Comments shared under the Fair Use Doctrine

coverage analyzed throughout this book, these videos enact processes of vertical mediation by using aero-orbital platforms to destroy, reorder, and/or control lifeworlds on the ground.

Drone sensor operators wage aerial assaults based upon *optics of suspicion*. Bombings and killings are authorized again and again because people on the ground "appear to be" or "look like" or are "believed to be" carrying objects or moving in ways that "look suspicious." In other words, the most tentative kind of knowledge is met with the most fatal kind of act. Though sensor operators often monitor a potential target for weeks to determine whether and when to strike, such vertical viewing and predictive analytics have led to a series of "accidental" aerial assaults, whether on two Reuters journalists killed from above while walking on a street in Baghdad in 2007[50] or nine Afghani boys gunned down and killed by two Apache helicopters while they were gathering firewood in Eastern Afghanistan in March 2011. As Derek Gregory suggests, the permissible scope of "the target" has been widened in the context of late modern warfare, leading to a displacement of the concept of "the civilian."[51] Such conditions, I argue, have led to the emergence of a *targeted class*. Particular inhabitants of Pakistan, Somalia, Yemen, and the Palestinian Occupied Territories, for instance, have become part of a disenfranchised "targeted" class simply because they live in areas in which terror *suspects may operate*.[52] A 2009 Brookings Institution study estimated that for every "militant" killed by a drone, there were 10 civilian casualties.[53] A 2010 report from the New America Foundation indicated that since 2004 32% (or approximately 1 in 3) of those killed in drone attacks were civilians.[54] In areas of US military drone operations anyone and everyone is at risk and daily life is haunted by the specter of aerial bombardment. As coverage visualizes "the targeted"—whether in a drone attack photo or an aerial assault video—it reveals that asymmetric warfare creates new forms of disenfranchisement for some and greater precariousness for all. These intractable conditions have catalyzed an international anti-drone war protest movement fueled by networked solidarities and counter-hegemonic critique.

Drone Protest Media

As the frequency and death tolls of drone attacks in Pakistan escalated in 2009–2011, they were met with major demonstrations in Islamabad, Karachi, Peshawar, Multan, Lahore, and in London, Dublin, and Washington, DC. The Pakistani demonstrations were organized by a variety of political organizations such as Pakistan's National Trade Union Federation, Labour Party, and Foundation for Fundamental Rights, among others, and have been documented by photojournalists, news agencies, and activists alike. Drone protest photos not only conveyed Pakistani citizens' widespread discontent with President Asif Ali Zadari's administration (2008–2013), they also sent a bold message to Barack Obama's administration (2008–2016) and US citizens. This coverage included many signs and banners written in English, including phrases such as "Down with American Drones," "Stop Drone Attacks," "Stop Killing of Innocent Trible (sic) Peoples. Victims of Drones," "Obomba—Hands off Muslim Lands!" "USA Leave Us Alone," "Thousands of Innocent Civilians Died of Drone Attacks. Who is Responsible??" No to American Interference & Drone Attacks," "Terrorist? CIA or Taliban? Ask the Victims of Drone Attacks!" "No to Drones. No to USA Aid. We can stand by ourselves." "Bombing on Tribs (sic) Obama's First Gift to Pakistan." As these signs were proudly brandished in the air above and around protesters bodies, the placards projected succinct and powerful messages, and in so doing reclaimed Pakistani air space to communicate collective opposition to US military drone maneuvers overhead.

In some drone protest photos, drawings and models are used to publicize opposition to the attacks. A June 2011 photo from a Karachi protest shows

FIGURE 4.3 During the US drone wars under the Obama administration, many photographs of drone protests in Pakistan and beyond appeared online.

Source: Google image search. Screen capture used under the Fair Use Doctrine

several male protesters gathered in front of a painting featuring a drone that hovers over a village and is targeted by a surface-to-air missile with "Pakistan" inscribed on it. Text dripping in blood and written in Urdu reads, "Give us permission to bring down the drones of cruel rulers/overlords."[55] A July 2011 protest photo from Peshawar shows a hand-made model of a Predator mounted on a stake and set ablaze as a fake missile plunges into it. Yet another photo features an effigy of President Obama wearing an American flag t-shirt and blue jeans, and as the effigy is set on fire the crowd cheers.

Many drone protest photos were taken during demonstrations in the spring of 2011, the notorious Arab Spring, when most of the world's attention was directed to mass demonstrations in Tunisia, Egypt, Bahrain, Libya, and Syria. While the Arab Spring uprisings, which attempted to oust the longstanding leaders of corrupt regimes, were celebrated as showcasing democracy in action, anti-drone demonstrations in Pakistan were largely ignored by Western media, despite the fact that Pakistanis, too, had been fighting a corrupt regime. Indeed, Pakistani citizens found themselves between a rock and a hard place as their government has authorized, and partnered in, US drone attacks resulting in the killing of hundreds of civilians and injury of untold others in the FATA.[56] The particularities of the political situation in Pakistan, of which I have barely scratched the surface, make the online circulation of drone attack and protest photos all the more significant for they carry and transmit Pakistanis' urgent objections to the US drone war across nation-state borders and within the informational milieu. As we have witnessed in other countries in recent years, this capacity has become a crucial tactic in political movements against oppressive regimes, though it can also lead to a situation in which the world knowingly watches on, from above and below, as state-sanctioned violence against civilians persists (as we have seen in Darfur, Syria, and elsewhere).[57]

In her book *Digital Media and Democracy*, Megan Boler argues that the historical conjuncture of the war on terror is characterized, on the one hand, by "a radical democratization of knowledge and multiplication of sources and voices afforded by digital media," and, on the other by "blatant and outrageous instances of falsified national intelligence shielded from scrutiny."[58] She continues, "Because much footage is accessible in digital form (whether through official news sites or individuals posting footage), we have a new way of 'constructing' accounts to assuage our sense of having been lied to but having few ways to 'prove' it."[59] Drone media enable viewers/users to imagine and speculate about covert US drone attacks in Pakistan through multiple positions and modalities—the air or ground, perpetrator or victim, documentary or parody—as part of the process of grappling with the targeted killing and injury of thousands of people, including Pakistani civilians and children, which US officials have refused to account for. Drone coverage registers shifting the relations between security states and citizens in the midst of the war on terror. Invoking exceptional circumstances, the US state neither seeks authorization to conduct drone wars, nor does it circulate media to inform citizens about them. Thus, coverage must either be acquired surreptitiously or with risk, leaked online, or produced during demonstrations.

While Behram's photos stand as some of the most "authentic" visual accounts of drone violence in Pakistan, parodic and fictional protest media can be as poignant and revelatory. India-based YouTube user sandeepsb1 produced a 56-second video *Death by Drone-In the Still of the Night* and posted it on January 28, 2011. The video draws upon a repertoire of images found online to construct a fictional romance between a drone operator and a person on the ground. This air-to-ground romance is articulated through a rewriting of the 1956 doo-wop song "In the Still of the Night" by the Five Satins. On the soundtrack a male voice sternly utters, "In the still of the night, watch me my love as I circle over you with caress. In the still of the night while you sit by your fire watch me, my love, hover over your darling face from Arizona with a joystick in my hand, soundless over you with love. And then I squeeze the red button and the hell-fire slides out and cuts into your crosswired face. Such is my love. Such is my precision." The visual track opens with scenes of drones floating harmlessly through the sky and, after a round of gunfire is heard, a more cataclysmic vision appears. A massive hellfire explosion is followed by a series of photographs of drone attack victims' funerals and dead bodies. The sequence closes with a photo of Barak Obama with the words "Yes!! We can" inscribed upon it.

While drone attack and protest photos use conventions of realism to generate and extend political affection, this video functions in a highly self-conscious manner, using the saccharine spirit of the American pop song and the subversive sensibilities of mash-up to architect its romantic nightmare. In what feels like a happenstance homage to *Hiroshima Mon Amour* and *La Jetée*, the video confronts the psychic dimensions of drone warfare by casting the targeter and the targeted in an uncanny love that is orchestrated as a fatal air-to-ground affair. Here documentary drone attack and protest photos become a kind of raw material for a meta-level critique that points to their limitations and insufficiencies. If drone attack and protest photos have not changed the course of US drone policy by now, so the logic goes, then what will? This question leads sandeepsb1 to invent a more caustic drone media discourse.

Documentary forms of drone protest media have helped to make transnational opposition to US drone attacks legible by highlighting its various locations, scattered constituencies, and array of positions. While the political specificities of these positions remain uncertain, the collective signage and bodies in drone protest photos place the US drone war in Pakistan into the digital public record, making it harder and harder to deny. When drone protest photos circulate online they can also build solidarities and activate speculative imaginaries. For instance, networked drone protest photos have the potential to link Pakistani demonstrators with American activists John Heid and Gretchen Nielsen, who were arrested after they unfurled a banner declaring "War is Not a Show" as they quietly stood near the Predator on display at Davis–Monthan Air Force Base in March 2010.[60]

FIGURE 4.4 The "Creech 14" activists entered the Creech Air Force base outside of Las Vegas on April 9, 2009, started a vigil to end the US military's use of drones, and were arrested.

Source: www.ncronline.org/news/justice/antiwar-defendants-get-unexpected-hearing—screen capture used under the Fair Use Doctrine

They forge alliances between Pakistani demonstrators and Peace of Action members who marched to CIA headquarters in Langley, Virginia in January 2010 to protest the US drone program[61] and with the so-called Creech 14, who were found guilty of trespassing during an April 2009 protest Creech Air Force base in Nevada (see Figure 4.4).[62] Drone protest images connect survivors' families in Waziristan with protesters at General Atomics Predator manufacturing plant in San Diego, the 200 Americans who swarmed the National Air and Space Museum in Washington, DC in October 2011 to protest a drone exhibit and were forced out of the museum and covered with pepper spray,[63] and CODEPINK activists who gathered for the Drone Summit in Washington, DC and sent delegation to Pakistan in 2012.[64]

By drawing attention to the grounded dimensions of drone warfare in Pakistan, drone media have become important sites for interrogating and contesting US vertical hegemony and targeted killing. While this coverage has helped to fuel the political (dis)affection that brings protesters together, drone attack photos, aerial assault videos, and protest media all constitute different ways of responding to epistemological and political uncertainty. While Behram's work relies upon familiar journalistic aesthetic conventions to assert its truth claims, the aerial assault videos reveal the remote views and optics of suspicion that determine fates on the ground. In contrast, the *Death by Drone* parody resorts to bitter exaggeration to spotlight the inescapable uncertainties that emerge when states keep secrets and public speculation runs amok.

As drone media generate a spectrum of epistemologies, they also reveal that decisions to kill from the air are often based upon logics of suspicion, speculation, and uncertainty. Like state and military officials who use satellite images to monitor conditions on the ground, drone pilots make decisions to strike targets based on *close readings* of *distant views*, and after conversations with parties situated within and beyond the designated mission area. Although targets are typically confirmed by intelligence on the ground, it is often difficult for remote decision-makers to differentiate "enemies" from "friendlies," to discern a weapon from a piece of farming equipment, or to distinguish a boy from a man, and there have been numerous civilian casualties and injuries resulting from such confusions. Another video parody called *The Ethical Governor* resolves such errors by forecasting a future that removes the human element from drone warfare, delegating all decision-making to the drone itself. In these futurist scenarios drones select and destroy targets using a decision matrix, intervene only according to the rules of engagement, and assess guilt levels after an attack, deactivating weapon systems if the drone has killed too many people.[65] What this parodic commentary suggests is the need to investigate further the infrastructural and perceptual dimensions of drone warfare—to explore and evaluate the systems remote pilots use, how they see, and what can go wrong.

War Theater Two: The Horn of Africa Region

As the US has waged a war on terror, not only in Afghanistan, Iraq, and Pakistan, but also in countries in the Middle East and Africa, satellites and drones have been cornerstones of these efforts. Aero-orbital platforms have enabled US forces to jam enemy airwaves, monitor movements from above, and target terror suspects. Technologies ranging from signal intelligence to satellite imaging to drone strikes have been used to assert persistent US presence above particular "areas of concern." It would not be possible to track the multiple fronts and extensive global terrain of the war on terror without aerial views. As the war on terror has taken shape across different territorial sites, US monitoring of and intervention in these sites has occurred through the same windows. Its fleet of satellites and drones has been flexibly redeployed across continents to conduct surveillance, apply force, and fight terror from above.

While the US was fighting a drone war in the FATA region of Pakistan, the US Joint Special Operations Command (JSOC) and the Central Intelligence Agency (CIA) have fought a covert drone war from Camp Lemonnier in the tiny African country of Djibouti, monitoring and striking alleged al-Qaeda and Al-Shabaab suspects in Yemen and Somalia since 2004. This camp is one of many used by the US to fight a "shadow war" in Africa against al-Qaeda in the Islamic Maghreb in North Africa, Boko Haram in Nigeria, and al-Shabaab in Somalia, among others. As Nick Turse explains, "to support these mushrooming missions, near-constant training operations, and alliance-building joint exercises, outposts of all sorts are sprouting continent-wide, supported by a sprawling shadow logistics network."[66] Camp Lemmonier in Djibouti is the centerpiece of this network, which extends across the continent, and has been used to coordinate such activities.[67]

A small nation on the east coast of Africa, Djibouti is bordered by Eritrea, Ethiopia, and Somalia. Its capital city, Djibouti City, sits on the Red Sea and the Gulf of Aden, along a key shipping corridor targeted by Somali pirates over the past decade. A former French colony, Djibouti asserted its independence in 1977 and over the past forty years has had only two presidents. Of the country's 828,000 citizens, 94% are Muslim and 60% are unemployed.[68] A country with scant natural resources, Djibouti lives off the "bonanza rents" it garners from its geostrategic location, and this situation has created a "government inclined toward authoritarianism, highly consolidated power, repressive tactics," and a corrupt administrative apparatus.[69] Djibouti also has a poor record on human rights and civil liberties, and the state tightly restricts media and civil society organizations, though there have been major demonstrations against the ruling regime since 2011 due to allegations of election fraud. Far from being democratic, political and economic mobility in Djibouti are based on an individual's position within a system of racial/ethnic hierarchy and are characterized as client–patron relationships in which citizens have very few rights.[70]

From March to May 2001, the US military entered into conversations to establish a base in Djibouti as part of an effort to address humanitarian, demining, and counterterrorism in the region.[71] After the 9/11 attacks, the US also used the base to respond to al-Qaeda groups allegedly operating training centers in Yemen and Somalia. Described by the Pentagon as the "backbone" of counter-terrorism in the region, Camp Lemonnier is a 500-acre base located next to Djibouti's international airport. In 2010 the annual budget for Lemonnier was $238 million,[72] and by 2016 the United States was paying Djibouti $70 million to lease the space for the base each year.[73] In 2017 the US announced plans to invest more than $1 billion to upgrade the installation.[74] Working with the CIA, Combined Joint Task Force—Horn of Africa leads these counterterrorism efforts and serves as the "organizational hub" or "revolutionary motor" of networked warfare in the region, often using the drone as a centerpiece.[75] As Steve Niva suggests, JSOC and CIA "share information, compile target lists, and then hunt, kill and capture enemies worldwide through shadowy operations in which violence is largely disappeared from media coverage and political accountability."[76]

Indeed, the US drone war in the Horn of Africa has been particularly challenging for reporters and human rights organizations to document, given restricted access to areas throughout the region, security risks, and limited net-work connectivity. While conditions on the ground are precarious, the war from above continues. US drones have been used in practices of vertical mediation, conducting surveillance, intelligence, and reconnaissance as well as targeted killings, and transforming the territories and lifeworlds of Yemenis and Somalis in the process. According to The Bureau of Investigative Journalism, drone strikes in Yemen between 2002 and 2017 killed an estimated 890–1,228 people.

In Somalia, strikes occurring between 2007 and 2017 killed between 325 and 482 people.[77] This section analyzes coverage to address other aspects of drone warfare's grounded materialities, focusing on views of drone infrastructure, the politics of infrared images, and drone crash scene photos. Here again, rather than approach these media as sites of representation, I treat them as demonstrations of the materializing capacities and effects of drone interventions—as sites where the drone's relation to the material world becomes intelligible, vivid, palpable, and contestable.

Views of Drone Infrastructure

While US drone operations in Djibouti remain classified, parts of their infrastructure can be seen in Google Earth. A search for Camp Lemmonier turns up DigitalGlobe satellite images that pinpoint the base as well as the Chabelley airstrip just outside Djibouti City (see Figures 4.5 and 4.6), where Predators and Reapers take off and land.[78] These infrastructural views help to clarify the fact that US drone operations rely not only on telecommunication networks and screen interfaces; they are also contingent on a variety of other material resources, including energy, ground space, cement, labor, air, spectrum, and orbit. In addition, acts of earthmoving, importation, construction, installation, and maintenance are required to build and operate drones. As an infrastructural inscription,

FIGURE 4.5 A Google Earth screen capture of Camp Lemonnier in Djibouti City, Djibouti, reveals dimensions of drone infrastructure on the ground.

Source: Google Earth. Screen capture used under the Fair Use Doctrine

FIGURE 4.6 A Google Earth screen capture reveals the Chabelley airstrip in Djibouti where some US drones take off and land.

Source: Google Earth. Screen capture used under the Fair Use Doctrine

a line in the sand, as it were, the airstrip is the staging ground for drone campaigns and vertical maneuvers. The airstrip not only marks the Earth's surface in ways that satellite images can uniquely convey, but also directs attention to the vertical conditions of geology, physics, energy, and weather that drones must negotiate in order to operate.

The Chabelley airstrip is only one of many infrastructural lines in the sand that supports US drone operations in east Africa.[79] As Predators and Reapers hopscotch their way around the region to conduct aerial campaigns in Somalia and Yemen, they circle back to runways for refueling or maintenance after a certain number of hours in flight. Flight routes are determined by both the capacity of the drone and the number of hours drone pilots are allowed to work. The range of a Predator is approximately 675 miles and the range of a Reaper is 1,150–3,600 miles depending on the size of the payload carried. Other airstrips in Nairobi and Mombasa (Kenya), Ethiopia's Arba Minch Airport, Mahé (Seychelles), and Saudi Arabia have also been constructed or repurposed for use by the JSOC and the CIA. The United States has twenty-nine agreements to use international airports in Africa as refueling stations for US military aircraft.[80]

While Google Earth spotlights US drone infrastructure in and around Djibouti, coverage such as military training manual diagrams also demonstrates the drone's vertical mediations. Designed to educate drone crews about operational scenarios, these diagrams portray drones performing defensive, offensive, stability, and civil support missions. In the military imaginary, the drone becomes the center point of coordinated activities fluidly orchestrated through aerial, orbital, spectral, and terrestrial domains. Here the drone is figured as a technology of vertical mediation and US vertical hegemony par excellence as it facilitates relations between terrain vehicles and satellites, provides aerial surveillance for ground operations, guides missiles to targets, and drops messages to civilians. This mediating machine, this extensive life and death support system, appropriates the vertical field as the medium of its movements, transmissions, inscriptions, and projections. As training diagrams suggest, the drone's theater of operations is contingent on a robust yet scattered constellation of communication and global positioning satellites, fiber optic Internet links, and computer-equipped Earth stations, all of which must be electrified. The "where" of drone operations is ultimately much more complex than any one image could suggest. As one analyst explains, a drone might be "piloted from Nellis Air Force Base in Nevada, USA, coordinate with an intelligence cell in Bagram, Afghanistan, tap into data stored in Nairobi, coordinate with a carrier launched ELINT [electronic intelligence] platform, be monitored in Washington and be hunting a target in Kismayo (in Somalia)."[81] Putting this extensive and multitiered infrastructure in place in the Horn of Africa not only takes time and money but also requires access to land, spectrum, and sky and is contingent on a dizzying array of contracts, agreements, and leases with host countries, who, by taking US money and offering land, implicitly authorize the US military to do what it does, even if it creates adverse conditions for civilians in the region.

Given the broad reach and capacities of US drone infrastructures, it is impossible to separate an understanding of them from other systems around the world, whether energy grids, airports, or telecommunications networks. In 2014, investigative journalists Jeremy Scahill and Glenn Greenwald published an exposé revealing that US military drones are equipped with "virtual base-tower transceivers" that enable them to intercept commercial mobile phone traffic and "suck up data" for the National Security Agency (NSA).[82] Continuous with the kinds of signal operations performed by Commando Solo, discussed in Chapter 1, these drone-based transceivers function as a fake cell phone tower that forces targeted mobile devices to lock onto an NSA receiver without the user's knowledge. Thus, as US military drones hover above, they conduct signals intelligence, intercepting the proprietary data of commercial mobile telephone providers and users and trafficking it into NSA clouds. In this scenario, the drone becomes part of an extractive information economy functioning as a digital vacuum cleaner or flying data miner. Although these transceivers were ostensibly put in place to help authenticate suspects before US drone strikes, Scahill and Greenwald reveal that attacks have been authorized again and again based on mobile phone metadata alone, leading to killings of unidentified suspects, a situation they call "death by metadata."[83] Their report cites a former drone pilot who explains, "It's really like we're targeting a cell phone. We're not going after people—we're going after their phones, in the hopes that the person on the other end of that missile is the bad guy."[84]

This practice emerged as part of a JSOC and CIA paradigm, first tested during the war in former Yugoslavia, known as "Feed" or F3EAD, which stands for Find, Fix, Finish, Exploit, Analyze, Disseminate. Feed involves monitoring mobile phone communications to find suspects' exact locations and positioning drones above to provide "deadly persistence" until the suspect emerges.[85] If the suspect is confirmed, lethal force is applied and helicopters drop ground crews in immediately after a drone strike to "exploit" any physical evidence on the scene.[86] The intelligence is "analyzed" and "disseminated" across the JSOC network.[87] Scahill describes the operational logic: "We can kill you if we don't know your identity, but once we kill you, we want to figure out who we killed."[88] Preemptive targeted killings are met with retrospective confirmations.

This F3EAD strategy positions Africans in general, and Yemenis and Somalis, as well as Afghanis, Iraqis and Pakistanis, in particular, at the treacherous infrastructural crossroads of mobile communications and US military drone operations. During Africa's first decade of mobile telephony, consumers could purchase multiple SIM cards from different mobile phone networks without registration; however, now most (all but three) African countries have adopted mandatory SIM card registration policies, requiring consumers to provide personal identification when purchasing a SIM card, which is needed to activate a mobile phone.[89] In Afghanistan there is a push for mobile telecom providers to implement biometrics with SIM card registration, and such programs have been implemented in Pakistan and Iraq.[90] Pakistani officials perceive state monitoring of SIM card registration as a counterterrorism strategy since mobile phones have frequently been used to detonate explosive devices in Pakistan. Given such state policies, there is growing concern about the potential for SIM card databases to be used in preemptive security and policing, including in the formation of JSOC and CIA target lists.[91] In Yemen, fifty-eight out of one hundred people use mobile phones with one of four providers. In Somalia, twenty-three out of one hundred people use mobile phones with one of six providers.[92] Pakistan has 136 million mobile phone subscribers, which amounts to 73% the population.[93] Simply by having a SIM card, using a mobile phone, or being in the vicinity of others using them, people in range of US drone wars increase the risk of being targeted by a drone.[94]

In response to these infrastructural intersections, people on the ground have devised various tactics to mitigate this risk, tactics that parallel the photo-documentation, parodic videos, and mass demonstrations discussed in the previous section. In an effort to encourage critical reflection on the "death by metadata" practice, web developer Josh Begley created an iPhone app called Metadata+ (which Apple rejected five times) that informs the user each time the United States conducts a drone strike, enabling people to track and respond to the strikes.[95] In regions of US drone operations, people use multiple SIM cards, up to six a day, to create confusion about users' identities.[96] Mandatory SIM card registration policies have catalyzed black market SIM card economies in places from Pakistan to Saudi Arabia, and some people use ten different SIM cards with twenty different numbers.[97] In Somalia, Al-Shabaab has reportedly stopped using mobile phones and has halted others' access as well. In early 2014 members of the organization stormed into the headquarters of one of Somalia's largest mobile Internet providers, Hormudd Telecom, with weapons and demanded that the network be shut down, claiming the organization was being used by Western spy agencies to collect information on Muslims.[98] Al-Shabaab has also confiscated and banned the use of camera-equipped smart phones, claiming they are used to spy on Muslims.[99]

Thus, while Google Earth interfaces demonstrate drone infrastructure's material transformation of the Earth's surface and training diagrams convey its vertical layers and extensions, the "death by metadata" scenario reveals how US use of drone infrastructure alters the status of mobile telephony systems on the ground, reshaping the policies of mobile phone providers, the behavior of their users, and the operations of their networks.[100] Just as geospatial images are used in efforts to materially transform systems and sites on earth—and to redefine their purpose and value—the drone's vertical mediations can work to reorganize conditions on the ground.

Infrared Imagery

In addition to reorganizing how countries allocate land and people communicate on the ground, drone operations remediate human perception of and interaction with material phenomena. Like remote-sensing satellites, discussed in Chapter 3, the drone is equipped with electro-optical (EO) and infrared sensors that can detect electromagnetic radiation reflected off of or emanating from the Earth's surface. As this imperceptible radiation is turned into data, rendered by software, and made legible and productive within an information economy, the drone participates in a radiographic episteme.[101] The infrared radiation that its sensors detect becomes coverage that can make various processes "known," including the vertical mediation of racial difference and death.

When drone crews begin their work in a designated mission area, they "build a picture" of conditions on the ground.[102] The sensor operator often begins this process by using Google Earth imagery to determine how a given mission area should look from above and then positions the drone's sensor ball to acquire optimal EO/IR views of the area. The goal, as one pilot puts it, is to "get the ball over the target."[103] While this process is often imagined as a simple act of button pushing, Tim Cullen's declassified yet heavily redacted ethnography of Reaper crews reveals that sensor operators are often completely overwhelmed by the multiple views and different kinds of information they must engage with during drone operations. He writes, "Coordinating the cacophony of displays and paper products at a work station required discipline and skill and sensor operators said it took up to half a year or more to master how to correlate information from [redacted] maps and imagery with objects on the [redacted] display and images in the HUD (head-up display)."[104] Those who manage to master the hand–eye coordination needed to acquire good overhead views become known as having "golden hands."[105] Like the CNN anchors who walked across maps of Afghanistan and Colin Powell who spun satellite images of Iraq before the UN Security Council, drone operators must learn to read images like a state.

Since US drone operations often occur at night, infrared sensors are useful because they allow crews to "see" through darkness and clouds. Caroline Holmqvist insists that such sensors and screens have "agential capacities" because their impacts far exceed acts of representation.[106] Although infrared drone imagery of US counterterrorism campaigns is classified, the CIA and JSOC have used IR imaging to track and target Osama bin Laden[107] and US citizens Anwar al-Awlaki and Samir Khan, as well as more than four thousand alleged terror suspects and civilians in Pakistan, Yemen, and Somalia during the past decade. In the United States, Homeland Security, border patrol, and law enforcement officers have used aerial infrared sensors to monitor activity along US borders, bolster urban and rural policing, and locate and apprehend Boston Marathon bombing suspect Dzhokhar Tsarnaev. As US law enforcers hunted Tsarnaev from above, this televised event enabled viewers to sense what it would be like to live in an area patrolled by military drones.

In such operations, the drone is mobilized in a hunt for heat, fixed on heat-bearing objects such as bodies, guns, missiles, explosives, tanks, anti-aircraft vehicles, trucks, and power generators.[108] Within such conditions, the universal human condition of body temperature becomes a liability. Drone imagery is calibrated to visualize infrared emissions such that human bodies pop out in the visual field as white or black blotches (depending on image processing selections) of stasis or movement. In low-light conditions, human bodies are not only easier to see in IR imagery but also easier to track and target. Within this radiographic episteme, visual surveillance practices are extended beyond epidermalization, as infrared imagery can be used to isolate suspects according to the energy emitted by their bodies. While other systems of human differentiation and social sorting are organized around skin color, personal information, or biometrics,[109] aerial infrared imagery turns all bodies into indistinct human morphologies that cannot be differentiated according to conventional visible light indicators, correlated with constructs of gender, race, or class. Seeing according to temperature turns everyone into a potential suspect or target and has the effect of "normalizing" surveillance since all bodies appear similar beneath its gaze.

At the same time, however, it is important to point out that temperature data has become visible precisely so that it can be made productive within existing regimes of power. Even as it displaces the visible light or epidermal registers of ethnic/racial difference, drone IR imaging reinforces already existing power hierarchies by monitoring and targeting certain territories and peoples—such as those in Pakistan, Yemen, and Somalia, or along the US borders—with greater frequency and intensity, designating these areas and people as "hot spots" that need to be preemptively contained. Strategies of ethnic/racial differentiation do not disappear within an aerial system of temperature-based visuality; rather, they are restructured along a vertical axis of power and recodified according to issues such as moving to or being in certain places at certain times, being in the vicinity of other suspects, driving certain vehicles, or carrying certain objects with certain temperatures or shapes or sizes. Racializing logics and social sorting persist as certain peoples' territories, bodies, movements, and information are selected for monitoring, tracking, and targeting day after day, month after month, year after year, such that they become *spectral suspects*—visualizations of temperature data that take on the biophysical contours of a human body while its surface appearance remains invisible and its identity unknown. Such processes reorganize the racialized gaze so that black African and brown Arab bodies once discriminated against and/or exoticized on the basis of skin pigment are digitally recast as white blotches of body heat that can be tracked from above. The effect of this vertical remediation of racial difference is to mainstay counterterrorism as a social order. For it is precisely the issue of not being able to verify or confirm the identities of suspects that fuels counterterrorism as a paradigm and drone warfare as its method. The recoding of racial difference as thermal abstraction thus becomes infrastructural as it rationalizes and drives the militarized drone economy.

This thermal imaging of bodies has other effects as well, including creating post-traumatic stress among drone sensor operators and altering the appearance of death. Former sensor operator Brandon Bryant publicly shared his experiences with reporters in 2013 after manning a sensor ball at Creech and Cannon from 2007 to 2011; working on US drone operations in Afghanistan, Iraq, and Yemen; and participating in the killing of 1,626 people. Working in twelve-hour shifts six days a week, drone crews partake in "an endless loop of watching: scanning roads, circling compounds, tracking suspicious activity," shifting between visible light and infrared registers to get the best possible view.[110] When the mission is to monitor a high-value target, a sensor operator might linger above a single house for weeks. Far from being an exercise in objectification, this focused monitoring, Derek Gregory has suggested, generates a "voyeuristic intimacy."[111] Bryant's perceptions of the thermal mediascape had a profound effect on him. He recounts his drone memories in infrared, detailing the first time he killed someone via drone and watching the body's "hot blood" "hit the ground" and "start to cool off." Tasked to linger above the site and conduct surveillance for an "after-action report," Bryant recalls, "It took him a long time to die. I just watched him. I watched him become the same color as the ground he was lying on."[112] Like race, death looks different in the thermal mediascape. When a body is killed, its motion stops and its temperature drops. As the body slowly takes on the temperature values of the matter surrounding it, it loses its contour and recedes into the visual field. Drone IR imagery depicts race as abstract whiteness and death as disappearance.

Just as people have responded to drone strikes and death by metadata practices with protest photos, parodic videos, apps and illicit economies, so too have they devised a plethora of counterinfrared imaging tactics. Some have created drone survival guides that encourage people to avoid becoming part of drone views. Others have experimented with deflective and insulating material such as glass, wool blankets, rugs, tin foil, and synthetically designed fabrics that trap or hide heat, even if temporarily, so that it cannot be detected when drones are hovering above. New York artists Adam Harvey and Johanna Bloomfield designed a drone-proof clothing line called "Stealth Wear" made of nickel-metalized fabric, and German company Blucher sells a special outfit called "Ghost," which makes the body invisible to infrared sensors and is made from a patented material called spectralflage.[113] In rural Mali, where al-Qaeda in the Islamic Maghreb operates, vendors sell woven reed mats, which are reportedly used to cover jihadi vehicles or form makeshift carports to prevent detection by thermal infrared drone sensors.[114] Still others in rural Pakistan have created massive art installations called "not a bug splat," placing giant images of children's faces on the Earth's surface to show drone operators that the anonymous white blobs seen from afar are anything but "bug splats"—they are humans, including children.[115] Such practices contest US vertical hegemony through tactics of concealment and confrontation, using materials and bodies on the earth's surface to evade or defy drone sensors. Some of these practices are designed to insulate the body from infrared sensors and, in doing so, refuse the drone's racialization from above.[116] Even as those in drone war theaters transform everyday behaviors to avoid drone strikes and surveillance, sometimes drone operations go awry.

Drone Crash Scenes

While infrared drone coverage reorganizes racial difference as spectral suspects and death as disappearance, the technology is not foolproof. Drones sometimes fail. And crash sites bring their vertical mediations into dialogue with the forensic.[117] Since 2007, the organization Drone Wars UK has maintained a drone crash database compiled by gleaning details from USAF Accident Investigation Board (AIB) Reports, the WikiLeaks War Logs, and press reports.[118] While this database is not totally comprehensive due to the classification of information, it serves as a useful starting point for extending this discussion of the material contingencies of drone operations. Failures and accidents bring drones plummeting fatefully back to Earth, etching their inadvertent effects into grounded lifeworlds and biomatter. In these situations, airborne maneuvers suddenly become dirtborne ruins and sites of forensic investigation. As Greg Siegel suggests, forensics are "called upon to search for telltale clues, to trace hidden causal nexuses, to provide reliable evidence, to identify sources of misfortunes, to solve puzzles of physical destruction . . . to logically reconstruct and accurately recount the essence of 'what went wrong.' "[119]

Since 2011, there have been at least ten US military drone crashes in or around Djibouti.[120] Accident reports link these events to a multitude of circumstances, ranging from component anomalies to faulty parts, weather conditions to pilot inexperience, software glitches to intentional destruction. On March 15, 2011, a Predator returning from a classified mission overran the runway at Djibouti airport and crashed through a fence, causing almost $1.4 million in damages.[121] Nearly two months later, on May 7, 2011, a Predator plummeted into the Gulf of Aden one and a half hours after takeoff due to component failure, resulting in a $4.4 million loss.[122] Ten days later, on May 17, 2011, a Predator that had flown for 16.9 hours was directed to return to base early because of an oil leak, yet pilots had trouble identifying the runway on the approach at night because of low clouds and high humidity. The Predator and Hellfire missile onboard exploded on impact for a total loss of nearly $3 million.[123] On February 21, 2012, a Predator returning to Djibouti experienced engine anomalies and made an uncommanded gradual descent while on a target during an operation. Commanders directed the drone to return to Djibouti, but when it malfunctioned en route, the pilot was ordered to perform a "hard-ditch," intentionally sending it into the Indian Ocean at a high speed so that the drone and Hellfire missile onboard would be destroyed, costing the US government $4.4 million.[124]

Declassified US Air Force accident reports contain some of the most detailed publicly available information about US drone operations in the Horn of Africa. As they recount accidents, they convey information about the drone's technical specifications, the personnel and bases involved, the maintenance history of the drone, the training, work, and medical history of the pilots, weather conditions, and the cost of damages and losses.[125] As the accident report establishes the parties involved, what went wrong, and who is at fault, it becomes a part of the US military's audit culture. Failure analysis is conducted from the perspectives of US military personnel to refine drone crew performance, improve technical standards in manufacturing, and assess costs, not to question the effectiveness of drone operations.

Photos and cockpit video accompanying accident reports remain classified, but on September 24, 2013, the *Washington Post* published eight US Air Force photos of two drone crash scenes in Djibouti with an article that expressed dismay over the frequency of US drone accidents there.[126] Seven of the photos show a Predator crash near a residential area in Djibouti city. A wide shot of the crash site shows the smashed Predator belly up in the dirt with its casing punctured and bent (see Figure 4.7). Four other photos show close-ups of the object in ruins, honing in on its frayed interior circuitry, damaged landing gear,

FIGURE 4.7 A Predator MQ-1B crashed while trying to return to Camp Lemonnier, the US military base in Djibouti, on May 17, 2011 and landed in a vacant lot near a residential area of Djibouti City. These photographs, taken by US Air Force investigators, were released as part of an unclassified Accident Investigation Board report into the crash (US Air Force).

Source: www.washingtonpost.com/world/national-security/remote-us-base-at-core-of-secret-operations/ 2012/10/25/a26a9392-197a-11e2-bd10-5ff056538b7c_story.html?utm_term=.b8b9553241e5

and crunched mechanical parts (see Figure 4.8). These grounded views exceed the logics of the audit-oriented accident report and demonstrate the fragility of the Predator. Two of the photos feature human onlookers, delineating different epistemological positions in relation to the drone crash scene. The first shows a team of investigators huddled near their SUVs with the crash scene marked off by yellow police tape as if part of an official forensic unit (see Figure 4.9). Another photo reveals about seventy curious Djiboutian onlookers standing on the site perimeter and staring at the dead drone in the distance, positioning the drone crash as an experience that punctuates the lifeworlds of Djiboutian citizens and residents (see Figure 4.10). The photo situates them as silhouettes on the horizon, as remote sensors of a US drone accident in their own backyard.[127]

While drone attack scene photos from the FATA region, discussed earlier, highlight the human costs of drone warfare, these crash scene photos present the drone itself in ruins. A fallen drone is certainly not as horrifying as a bombed building or a targeted killing, but coverage of these vertical maneuvers often places the viewer at the epicenter of the drone's earthly destruction. By featuring human survivors amidst grounded debris, these images raise broader questions about the politics of failure—not just technical, but social failure, and call for a critique that exceeds the bureaucratic logic of the military audit. This coverage of people living amidst drone ruins prompts us to ask how the US can continue to produce and proliferate such a violent form of social hierarchy—one that mobilizes aero-orbital platforms to control and transform vast stretches of sovereign nations. The media I have discussed throughout this book are not simply documentary or evidentiary; rather, they communicate and bring forth a socio-technical order of vertical mediation, an order that uses techniques from global surveillance to targeted killing to reassert US vertical hegemony.

While there are many online photos of protests of the US drone war in Pakistan, such as those analyzed earlier, few exist in Djibouti or the Horn of Africa region. Numerous news reports indicate the Arab Spring protests had a radiating effect on Djiboutian youth, inspiring them to organize demonstrations against their president in an effort to reclaim their nation's political future.[128] Yet press freedoms in the country have been under serious attack, limiting public discussion of important political issues.[129] Djibouti is one of the only countries in Africa without any independent press.[130] As of 2016, only 17.7% of Djiboutians had Internet access and Facebook accounts. It is risky for Djiboutians to express

FIGURE 4.8 A view of the engine and propeller area of the Predator that crashed in Djibouti (US Air Force).

Source: www.washingtonpost.com/world/national-security/remote-us-base-at-core-of-secret-operations/2012/10/25/a26a9392-197a-11e2-bd10-5ff056538b7c_story.html?utm_term=.b8b9553241e5

opposition to state policies such as the hosting of Camp Lemmonier. Journalists have been detained without charge, intimidated, and tortured, and police have used excessive force to quell demonstrations.[131] Foreign journalists who have visited the country have been followed and interrogated by state officials. When one journalist tried to interview activists, locals warned him that their phones were tapped.[132]

Suffice it to say, I have not found extensive online evidence of Djibouti opposition to US drone operations, but in 2013 six hundred janitorial and food service workers waged a strike outside Camp Lemonnier after hundreds of jobs were terminated by new private contractor KBR.[133] While some Djiboutians have come to rely on employment opportunities brought by their country's geo-strategic location, others may be less enthusiastic about Djibouti's role in regional militarization. Chairman of the Djibouti Human Rights League, Farah Abdillahi Miguil, has asked, "Have we become an aircraft carrier?" and indicated, "This huge military presence hasn't translated to something positive on issues like democracy."[134] According to Djibouti's foreign minister, Mahmoud Ali Youssouf, such conditions have positioned his country as "one of the top targets of al-Shabaab in the region."[135] Indeed, some experts have argued that US drone wars have only strengthened the resolve of terrorist organizations to perpetrate violent attacks on the US and its allies. On May 27, 2014 a suicide bombing in

FIGURE 4.9 US Air Force investigators demarcate the crash scene of the Predator that collided as it descended toward Camp Lemonnier (US Air Force).

Source: www.washingtonpost.com/world/national-security/remote-us-base-at-core-of-secret-operations/2012/10/25/a26a9392-197a-11e2-bd10-5ff056538b7c_story.html?utm_term=.b8b9553241e5

FIGURE 4.10 Hundreds of Djiboutians gathered at the scene to gaze at the drone wreckage (US Air Force).

Source: www.washingtonpost.com/world/national-security/remote-us-base-at-core-of-secret-operations/2012/10/25/a26a9392-197a-11e2-bd10-5ff056538b7c_story.html?utm_term=.b8b9553241e5

a Djibouti City restaurant frequented by Western military personnel killed three people and injured eleven others. Al-Shabaab claimed responsibility for the attack.[136] US drone operations not only turn individuals into spectral suspects, they make host countries targets.[137]

Despite Djiboutians' reluctance to report or publicly discuss the adverse effects of US drone operations upon their country, groups in Somalia and Yemen have loudly protested US drone strikes.[138] Members of Al-Shabaab have actually targeted and shot down US drones, though information about most such incidents is classified. On May 27, 2013, an S-100 Camcopter drone crashed in Somalia near the Lower Shabelle region/shoreline of Mogadishu.[139] The drone's mission is classified, but the manufacturer's press release and technical demonstration on YouTube indicates its aerial sensor, loudspeaker, and leafleting systems are used for psychological operations (PSY-OPS)—to communicate with civilians during US military apprehension of a terrorist cell. The video based on a demonstration at Fort Bragg shows the camcopter drone flying above a mock village as armed personnel carriers and a UGV (unmanned ground vehicle) enter the area to apprehend a terrorist cell. A loudspeaker onboard the camcopter drone informs the public about the operation and then drops informational pamphlets into the area.[140] Whether the downed drone was performing PSY-OPS in Somalia remains an open question. After the incident, members of Al-Shabaab posted several photos of the drone's ruins on its English-language Twitter account, boasting: "This one won't spy on Muslims again. So much for the empty rhetoric on the drone program!"[141] Alongside another picture, the militant group added: "This one is off to the scrap yard, Schiebel! You are fighting a losing battle. Islam will prevail."[142]

The drone crash and the documentations of and responses to it are crucial aspects of vertical mediation. These practices range from official accident reports to civilians viewing crash scenes in their neighborhoods to militants posting ruined drone photos on Twitter. They are important for multiple reasons. First, they expose the kinds of drones being operated and where they are being operated. Second, they highlight drone materialities, reminding viewers that un-manned and autonomous technologies are still subject to the laws of gravity, software glitches, and bad weather, and they also have enemies. Finally, given that drone strike photos and assessments in the Horn of Africa do not circulate and there is limited reporting at such sites, the drone crash scene stands in as a symbolic reminder of these concealed sites as well as the injured or dead bodies that remain invisible or uncounted and have been subjected to a strategy of dis-appearance. This strategy, I suggest, is symptomatic of the U.S. drone program more generally—it is achieved not only by using infrared images to watch bodies die and slowly disappear but also by using Hellfire missiles to incinerate bodies on contact so there are no remains left to identify or count (except with DNA analysis), by directing troops to sweep in to remove remains from strike scenes so locals are unable to confirm who is missing or honor the dead, and by waging US drone wars in secret so that no one knows where or when strikes occur. Within this context, drone crash scene documentation serves a vital function as it puts material traces of these operations into mediated forms that can catalyze public inquiry and responses.

Although Pakistan, Djibouti, Somalia, and Yemen have distinct histories and cultures, in the aftermath of 9/11 all of these countries became theaters of US counterterrorism and drone warfare. This chapter has analyzed how various forms of drone coverage work to communicate, enact, or challenge US vertical hegemony. I have conceptualized these dynamics as vertical mediations—power relations and actions that are materialized through and between the air, spectrum, and ground. Coverage materializes vertical mediations to the extent that it can signal or register processes that are kept secret, left invisible, and thus must be inferred or imagined, such as the earthmoving required to build drone infrastructure, the labor of aerial monitoring of targets on the earth's surface, and the grim scenes found by survivors and photographers at drone attack sites. Such mediations reveal that the vertical field has not only been commandeered by dominant military organizations, but also has been seized from the ground up. It takes the form of bottom-up responses from those who document the effects of, comment on, and seek to stop US military drone operations.

Of the practices discussed in this book, targeted killing by drone is the most forceful and violent practice of vertical mediation. This practice not only involves automating a logistics of perception—the temporal coordination of movement and vision—but adds to it the power of ballistics. As drones assemble the capacities to communicate, transport, sense, and destroy, they equip operators with the power to reorder, reform, and remediate life on earth in most material way. As I have discussed throughout this chapter, drones are used to kill certain people while turning others into spectral suspects, to turn homes into holes and countries into targets, and to imprint foreigners' futures onto sovereign surfaces of the earth. The drone's vertical mediations involve much more than gaming or sensing: these practices range from the building of airstrips in others' territories to the transmission of signals through spectrum, from drone navigation via global positioning satellites to the guiding of missiles to targets, from the burials of the dead to the mass uprisings of the living. Drone media enable a mapping of vertical power that exceeds acts of imaging, sensing, and simulation. Though drone maneuvers may be guided by the screen interface, they are not bound by it.

Vertical mediation is entangled with dirt, air, orbit, and spectrum. US military drone operations participate in vertical mediation by using airborne sensors, transmitters/receivers, loudspeakers, and leafleting, but they also do so by requiring the construction of airstrips on the Earth's surface, altering the status of commercial mobile telephone networks, creating craters and losses of life with Hellfire missiles, and plummeting unpredictably to Earth when they fail. These too are vertical mediations—ways in which drone use rewrites the surface of and life upon Earth. The material dimensions of US drone operations are much more extensive than I have delineated in this chapter. Ultimately, I argue that the power of the drone is not just to hunt and kill from afar but to "secure territories" and "administer populations" from the sky, to reorder, reform, and remediate life on Earth in a most material way.[143]

Since drone warfare is here to stay and is likely to be deployed more frequently, it is vital that vertical fields of biopower continue to be critically delineated and analyzed. This analysis needs to extend beyond Paul Virilio's important recognition of the technological fusion of the airplane, the camera, and the gun[144] to include more careful consideration of the biopolitical organization of resources (fuel, labor, lands, hardware, networks, data, sky, orbit) and hierarchies of command that enable targeted killings and the aerial restructuring of life on earth. Just as it is important to recognize how drone warfare is defined by remote control, simulation, and gaming, it is equally important to acknowledge its grounded dimensions, the landscapes and topographies that register and archive the drone's uses and effects. During the past century the world has witnessed a devastating flurry of air raids, carpet bombings, and surgical strikes. US drones have killed thousands of people since 9/11. That the drone has been heralded by some as a technology of "humane warfare" is not only deeply troubling, but perverse.

As drone use supplements the "dark side" of the war on terror—the profiling, capturing, transporting, detention, and torturing of terror suspects—with practices of targeted killing, it has also generated a *new disenfranchised class of "targeted" people*. Derek Gregory has pointed out that the permissible scope of "the target" has been widened in the context of late modern warfare, leading to a displacement of the concept of "the civilian." I would suggest that these conditions have also led to the emergence of a *targeted class*.[145] Particular inhabitants of Pakistan, Yemen, and Somalia, for instance, have become part of a "targeted" class simply because they live and move in areas in which *terror suspects may operate*. In such areas anyone and everyone is at risk and daily life is haunted by the specter of aerial monitoring and bombardment. Drones may sidestep the dirty work of torture, but they advance other kinds of PSY-OPS, using the sky to delineate and administer zones of surveillance and fear, death and destruction. Within this context, asymmetric warfare creates new forms disenfranchisement for some and greater precariousness for all.[146]

Though drones are currently controlled by aero-orbital elites, they are likely to be used by a wider array of political entities in the future given their relatively low cost and ease to develop. Witness, for instance, the emergence of DIY Drone websites or the home-made drone used to monitor police at an Occupy protest in Warsaw, Poland in November 2011, or the fact that online hobby stores sometimes sell out of drone models.[147] While "the targeted" may appear to be isolated to certain "lawless regions" or "rogue states," the expansion of drone use, including by local law enforcers from New York to Houston, on the US–Mexico border, and against US citizens (Anwar al-Awlaki and his 16 year-old son in Yemen) reveals that people across the planet (including citizens of democratic nation-states) are becoming part of a targeted class.[148]

Notes

1 As Lisa Hajjar shows, drones have also been used by the Israeli government since the 1990s. See her article, "Lawfare and Targeted Killing: Developments in the Israeli and US Contexts," *Jadaliiya*, January 15, 2012, accessed February 15, 2014, www.jadaliyya.com/pages/index/4049/lawfare-and-targeted-killing_developments-in-the-I

2 John Keller, "DOD Plans to Spend $5.78 Billion for Unmanned Vehicles Procurement and Research in 2013," *Military & Aerospace Electronics*, February 14, 2012, www.militaryaerospace.com/articles/2012/02/dod-unmanned-vehicle-spending-requiest-for-2013-announced.html

3 Jane Mayer, "The Predator War," *The New Yorker*, October 26, 2009, accessed August 2, 2011, www.newyorker.com/reporting/2009/10/26/091026fa_fact_mayer

4 Ibid.

5   Jay Solomon, Siobhan Gorman, and Matthew Rosenberg, "U.S. Plans New Drone Attacks in Pakistan," *The Wall Street Journal*, March 26, 2009, accessed July 21, 2011, http://online.wsj.com/article/SB123803414843244161.html

6   "Predators and Civilians," editorial, *The Wall Street Journal*, July 14, 2009, accessed July 28, 2017, http://online.wsj.com/article/SB124743959026229517.html#mod= djemITP

7   Elizabeth Mumiller and Thom Shanker, "War Evolves With Drones, Some Tiny as Bugs," *The New York Times*, June 19, 2011, accessed July 21, 2011, www.nytimes. com/2011/06/20/world/20drones.html?

8   "The C.I.A. and Drone Strikes," *The New York Times*, August 13, 2011, accessed August 20, 2011, www.nytimes.com/2011/08/14/opinion/sunday/the-cia-and-drone-strikes.html

9   "Flight of the Drones," *The Economist*, October 8, 2011, accessed November 1, 2011, www.economist.com/node/21531433

10 Text of Freedom of Information Act Request can be found here: www.aclu.org/national-security/predator-drone-foia-request

11 Peter Beaumont, Campaigners seek arrest of former CIA legal chief over Pakistan drone attacks," *The Guardian*, July 15, 2011, www.theguardian.com/world/2011/jul/15/cia-usa

12 Jonathan Adams, "US Defends Unmanned Drone Attacks after Harsh UN Report," *The Christian Science Monitor*, June 3, 2010, accessed July 21, 2011, www.csmonitor. com/World/terrorism-security/2010/0603/US-defends-unmanned-drone-attacks-after-harsh-UN-report. Also see Alston's report linked in pdf to this news report; Philip Alston, "Report of the Special Rapporteur on Extrajudicial, Summary or Arbitrary Executions," UN Human Rights Council, May 28, 2010, accessed November 1, 2011, www2.ohchr.org/english/bodies/hrcouncil/docs/14session/A.HRC.14.24.Add6.pdf

13 Nathan Hodge, "Drone Pilots Could Be Tried for 'War Crimes,' Law Prof Says," *Wired*, April 28, 2010, accessed August 1, 2011, www.wired.com/dangerroom/2010/04/drone-pilots-could-be-tried-for-war-crimes-law-prof-says/

14 See, for example, Elisabeth Weber, *Kill Boxes: Facing the Legacy of US-Sponsored Torture, Indefinite Detention, and Drone Warfare* (New York: Punctum Books, 2017); G. Chamayou and J. Lloyd (trans.), *A theory of the drone* (New York, The New Press, 2013); Medea Benjamin, *Drone Warfare: Killing by Remote Control* (New York, OR Books, 2012); Adam Rothstein, *Drone* (London: Bloomsbury, 2015); John Kaag and Sarah Kreps. *Drone Warfare* (Cambridge, UK: Polity Press, 2014); Ann Rogers and John Hill, *Unmanned: Drone Warfare and Global Security* (London: Pluto Press, 2014); M. Shane Riza, *Killing without Heart: Limits on Robotic Warfare in an Age of Persistent Conflict* (Washington, DC: Potomac Books, 2013); Lloyd C. Gardner, *Killing Machine: The American Presidency in the Age of Drone Warfare* (New York: New Press, 2013); Marjorie Cohn, Ed., *Drones and Targeted Killing: Legal, Moral, and Geopolitical Issues* (Northampton, MA: Olive Branch Press, 2015); and Hugh Gusterson, *Drone: Remote Control Warfare* (Cambridge, MA: MIT Press, 2016).

15 Scott Horton, "Lawfare Redux," *Harper's Magazine*, March 12, 2010, accessed July 28, 2017, http://harpers.org/blog/2010/03/lawfare-redux/

16 Sarah Kember and Joanna Zylinksa, *Life after New Media: Mediation as a Vital Process* (Cambridge, MA: MIT Press, 2012).

17 This analysis is based on the collection and study of 72 drone attack and 183 drone protest photos using Google image search in 2011 and 10 aerial assault videos on YouTube, Dvids and Live Leak.

18 Mayer, "The Predator War." In addition, Western news institutions have severely reduced budgets for international reporting in recent years, and are wary about sending correspondents to this region.

19 Farhat Taj, "The Year of the Drone Misinformation," *Small Wars & Insurgencies* 21, no. 3 (2010): 530.

20 Taj, "The Year of the Drone Misinformation," 531. For further discussion of the lack of access to credible information about drone attack casualties and the treatment of targets as "militants" or "civilians," see Daphne Eviatar, "CIA Drones Gone Wild?," *The Huffington Post*, January 8, 2012, accessed July 28, 2017, www.huffingtonpost.com/daphne-eviatar/cia-drones-gone-wild_b_1080310.html? ref=tw; and Susan Breau, Marie Aronsson, and Rachel Joyce, "Discussion Paper 2: Drone Attacks, International Law, and the Recording of Civilian Casualties of Armed Conflict," Oxford Research Group, June 2011, accessed July 28, 2017, http://reliefweb.int/node/421916, 1

21 "Drone Warfare: Current Statistics," Bureau of Investigative Journalism website, 2017, www.thebureauinvestigates.com/projects/drone-war

22 Clive Stafford Smith, "For Our Allies: Death From Above," *The New York Times*, November 3, 2011, accessed July 28, 2017, www.nytimes.com/2011/11/04/ opinion/in-pakistan-drones-kill-our-innocent-allies.html

23 Ibid. Also see Pratap Chatterjee, "Bureau Reporter Meets Sixteen-Year-Old Three Days before US Drone Kills Him," *The Bureau of Investigative Journalism*, November 4, 2011, accessed July 28, 2017, www.thebureauinvestigates.com/ 2011/11/04/bureau-reporter-meets-16-year-old-just-three-days-before-he-is-killed-by-a-us-drone/

24 Sahil Kapur, "67% of Pakistani Journalists Say US Drones Attacks are Acts of Terrorism: Survey," *The Raw Story*, February 14, 2011, accessed July 28, 2017, www.rawstory.com/rs/2011/02/14/67-of-pakistani-journalists-say-us-drones-attacks-are-acts-of-terrorism-survey/. Photos have been removed from the story since the time of publication.

25 Bob Crilly, "168 Children Killed in Drone Strikes in Pakistan Since Start of Campaign," *The Telegraph*, August 11, 2011, accessed July 28, 2017, www.telegraph. co.uk/news/worldnews/asia/pakistan/8695679/168-children-killed-in-drone-strikes-in-Pakistan-since-start-of-campaign.html

26 On the Getty website the full caption reads: "Pakistani residents stand amongst the rubble of a classroom after militants blew up a girls' school on the outskirts of Peshawar on June 22, 2009. Pakistan has been hit by a wave of deadly suicide bombs in recent weeks, attacks blamed on Taliban rebels seeking to avenge the campaign against them. The army confirmed that the offensive would be expanded into the lawless tribal areas along the Afghan border, the stronghold of feared Pakistan Taliban chief Baitullah Mehsud and his fighters." See: www.gettyimages.com/detail/ news-photo/pakistani-residents-stand-amongst-the-rubble-of-a-classroom-news-photo/88615345#pakistani-residents-stand-amongst-the-rubble-of-a-classroom-after-picture-id88615345

27 "Pakistan Drone War Photo Gallery," *Channel 4 News*, December 14, 2010, www. channel4.com/news/pakistan-drone-warfare-photo-gallery/display/image/drone7. Original page no longer available, but image can be found here: www.nbcnews.com/ slideshow/pakistans-year-turmoil-34067531

28 Howard LaFranchi, "US Message in Drone Strikes: If Pakistan Doesn't Take on Taliban, We Will," *The Christian Science Monitor*, June 28, 2011, accessed July 28, 2017, www.csmonitor.com/USA/Foreign-Policy/2011/0628/US-message-in-drone-strikes-If-Pakistan-doesn-t-take-on-Taliban-we-will

29 Derek Gregory, "'In Another Time-Zone the Bombs Fall Unsafely . . .': Targets, Civilians and Late Modern War," *The Arab World Geographer* 9, no. 2 (2006): 88–111. Also see, Susan Breau, Marie Aronsson, and Rachel Joyce, "Discussion Paper 2: Drone Attacks, International Law, and the Recording of Civilian Casualties

of Armed Conflict," Oxford Research Group, June 2011, accessed July 28, 2017, http://reliefweb.int/node/421916

30 "U.S. Passes up Chance to Strike Taliban," *NBC News*, September 13, 2006, accessed July 28, 2017, www.nbcnews.com/id/14823099/ns/world_news-south_and_central_asia/t/us-passes-chance-strike-taliban/#.V41TrK6-sXk; also see, David Hambling, "Why Was Pakistan Drone So Deadly?" *Wired*, June 24, 2009, accessed July 28, 2017, www.wired.com/dangerroom/2009/06/why-was-pakistan-drone-strike-so-deadly/

31 Nathan Hodge, "Deadliest Strike Yet in Pakistan Drone War, *Wired*, June 24, 2009, accessed July 28, 2017, www.wired.com/dangerroom/2009/06/deadliest-strike-yet-in-pakistan-drone-war/. Also see Pir Zubair Shah and Salman Masood, "U.S. Drone Strike Said to Kill 60 in Pakistan," *The New York Times*, June 23, 2009, accessed July 28, 2017, www.nytimes.com/2009/06/24/world/asia/24pstan.html. This particular drone attack even has its own Wikipedia entry available at http://en.wikipedia.org/wiki/23_June_2009_Makeen_airstrike

32 Adam Entous, Siobahn Gorman, and Julian E. Barnes, "US Tightens Drone Rules," *The Wall Street Journal*, November 4, 2011, accessed July 28, 2017, online.wsj.com/article/SB10001424052970204621904577013982672973836.html

33 See image here: "Who Will Avenge the Blood of These Pakistanis?," from discussion "CIA Islamabad Station Chief Sued for Murder and Terrorism," *Pakistan Defence*, posted by "AstanoshKhan," December 15, 2010, accessed July 31, 2017, http://defence.pk/threads/cia-islamabad-station-chief-sued-for-murder-and-terrorism.84845/

34 Anna Doble, "Drone Attacks in Pakistan are Next Guantanamo," *Channel 4 News*, May 9, 2011, accessed July 28, 2017, www.channel4.com/news/drone-attacks-in-pakistan-are-next-guantanamo

35 Chris Woods, "The US has Killed More than 168 children in Pakistan," *Another World Is Possible . . .* blog, August 12, 2011, accessed July 28, 2017, www.a-w-i-p.com/index.php/2011/08/12/the-us-has-killed-more-than-168-children

36 Asim Qureshi, "Interview with Family Devastated by US Drone Attack," *Global Research*, September 26, 2010, accessed July 28, 2017, www.globalresearch.ca/interview-with-family-devastated-by-us-drone-attack-the-dead-were-completely-unrecognisable/21199?print=1

37 Breau, Aronsson, and Joyce, "Discussion Paper 2: Drone Attacks."

38 Shah and Beaumont, "US Drone Strikes in Pakistan."

39 "Gaming in Waziristan," July 19—August 5, 2011, Beaconsfield Gallery website, accessed July 28, 2017, http://beaconsfield.ltd.uk/projects/gaming-in-waziristan/; Zofeen Ebrahim, "PAKISTAN: Videogames Pictured Killing the Innocent," *Inter Press Service*, August 11, 2011, www.ipsnews.net/2011/08/pakistan-videogames-pictured-killing-the-innocent/

40 Press articles featuring Behram's work include, Spencer Ackerman, "Rare Photographs Show Ground Zero of the Drone War," *Wired*, December 12, 2012; Hasnain Kazim, "Drone War in Pakistan: Photos from the Ground Show Civilian Casualties," *Spiegel Online International*, July 18, 2011; Jemima Khan, "Under Fire from Afar: Harrowing Exhibition Reveals Damage Done by Drones in Pakistan," *The Independent*, July 29, 2011; and Saeed Shah and Peter Beaumont, "US Drone Strikes in Pakistan Claiming Many Civilian Victims, Says Campaigner," *The Guardian*, July 17, 2011.

41 Bureau of Investigative Journalism, "Obama 2009 Pakistan Strikes," *Bureau of Investigative Journalism*, August 10, 2011, www.thebureauinvestigates.com/2011/08/10/obama-2009-strikes/

42 Ibid.

43 Chris Woods, "Over 160 Children Reported Among Drone Deaths," *Bureau of Investigative Journalism*, August 11, 2011, accessed July 28, 2017, www.thebureau investigates.com/2011/08/11/more-than-160-children-killed-in-us-strikes/

44 Tiziana Terranova, *Network Culture: Politics for the Information Age* (London: Pluto Press, 2004), 142.

45 For further discussion of infrared drone imagery, see Lisa Parks, "Drones Infrared Imagery and Body Heat," *International Journal of Communication* 8 (2014): 2518–2521.

46 As Obama counterterrorism advisor Lisa Monaco puts it, "Because the threats and enemies we face evolve and adapt, we must be flexible in confronting them where they are—always doing so consistent with our laws and our values." Quoted in Charlie Savage, Eric Schmitt, and Mark Mazzetti, "Obama Expands War With Al Qaeda to Include Shabab in Somalia," *The New York Times*, November 27, 2016, accessed July 28, 2017, www.nytimes.com/2016/11/27/us/politics/obama-expands-war-with-al-qaeda-to-include-shabab-in-somalia.html. Also see David Harvey, "Flexible Accumulation Through Urbanization: Reflections on 'Post-modernism' in the American City," *Antipode* 19, no. 3 (1987), 260–286.

47 "Taliban Hits Taliban Column," YouTube video, posted by "Andrew Fell," June 20, 2009, www.youtube.com/watch?v=2bgX9J_ZBC0

48 "Afghanistan War: Proof of care taken note to injure civilians. UAV Aborted Attack. (HiDef)," YouTube video, 1:20, posted by "US Military Videos By OpsLens," August 10, 2010, www.youtube.com/watch?v=D3e7hB65Dv0

49 Butler, *Frames of War*, 54.

50 Wikileaks produced a video related to this incident entitled *Collateral Murder*, available here: https://collateralmurder.wikileaks.org/

51 Derek Gregory, "'In Another Time-Zone the Bombs Fall Unsafely . . .': Targets, Civilians and Late Modern War," *The Arab World Geographer* 9, no. 2 (2006): 88–111. Also see, Derek Gregory, "The Everywhere War," *The Geographical Journal* 177, no. 3 (2011): 238–250.

52 Lisa Parks, "Drones, Vertical Mediation, and the Targeted Class," *Feminist Studies* 42, no. 1 (2016): 227–235.

53 Daniel L. Byman, "Do Targeted Killings Work?," *Brookings Institute*, July 14, 2009, www.brookings.edu/opinions/2009/0714_targeted_killings_bymanaspx?p=1; http://returngood.com/2009/07/21/brookings-report-confirms-high-civilian-death-rate-and-misses-the-point/

54 Peter Bergen and Katherine Tiedemann, "The Year of the Drone: An Analysis of U.S. Drone Strikes in Pakistan, 2004–2010," Counterterrorism Strategy Initiative Policy Paper, *New America Foundation*, February 24, 2010, https://perma-archives. org/media/2014/8/16/18/22/XSE6-SWPR/cap.pdf. Also see, Dean Nelson, "One in Three Killed by US drones in Pakistan is a Civilian, Report Claims," *The Telegraph*, March 4, 2010, accessed July 28, 2017, www.telegraph.co.uk/news/world news/asia/pakistan/7361630/One-in-three-killed-by-US-drones-in-Pakistan-is-a-civilian-report-claims.html

55 Thank you to Afzal Shah and Bashkar Sarkar for this translation.

56 Derek Gregory, "Dirty Dancing: Drones and Death in the Borderlands," in *Life in the Age of Drone Warfare*, Ed. Lisa Parks and Caren Kaplan (London and Durham, NC: Duke University Press, 2017), 25–58.

57 For discussion of this issue, see, for instance, Alex de Waal, "Darfur and the Failure of the Responsibility to Protect," *International Affairs* 83, no. 6 (2007): 1039–1054, www.jstor.org/stable/4541909?seq=4#page_scan_tab_contents; Cristina G. Badescu and Linnea Bergholm, "The Responsibility to Protect and the Conflict in Darfur: The Big Let-Down," *Security Dialogue* 40, no. 3 (2009): 287–309, http://journals. sagepub.com/doi/pdf/10.1177/0967010609336198; Carsten Stahn, "Between Law-

breaking and Law-making: Syria, Humanitarian Intervention and 'What the Law Ought to Be,'" *Journal of Conflict & Security Law* 19, no. 1 (2014): 25–48, https://academic.oup.com/jcsl/article/19/1/25/1095195/Between-Law-breaking-and-Law-making-Syria

58 Megan Boler, "Introduction," in *Digital Media and Democracy: Tactics in Hard Times*, Ed. Megan Boler (Cambridge, MA: MIT Press, 2008), 14.

59 Ibid, 6.

60 "What Happens When You Protest Predator Drones," *Public Intelligence* blog, October 30, 2010, accessed July 28, 2017, http://publicintelligence.net/what-happens-when-you-protest-predator-drones/

61 "Outside C.I.A. Headquarters, Protesting U.S. Drone Attacks," *Debra Sweet* blog, Janruary 17, 2010, accessed July 28, 2017, http://debra.worldcantwait.net/2010/01/outside-c-i-a-headquarters-protesting-u-s-drone-attacks/. Also see photos from the protest available here: www.facebook.com/media/set/?set=a.293206967563.191705.744057563

62 "DRONE-Resisting Sanitized Remote-Control Death," *Voices for Creative Non-Violence* blog, http://vcnv.org/drone-resisting-sanitized-remote-control-death

63 Emma Brown and Del Quentin Wilber, "Air and Space Museum Closes after Guards Clash with Protesters," *The Washington Post*, October 8, 2011, accessed July 28, 2017, www.washingtonpost.com/blogs/post_now/post/2011/10/08/gIQAx0x 2VL_blog.html; Christopher Santarelli, "Protesters Pepper Sprayed at Air and Space Museum in Washington DC," *The Blaze*, October 8, 2011, accessed July 28, 2017, www.theblaze.com/stories/2011/10/08/protesters-pepper-sprayed-at-air-and-space-museum-in-dc/; and Deborah Dupre, "Drones Kill Kids: Occupy D.C. Rights Defenders Shut Museum with Drone Exhibit," *Examiner.com*, October 8, 2011, www.examiner.com/article/drones-kill-kids-occupy-d-c-rights-defenders-shut-museum-with-drone-exhibit

64 Code Pink, "Drone Summit: Killing and Spying by Remote Control," April 28–29, 2012, www.codepinkarchive.org/article.php?id=6065; Code Pink, "Code Pink Peace Delegation to Pakistan," www.codepinkarchive.org/article.php?id=6174

65 "The Ethical Governor," YouTube video, 8:00, posted by "johnbutlerA," November 27, 2010, www.youtube.com/watch?v=96oR36im7cY

66 Nick Turse, Tomorrow's Battlefield: U.S. Proxy Wars and Secret Ops in Africa (Chicago, IL: Haymarket Books, 2015).

67 Craig Whitlock, "U.S. Expands Secret Intelligence Operations in Africa," *The Washington Post*, June 13, 2012, accessed July 28, 2017, www.youtube.com/watch?v =96oR36im7cY

68 Central Intelligence Agency (CIA), "Djibouti," *The World Factbook*, accessed July 29, 2017, www.cia.gov/library/publications/the-world-factbook/geos/dj.html

69 Jennifer N. Brass, "Djibouti's Unusual Resource Curse," *Journal of Modern Africa Studies* 46, no. 4 (2008): 525, 529.

70 Samson A. Bezabeh, "Citizenship and the Logic of Sovereignty in Djibouti," *African Affairs* 110, no. 441 (2011): 1–20; Human Rights Watch, "Djibouti: Allow Peaceful Protests," April 4, 2011, accessed July 29, 2017, www.hrw.org/news/2011/04/04/djibouti-allow-peaceful-protests

71 "Camp Lemonnier, Djibouti," *naval-technology.com*, accessed July 29, 2017, www.naval-technology.com/projects/camplemonnier/; also see "Defense Management: DOD Needs to Determine the Future of Its Horn of Africa Task Force," Report to the Subcommittee on National Security and Foreign Affairs, Committee on Oversight and Government Reform, House of Representatives, *US Government Accountability Office*, April 2010, accessed July 29, 2017, www.gao.gov/products/GAO-10-504.

72 "Defense Management."

73 David Vine, "The Pentagon's New Base Plan Will Achieve the Exact Opposite of Its Goal," *The Nation*, January 14, 2016, accessed July 29, 2017, www.thenation.com/article/the-pentagons-new-base-plan-will-achieve-the-exact-opposite-of-its-goal/

74 Andrew Jacobs and Jane Perlez, "U.S Wary of Its New Neighbor in Djibouti: A Chinese Naval Base," *The New York Times*, February 25, 2017, accessed July 29, 2017, www.nytimes.com/2017/02/25/world/africa/us-djibouti-chinese-naval-base.html; Shashank Bengali, "U.S. Military Investing Heavily in Africa," *Los Angeles Times*, October 20, 2017; Andrei Akulov, "Asia Pivot Declared, US Army Eyes Africa," *Global Research*, November 21, 2013, accessed July 29, 2017, www.globalresearch.ca/asia-pivot-declared-us-army-eyes-africa/5358964; Department of the Navy and CIA World Factbook, "An End to Drone Flights from Camp Lemonnier, Djibouti," *Washington Post*, September 24, 2013.

75 Steve Niva, "Disappearing Violence: JSOC and the Pentagon's New Cartography of Networked Warfare," *Security Dialogue* 44, no. 3 (2013): 186.

76 Ibid, 197.

77 "Project Drone: Current Statistics," The Bureau of Investigative Journalism website, 2017, www.thebureauinvestigates.com/projects/drone-war

78 Tabatha Zarrella, "Working Together, Sharing a Common Mission, Bond," Combined Task Force, Horn of Africa, January 27, 2014, accessed July 29, 2017, www.hoa.africom.mil/story/7844/working-together-sharing-a-common-mission-bond; Department of the Navy and CIA World Factbook, "An End to Drone Flights."

79 Nick Turse, "The Increasing US Shadow Wars in Africa," *Mother Jones*, July 12, 2012, accessed July 29, 2017, www.motherjones.com/politics/2012/07/us-shadow-wars-africa

80 Nick Turse, "Behind the Veil of Secrecy over US Military Operations in Africa," *Mother Jones*, April 14, 2014, accessed July 29, 2017, www.motherjones.com/politics/2014/04/us-military-africa-secrecy-operations; see also Nick Turse, "The Startling Size of US Military Operations in Africa," *Mother Jones*, September 6, 2013, accessed July 29, 2017, www.motherjones.com/politics/2013/09/us-military-bases-africa

81 Robert Young Pelton, "Enter the Drones: An In-Depth Look at Drones, Somali Reactions, and How the War May Change," *Somalia Report*, July 6, 2011, www.somaliareport.com/index.php/post/1096

82 Amy Goodman, "Death by Metadata: Jeremy Scahill and Glenn Greenwald Reveal NSA Role in Assassinations Overseas," *Democracy Now!*, February 10, 2014, www.democracynow.org/2014/2/10/death_by_metadata_jeremy_scahill_glenn. According to Scahill in his interview with Amy Goodman, these transceivers can locate a mobile phone within thirty feet of its position.

83 A. Goodman, "Death by Metadata"; see also Jeremy Scahill and Glenn Greenwald, "The NSA's Secret Role in the U.S. Assassination Program," *Intercept*, January 9, 2014, accessed July 29, 2017, https://theintercept.com/2014/02/10/the-nsas-secret-role/; David Cole, "We Kill People Based on Metadata," *New York Review of Books*, May 10, 2014.

84 A. Goodman, "Death by Metadata."

85 Charles Faint and Michael Harris, "F3EAD: Ops/Intel Fusion 'Feeds' the SOF Targeting Process," *Small Wars Journal*, January 31, 2012, http://smallwarsjournal.com/jrnl/art/f3ead-opsintel-fusion-"feeds"-the-sof-targeting-process

86 Pelton, "Enter the Drones."

87 This targeted method, also known as the "unwavering eye," stresses "massing all elements of intelligence, surveillance and reconnaissance on 'selected parts of the enemy's network.' " See Niva, "Disappearing Violence," 193. The decision-making

protocols for targeted killings require two forms of intelligence, but in areas where it is risky to deploy boots on the ground, such as Yemen and Somalia, it is increasingly common for commanders to authorize drone strikes based on aerial and signal intelligence alone. See also "Raytheon AST Surveillance and Reconnaissance Solutions," YouTube video, 0:53, posted by "Raytheon," November 8, 2011, www.youtube.com/watch?v=UtpURMoT1Qg

88 A. Goodman, "Death by Metadata." A program called Geolocation Cell or Geo Cell allowed the NSA to track and locate someone in real time, which generated a motto within the NSA: "We track 'em. You whack 'em." Dana Priest, "NSA Growth Fueled by Need to Target Terrorists," *Washington Post*, July 21, 2013.

89 Kevin P. Donavan and Aaron K. Martin, "The Rise of African SIM Registration: The Emerging Dynamics of Regulatory Change," *First Monday* 19, no. 2 (2014), http://firstmonday.org/ojs/index.php/fm/article/view/4351/3820

90 "ATRA Urges Cellcos to Implement Biometrics for SIM Registration," *TeleGeography*, August 18, 2016, accessed July 29, 2017, www.telegeography.com/products/commsupdate/articles/2016/08/18/atra-urges-cellcos-to-implement-biometrics-for-sim-registration/; AntiMedia, "New Cell Phone Policy Coming Soon: Register Fingerprints or Lose Service," *Aiqus*, accessed July 29, 2017, www.aiqus.com/new-cell-phone-policy-coming-soon-register-fingerprints-or-lose-service/

91 Jacob Appelbaum et al., "Obama's Lists: A Dubious History of Targeted Killing in Afghanistan," *Spiegel Online*, December 28, 2014, accessed July 29, 2017, www.spiegel.de/international/world/secret-docs-reveal-dubious-details-of-targeted-killings-in-afghanistan-a-1010358.html

92 World Bank Group, "Mobile cellular subscriptions (per 100 people)—Somalia" 2016, http://data.worldban.org/indicator/IT.CEL.SETS.P2?locations=SO

93 Tim Craig and Shaiq Hussain, "Pakistanis Face a Deadline: Surrender Fingerprints or Give Up Cellphone," *Washington Post*, February 23, 2015, accessed July 29, 2017, www.washingtonpost.com/world/asia_pacific/pakistanis-face-a-deadline-surrender-fingerprints-or-give-up-cellphone/2015/02/23/de995a88-b932-11e4-bc30-a4e75503948a_story.html?utm_term=.1cdc606ba65b

94 Caren Kaplan's prophetic work on GPS shows how a technology designed to support US military precision targeting during the Persian Gulf War was transitioned into mass markets and used to track and target consumers. Caren Kaplan, "Precision Targets: GPS and the Militarization of U.S. Consumer Identity," *American Quarterly* 58, no. 3 (2006): 693–714.

95 Sydney Brownstone, "Your iPhone Can Now Alert You When a Drone Attacks," *Fast Company*, February 11, 2014, accessed July 29, 2017, www.fastcoexist.com/3026320/your-iphone-can-now-alert-you-when-a-drone-attacks

96 James Bamford, *The Shadow Factory* (New York: Double Day, 2008).

97 Doug Bernard, "Pakistani Cellphone Crackdown May Fuel Black Market," *Voice of America News*, February 25, 2015, accessed July 29, 2017, www.voanews.com/a/pakistani-cellphone-crackdown-may-fuel-black-market/2659199.html; Fouzia Khan, "SIM Cards With IDs Are On Sale in Black Market," *Arab News*, July 26, 2013, accessed July 29, 2017, www.arabnews.com/news/459231; Nadim Al-Hamid, "Jeddah's SIM Card Black Market Thriving," *Arab News*, August 22, 2014, accessed July 29, 2017, www.arabnews.com/news/saudi-arabia/619206

98 Ahmed Osman, "Somalia Powerless to Stop Al-Shabaab Mobile Internet Shutdown," *Inter Press Service*, February 16, 2014, accessed July 29, 2017, www.ipsnews.net/2014/02/somalia-powerless-stop-al-shabaab-mobile-internet-shutdown/; see also "Hormuud Telecom services disrupted by militant group," *TeleGeography*, February 4, 2014, accessed July 31, 2017, www.telegeography.com/products/commsupdate/articles/2014/02/04/hormuud-telecom-services-disrupted-by-militant-group/

99 Alice Speri, "Al-Shabaab is Confiscating Camera-Equipped 'Spy' Phones," *Vice News*, March 20, 2014, accessed July 31, 2017, https://news.vice.com/article/al-shabaab-is-confiscating-camera-equipped-spy-phones. For detail on Al-Shabaab's control of social media and messaging, see Ken Menkhaus, "Al-Shabaab and Social Media: A Double-Edged Sword," *Brown Journal of World Affairs* 20, no. 11 (2014): 309–327.

100 Niva, "Disappearing Violence," 199.

101 Jeremy Packer, "Screens in the Sky: SAGE, Surveillance, and the Automation of Perceptual, Mneumonic, and Epistemological Labor," *Social Semiotics* 23, no. 2 (2013): 173–195.

102 Tim Cullen, "The MQ-9 Reaper Remotely Piloted Aircraft: Humans and Machines in Action," Ph.D. diss., Massachusetts Institute of Technology, 2011.

103 Bryan Williams Jones, "Creech AFB UAV Operations," *Jonesblog*, February 22, 2008, accessed July 29, 2017.

104 Cullen, "The MQ-9 Reaper," 96.

105 Ibid.

106 Caroline Holmqvist, "Undoing War: War Ontologies and the Materiality of Drone Warfare," *Millennium: Journal of International Studies* 41, no. 3 (2013): 543–544.

107 G. Miller, "CIA Flew Stealth Drones into Pakistan to Monitor bin Laden House," *Washington Post*, May 17, 2011.

108 Tyler Wall and Torin Monahan, "Surveillance and Violence from Afar: The Politics of Drones and Liminal Security-Scapes," *Theoretical Criminology* 15, no. 3 (2011): 239–254.

109 Frantz Fanon, *Black Skin, White Masks* (New York: Grove Press, 1967); Simone Browne, "Digital Epidermalization: Race, Identity and Biometrics," *Critical Sociology* 36, no. 1 (2009): 131–150; David Lyon, "Everyday Surveillance: Personal Data and Social Classifications," *Information, Communication & Society* 5, no. 2 (2002): 242–257; Kelly A. Gates *Our Biometric Future: Facial Recognition Technology and the Culture of Surveillance* (New York: New York University Press, 2011).

110 Matthew Power, "Confessions of a Drone Warrior," *GQ*, October 22, 2013, accessed July 29, 2017.

111 Derek Gregory, "From a View to a Kill: Drones and Late Modern War," *Theory, Culture and Society* 28, nos. 7–8 (2011): 188–215.

112 Power, "Confessions of a Drone Warrior."

113 Adam Harvey, "Stealth Wear Summary," January 17, 2013, accessed July 29, 2017; David Crane, "Blucher Systems Ghost Soldier Camouflage and Spectralflage Vehicle Camo: Multispectral Combat Camouflage Fabric Technology That Provides Anti-Thermal/IR (Infrared) Camo for 21st Century Special Warfare (Specwar)," *Defense Review*, April 29, 2011, accessed July 29, 2017, www.defensereview.com/blucher-systems-ghost-and-spectralflage-multispectral-combat-camouflage-fabric-technology-anti-thermalir-infrared-soldier-camouflage-and-vehicle-camouflage-for-21st-century-warfare-operations/

114 Rukmini Callimachi, "Tipsheet on avoiding drones found," *Deseret News*, February 21, 2013, accessed July 29, 2017, www.deseretnews.com/article/765623148/Tipsheet-on-avoiding-drones-found.html?pg=all

115 A Giant Art Installation Targets Predator Drone Operators," April 6, 2014, accessed July 29, 2017, https://notabugsplat.com/2014/04/06/a-giant-art-installation-targets-predator-drone-operators/; Ashley Feinberg, "Giant Portrait Shows Drone Operators That People Aren't 'Bug Splats,'" *Gizmodo*, April 6, 2014, accessed July 29, 2017, http://gizmodo.com/giant-portrait-shows-drone-operators-that-people-arent-15594 60573

116 Keith Feldman, "Empire's Verticality: The Af/Pak Frontier, Visual Culture, and Racialization from Above," *Comparative American Studies* 9, no. 4 (2011): 325–341.

117 For an excellent discussion of the forensic, see Greg Siegel, *Forensic Media: Reconstructing Accidents in Accelerated Modernity* (Durham, NC: Duke University Press, 2014). The accident is "not just an occasion for scientific inquiry but an opportunity for practical technical instruction; not just an occurrence that government and industry learned about but one that engineers and designers learned from. Forensic discourse thereby recast dystopian catastrophe as utopian possibility" (38).

118 Drone Wars UK, "Drone Crash Database," accessed July 29, 2017, http://dronewars. net/drone-crash-database/. The Predator, made by General Atomics, has had 9.26 accidents per 100,000 flight hours, while its Reaper has had 7.96. The Global Hawk has an accident rate of 15.16 per 100,000 flight hours, almost three times that of the aircraft it is designed to replace, the Cold War–era U-2 spy plane. Brendan McGarry, "Drones Most Accident-Prone U.S. Air Force Craft: BGOV Barometer," *Bloomberg Business*, June 17, 2012, accessed July 29, 2017, www.bloomberg.com/news/articles/ 2012-06-18/drones-most-accident-prone-u-s-air-force-craft-bgov-barometer

119 Siegel, *Forensic Media*, 31.

120 Chris Whitlock and Greg Miller, "U.S. Moves Drone Fleet from Camp Lemonnier to Ease Djibouti's Safety Concerns," *Washington Post*, September 24, 2013.

121 United States Air Force, Accident Investigation Board, "Summary of Facts and Statement of Opinon Aircraft Accident Investigation MQ-1B Predator, T/N 04–3126 Near Horn of Africa (HoA)," March 15, 2011, http://usaf.aib.law.af. mil/ExecSum2011/MQ-1B%2C%20Near%20Horn%200f%20Africa%2C%2015% 20Mar%2011.pdf

122 United States Air Force, Accident Investigation Board, "MQ-1B T/N 06–3173 432D Wing Creech Air Force Base, Nevada," July 28, 2011, http://usaf.aib. law.af.mil/ExecSum2011/MQ-1B_Djibouti_7%20May%2011.pdf

123 United States Air Force, Accident Investigation Board, "Executive Summary: Abbreviated Aircraft Accident Investigation MQ-1B, 07–3249, Republic of Djibouti 17 May 2011," May 2011, http://usaf.aib.law.af.mil/ExecSum2011/MQ-1B_ Djibouti_ExecSum_17%20May%2011.pdf

124 United States Air Force, Accident Investigation Board, "Executive Summary: MQ-1B, T/N 04–3125."

125 The reports also regularly refer to cockpit video and photographs, but since they are not included, they are presumably classified.

126 Whitlock and Miller, "U.S. Moves Drone Fleet."

127 On February 3, 2013, a surveillance drone reportedly crashed into a Badbado refugee camp in Mogadishu, Somalia, but there was no accident report detailing this crash and no pictures were released. Associated Press, "Surveillance Drone Crashes in Somali Capital," *Yahoo News*, February 3, 2012, http://news.yahoo.com/ surveillance-drone-crashes-somali-capital-134652928.html; see also Associated Press, "Unidentified Drone Crashes in Mogadishu," *Army Times*, February 3, 2012, www.armytimes.com/article/20120203/NEWS/202030310/Unidentified-drone-crashes-Mogadishu

128 Anthony Alessandrini, "A Word on Africa: Djibouti," *Jadaliyya*, February 19, 2011, accessed July 29, 2017, www.jadaliyya.com/pages/index/684/a-word-on-africa_ djibouti; "Djiboutians rally to oust president."; Abdourahim Arteh, "Protests Hit Djibouti as Opposition Leaders Held," *Reuters*, February 19, 2011, accessed July 31, 2017, www.reuters.com/article/us-djibouti-protests-idUSTRE71I1BQ20110219; *afrol News*, "Mass arrests stopped further Djibouti Protests," *afrol News*, February 27, 2011, accessed July 31, 2017, www.afrol.com/articles/37449

129 "Africa: Djibouti"; Committee to Protect Journalists, "Police Arrest Djibouti Journalist Covering Demonstration," *Committee to Protect Journalists*, August 12, 2014, accessed July 31, 2017, https://cpj.org/2014/08/police-arrest-djibouti-journalist-covering-demonst.php; Reporters Without Borders, "Djibouti Authorities Step Up Harassment

of Journalists," *Reporters Without Borders*, March 8, 2016, accessed July 31, 2017, https://rsf.org/en/news/djibouti-authorities-step-harassment-journalists

130 "Djibouti," *Freedom House*, accessed July 29, 2017, https://freedomhouse.org/report/freedom-press/2015/djibouti

131 Ibid; United States Department of State, "Djibouti 2014 Human Rights Report," accessed July 29, 2017, http://photos.state.gov/libraries/djibouti/304020/PDF/2014 human-rights-report.pdf

132 See, for instance, Katrina Manson, "Jostling for Djibouti," *Financial Times*, April 1, 2016, accessed July 29, 2017, www.ft.com/content/8c33eefc-f6c1-11e5-803c-d27c7117d132?mhq5j=e1; Tim Mak, "Djibouti: Insida the Tiny Police State with Seven Armies," *Horn Future*, January 2, 2016, accessed July 29, 2017, http://hornfuture.com/aragtida-qoraaga/djiboutiinsida-the-tiny-police-state-with-seven-armies/

133 John Vandiver, "Workers Protesting Work Force Cuts at US Base in Africa," *Stars and Stripes*, July 10, 2013, accessed July 29, 2017, www.stripes.com/news/africa/workers-protesting-work-force-cuts-at-us-base-in-africa-1.229711. Diplomatic cables found in the WikiLeaks archive indicate that the US embassy has been tracking protests and demonstrations in Djibouti over the past several years. See WikiLeaks, "Press Release: Secret US Embassy Cables," *WikiLeaks*, September 12, 2011, accessed July 29, 2017, https://wikileaks.org/Press-Release-Secret-US-Embassy.html.; afrol News, "Djibouti Opposition Boycotts Election," *afrol News*, March 11, 2011, http://afrol.com/articles/37560; *afrol News*, "Mass Protests Shake Djibouti," *afrol News*, February 26, 2011, http://afrol.com/articles/38194; and Kevin Gosztola, "Contemporary Colonialism: The Permanent US Drone War Base in Djibouti," *Shadow Proof*, October 26, 2012.

134 Mak, "Djibouti: Insida the Tiny Police State."

135 Frank Gardner, "US Military Steps Up Operations in the Horn of Africa," *BBC*, February 7, 2014, accessed July 29, 2017, www.bbc.co.uk/news/world-africa-26078149

136 Hamza Mohamed, "Al-Shabab Claims Deadly Djibouti Blasts," *Aljazeera*, May 27, 2014, accessed July 29, 2017, www.aljazeera.com/news/africa/2014/05/al-shabab-claims-deadly-djibouti-blasts-2014527154632977410.html; Feisal Omar, "Al Shabaab Claims Responsibility for Djibouti Suicide Attack," *Reuters*, May 27, 2014, accessed July 29, 2017, www.reuters.com/article/uk-djibouti-attacks-idUSKBN0E72AA 20140527; Because of such incidents the US intensified its attacks on Al-Shabaab in 2016—see Savage, Schmitt, and Mazzetti, "Obama Expands War With Al Qaeda."

137 Brass, "Djibouti's Unusual Resource Curse," 543.

138 Abdi Sheikh, "U.S. accused of killing 22 in misdirected Somali air strike," *Reuters*, September 28, 2016, www.reuters.com/article/us-somalia-security-idUSKCN11 Y0UC; Kevin Sieff, "The Pentagon said it killed Islamic militants in Somalia. Turns out they were allies," *Washington Post*, November 10, 2016, www.washingtonpost.com/world/africa/after-initial-denial-pentagon-discovers-it-killed-10-allies-in-drone-strike-in-somalia/2016/11/10/8231421e-a770-11e6-ba46-53db57f0e351_story.html?utm_term=.5dba0dfb85cb; "U.S. drone strike kills five suspected al-Qaeda fighters," *Al Jazeera*, April 30, 2017, www.aljazeera.com/news/2017/04/drone-strike-kills-suspected-al-qaeda-fighters-170430082159413.html; Lucy Draper, "The Wedding that Became a Funeral: U.S. Still Silent One Year on from Deadly Yemen Drone Strike," *Newsweek*, December 12, 2014, www.newsweek.com/wedding-became-funeral-us-still-silent-one-year-deadly-yemen-drone-strike-291403

139 David Cenciotti, "Pentagon Confirms Drone Crash in Somalia But It Doesn't Say It Was an Austrian Made Psyops-Capable Camcopter," *Aviationist*, May 29, 2013, accessed July 29, 2017, http://theaviationist.com/2013/05/29/schiebel-s-100/#.UcRf12ZwbIU

140 *Shephard News*, "Schiebel Demonstrates CAMCOPTER® S-100 Together with Boeing in Psychological Operations Role," *Shephard News*, December 16, 2009, accessed July 29, 2017, www.shephardmedia.com/news/uv-online/schiebel-demonstrates-camcopter-s-100-to/; see also "Schiebel CAMCOPTER® S 100 UAS PSYOP Capability Demo Fort Bragg," YouTube video, 2:34, posted by "Schiebel Group," February 27, 2013, www.youtube.com/watch?v=plbmgVU4U8E

141 Matt Blake, "'This One Won't Spy on Muslims Again': Somali Militants Publish Pictures of US Drones They 'Shot Down,'" *Daily Mail*, May 31, 2013.

142 Blake, "'This One Won't Spy on Muslims Again.'" It was also reported by additional media outlets: Feisal Omar, Abdi Sheikh and George Obulutsa, "Drone Crashes in Southern Somalia, May Have Been Shot Down," Reuters, May 28, 2013, accessed July 31, 2017, www.reuters.com/article/2013/05/28/us-somalia-conflict-idUSBRE94R0JP20130528; BBC, "Suspected US Drone Crashes in Somalia's Lower Shabelle," BBC, May 28, 2013; Hamza Mohamed, "Al-Shabab Say They Are Back on Twitter," *Al Jazeera*, December 16, 2013; Associated Press, "Al-Shabaab Showed Gruesome Social Media Savvy during Attack," CBS News, September 24, 2013, accessed July 31, 2017, www.cbsnews.com/news/al-shabab-showed-gruesome-social-media-savvy-during-attack/. When I checked the Twitter site several months later, the account had been suspended, but the photos had been posted on numerous news websites. Aislinn Liang, "US Drone 'Shot Down by al-Shabaab in Somalia,'" *Telegraph*, May 29, 2013. US ramped up attacks on Al-Shabaab in 2016: Barbara Starr, "U.S. Claims to Have Killed 150 Fighters from Al-Shabaab in Somalia," *CNN*, March 7, 2016, accessed July 31, 2017, www.cnn.com/2016/03/07/politics/somalia-us-claims-to-have-killed-150-fighters/index.html

143 Michel Foucault, *Security, Territory, Population: Lectures at the Collège de France, 1977–1978*, Ed. Arnold I. Davidson (New York: Palgrave Macmillan, 2007).

144 Paul Virilio, War and Cinema: The Logistics of Perception (London: Verso, 1989).

145 Gregory, "'In Another Time-Zone.'" Also see, Gregory, "The Everywhere War."

146 A 2009 Brookings Institution study estimated that for every "militant" killed by a drone, there were 10 civilian casualties. Daniel L. Byman, "Do Targeted Killings Work?," *Brookings Institute*, July 14, 2009, www.brookings.edu/opinions/2009/0714_targeted_killings_byman.aspx?p=1; http://returngood.com/2009/07/21/brookings-report-confirms-high-civilian-death-rate-and-misses-the-point/. A 2010 report from the New America Foundation indicated that since 2004 32% (or approximately 1 in 3) of those killed in drone attacks were civilians. Peter Bergen and Katherine Tiedemann, "The Year of the Drone: An Analysis of U.S. Drone Strikes in Pakistan, 2004–2010," Counterterrorism Strategy Initiative Policy Paper, *New America Foundation*, February 24, 2010, https://perma-archives.org/media/2014/8/16/18/22/XSE6-SWPR/cap.pdf. Also see, Dean Nelson, "One in three killed by US drones in Pakistan is a civilian, report claims," *Telegraph*, March 4, 2010, accessed July 31, 2017, www.telegraph.co.uk/news/worldnews/asia/pakistan/7361630/One-in-three-killed-by-US-drones-in-Pakistan-is-a-civilian-report-claims.html

147 "DIY Drones Homepage," *DIY Drones*, accessed July 31, 2017, http://diydrones.com/; David Edwards, "Warsaw Protester Launches Drone to Spay on Police," *Raw Story*, November 17, 2011, accessed July 31, 2017, www.rawstory.com/2011/11/warsaw-protester-launches-drone-to-spy-on-police/. When I first began writing this in 2011, I checked websites of hobby stores online and various drone models were sold out.

148 Lisa Parks, "Drones, Vertical Mediation, and the Targeted Class," *Feminist Studies* 42, no. 1 (2016): 227–235.

EPILOGUE

Since the 9/11 attacks, the US has elected three Presidents. George W. Bush, Barack Obama, and Donald Trump represent different parties and platforms, but the war on terror has been a geopolitical constant during their terms. Most of the coverage discussed in this book took shape while Bush and Obama led the country. Trump appears to be taking US vertical power to new heights. When Trump rose to power in late 2016, US struggles for vertical hegemony continued to play out through television airwaves, airport security, geospatial imaging, and drone warfare. Two days after his inauguration, Trump brazenly demonstrated where his administration stood on matters of vertical power and counterterrorism. On January 22 the new President authorized drone strikes in Yemen that killed three senior Al-Qaeda leaders.[1] A week later Trump approved an elite JSOC commando raid in the village of Yaakla, Yemen that killed US Navy Seal William "Ryan" Owens and injured three other Navy Seals. This helicopter attack also killed an estimated 14 civilians, including Anwar al-Awlaki's eight-year-old daughter, Nawar or "Nora" al-Awlaki, a US citizen.[2] Yemenis estimated that as many as 59 people were killed in the attack.[3]

While similar aerial attacks were carried out under Presidents Bush and Obama, Trump authorized these attacks during his first week in office, defining drone strikes and air raids as preferred military options. The second of these attacks went awry, killing an American girl, a US soldier, and Yemeni civilians. The father and brother of this American girl—Anwar and Abdulrahman al-Awlaki, both US citizens—had already been killed in US drone strikes in Yemen on September 30, 2011 and October 14, 2011, respectively. Obama authorized the targeted killing of Anwar al-Awlaki, a Yemeni-American cleric because he was an alleged leader of Al Qaeda. The rationale for killing two of al-Awlaki's children—both US citizens—demands further interrogation. The use of air power to kill terror suspects' family members was unspoken or incidental under Obama. Trump made his position on the matter loud and clear, telling Fox News when he was on the campaign trail, "The other thing with the terrorists is you have to take out their families, when you get these terrorists, you have to take out their families."[4]

Within his first 100 days of office, Trump authorized almost 100 drone strikes in Yemen alone, making vertical violence a defining characteristic of his Presidency.[5] The frequency of US drone strikes escalated 432% in the months following his inauguration, with a drone strike every 1.25 days compared to every 5.4 days under President Obama.[6] The difference between then and now is that there has since been an international public outcry and massive demonstrations against US drone strikes and targeted killings, as discussed in Chapter 4, as well as expert analyses indicating they are ineffective and illegal, which the Trump administration has chosen to ignore. In March 2017 Trump relaxed the targeting rules for counterterrorism operations and cleared the way for offensive attacks without intra-agency vetting. The administration also authorized US forces to intensify their drone campaign against Al-Shabaab in Somalia.[7] On June 11, a US drone strike killed eight Al-Shabaab militants and another on July 31 took out senior leader, Ali Muhammed Hussein, also known as Ali Jabal.[8] US drone strikes continue throughout the region.[9]

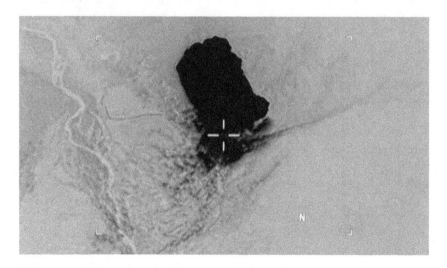

FIGURE E.1 A GBU-43/B Massive Ordnance Air Blast bomb, known as a "MOAB," strikes cave and tunnel systems in the Achin district of the Nangarhar Province in eastern Afghanistan on April 13, 2017 (screen capture from DoD video).

Source: https://commons.wikimedia.org/wiki/File:Aerial_Footage_of_MOAB_Bomb_Striking_ Cave,_Tunnel_System.webm—public domain, via Wikimedia Commons

Beyond escalating drone strikes, Trump has flaunted his vertical power in other ways as well. On April 10, 2017, he ordered the launch of 59 Tomahawk cruise missiles into Syria's Shayrat airbase as a response to the Syrian government's Khan Shaykhan chemical weapons attack on April 4.[10] And on April 13, 2017, Trump directed the Air Force to drop a GBU-43 MOAB, Massive Ordinance Air Blast, the largest non-nuclear bomb used in combat, on a cave and tunnel complex allegedly occupied by Islamic State fighters in the Achin district eastern province of Nangarha, Afghanistan. The 21,000-pound bomb, known as the "mother of all bombs," reportedly killed 92 ISIS militants and civilian casualties remain unknown.[11] Mohammad Shahzadah, a man from the area who witnessed the strike, stated, "It felt like the heavens were falling."[12] Cockpit video of the MOAB explosion played again and again in the world's media circuits, making it a visual signature of Trump's administration.[13] The black and white infrared footage highlights the bomb's lateral ballistics as they wipe out everything in their vicinity and generate a gigantic plume of black smoke and debris. The morning after the US dropped this massive bomb, *Fox and Friends* replayed the strike video to Toby Keith's song "Courtesy of the Red, White and Blue," and anchor Ainsley Earhardt quipped, "This is what freedom looks like."[14] The guest on the show that morning happened to be Geraldo Rivera. After the video played, Rivera declared, "One of my favorite things, in the 16 years I've been here at Fox News, is watching bombs drop on bad guys."[15] Bringing things full circle, Fox News' celebration of US aerial violence, airing of inflammatory remarks, and nationalist posturing, as discussed in Chapter 1, persist sixteen years after 9/11.

News media also used geospatial images to reinforce the power and impact of Trump's aerial assaults. After his Syria strike, CNN aired a series of three "before and after" satellite images from the Israeli company, ImageSat International, confirming destruction to aircraft hangers, "workshops," and a bunker at the Shayrat airbase.[16] Following the MOAB in Afghanistan, one headline boasted, "The Mother Of All Bombs Certainly Did Its Job Based On These New Satellite Images," claiming, "nearly all features built up on the targeted hillside were wiped off the face of the earth by the strike."[17] A more sober analysis of Digital Globe satellite images acquired 15 hours after the bombing confirmed "absolute destruction" of 20 compounds and trees in their vicinity yet suggested some damage was more likely due to a history of conflict in the area.[18] Nearly twenty years after 9/11, the use of commercial satellite images to monitor and reinforce counterterrorism campaigns by the US and its allies has been fully normalized. In July 2017, days after the US-supported Iraqi Security Forces defeated the Islamic State and won back the city of Mosul, Digital Globe released a series of "before and after" satellite images showing its utter devastation after months of fighting.[19] US forces were not engaged on the ground, but provided air support and monitored the conflict from above. Though these images raise questions about the extensive ruins and effects of war, Trump praised Iraqi

Security Forces for their victory in Mosul and vowed, "We will continue to seek the total destruction of ISIS."[20]

While the use of satellite images to monitor and reinforce counterterrorism campaigns resonates with discussions in Chapters 1 and 3, the Trump administration's disposition toward the geospatial image has been contradictory. On the one hand, the administration has embraced geospatial imagery that showcases its readiness to exercise aerial aggression in response to geopolitical conflicts, as described above. On the other hand, Trump's policies have attempted to obstruct the use of geospatial imagery in scientific climate research. In late 2016 Trump indicated plans to do away with NASA's climate research, cutting $2 billion from related programs, despite the fact that NASA's operates more than a dozen remote-sensing satellites.[21] In addition, Trump's administration proposed to slash the research funding and satellite programs of the National Oceanic and Atmospheric Administration (NOAA) by 17% and the US Geological Survey (USGS) by 15%.[22] Mashable published a story advising readers to "Enjoy NOAA's eye-opening satellite imagery while you still can," featuring a series of visuals used to analyze major storms and climate patterns.[23] Some perceive the use of budget cuts to prevent geospatial data from falling into the hands of climate scientists as a form of censorship that impedes scientific knowledge production. These issues hit a fever pitch on June 1, 2017, when Trump dramatically pulled the US out of the Paris Agreement, signaling his administration's denial of climate science and refusal to collaborate with international partners on such matters.[24]

The Trump administration's approach to vertical power is oriented less around environmental sustainability and more around intensifying the militarization and commercial development of orbit and outer space. His signing of the NASA Transition Act in March 2017 renewed support for the US space program while emphasizing opportunities for commercial engagement, including in areas of space technology and low earth orbit.[25] In June 2017 the US House Committee on Science, Space, and Technology unanimously approved the American Space Commerce Free Enterprise Act of 2017. According to Space Subcommittee Chair Brian Babin (R-Texas), the Act "streamlines regulatory processes, limits burdensome government intrusion, promotes American innovation and investment, protects national security, and satisfies our international obligations."[26] The bill also set out to reform commercial remote-sensing satellite licensing by removing oversight from NOAA and creating a single authority for administering non-governmental space activities within the Department of Commerce. The Satellite Industry Association, a major trade organization, and CEOs of companies ranging from Agile Aero to Digital Globe to Moon Express have enthusiastically endorsed this legislation. In June 2017 Trump also revived the long-dormant National Space Council with the goal of "restoring America's proud legacy and leadership in space."[27] Last functional during the Reagan and Bush terms, the council facilitates relations between the military, NASA, and the private sector.

Thus while Trump has actively suppressed climate science, his administration has enhanced the climate for deregulation and commercialization within the space sector.[28]

Some of Trump's most controversial vertical power plays have involved airports and immigration policy. Early in his Presidency, on January 29, 2017, Trump implemented an executive order, known as the Muslim ban, which prevented visitors from Iran, Iraq, Libya, Somalia, Sudan, Syria, and Yemen from entering the US for 90 days. Since people from these countries typically arrive in the US via airlines, this hastily implemented order created havoc at US airports, and many were unexpectedly denied entry or detained. (The order also halted the US refugee resettlement program for 120 days, indefinitely suspended resettlement of refugees from Syria, and reduced the cap of refugees in 2017 from 110,000 to 50,000.) Several federal district court judges ruled the order was unconstitutional, as it discriminated against people from Muslim-majority countries, and thus it was revised. Federal judges ruled against travel ban 2.0 as well, but on June 26, 2017 the Supreme Court held that a limited version of it could remain in effect.

The Muslim ban's implementation met fervent opposition and motivated protesters to flood US airports in cities from Boston to Los Angeles. They held signs that read, "No Muslim Ban," "My Muslim Family Pays More Taxes Than Trump," "He Will not Divide Us," "We are all immigrants," "No Wall/No Ban," and "I am being banned from seeing my grandma."[29] At Chicago O'Hare demonstrators chanted "Trump Out, Refugees In." At LAX they blocked the airport's main entrance. And in Philadelphia they sang Woody Guthrie's classic, "This Land is Your Land."[30] Claiming the US airport as a site of First Amendment protections, groups of Muslims quietly bowed down and prayed together in the Dallas airport's baggage claim area.[31] All the while, pro bono lawyers appeared at airports to assist travelers who were denied entry as well as their families.

If Trump's drone strikes and air raids aimed to kill Islamic terror suspects and their families in Yemen and Somalia, his travel ban attempted not only to block Muslim travelers from entering the US but to keep Muslim families physically separated. Trump's travel ban 2.0 tried to forbid grandparents, grandchildren, aunts and uncles, nieces and nephews, cousins and in-laws from visiting their relatives in the US.[32] Compounding the Muslim ban, Trump's Department of Homeland Security prohibited the use of personal electronics in the cabins of airplanes flying to the US from 10 major airports in the Middle East, preventing travelers from using their devices for work or entertainment during flights, as discussed in Chapter 2. Like the airport security checkpoint, these policies work to control which bodies enter US air and territory and what they are allowed to do in transit. What has become more explicit under Trump is that vertical power is applied not only to individual bodies but is used to immobilize, disrupt, or destroy the Muslim family. This is why the extremist group Al-Shabaab included in its recruitment videos a clip of Trump announcing his intention to implement a "complete and total shutdown" of Muslims entering the US during his 2016 campaign.[33] The political effects of Trump's inflammatory words and Muslim ban reverberated far beyond the airport and ironically unified US District Court judges and Islamic extremists in condemning his actions.

Even before Trump became President, it was possible to recognize his deep investments in vertical power. One needed only to glimpse the plethora of Trump Tower skyscrapers scattered across the globe—from to New York to Istanbul, from Manila to Toronto, from Las Vegas (see Figure E.2) to Vancouver.[34] Each one of these multi-million dollar buildings has also become a terrorism target.[35] Beyond his skyline real estate holdings, Trump owns a $100 million Boeing 757–000 airliner, which was turned into a private jet used on the campaign trail and dubbed "Trump Force One."[36] The Trump organization posted a video on YouTube to reveal its luxurious interior, including 24-carat gold seatbelt buckles, and demonstrate "what it is like to travel Trump style."[37] Since he became President, Trump has flown in Air Force One, often to his Mar-a-Lago resort in Florida. Though he has had no qualms about slashing the federal budgets of NOAA, NASA, the USGS, and more, each of Trump's trips

FIGURE E.2 Another kind of vertical power is encapsulated in Trump's skyscrapers around the world, including the golden Trump Hotel in Las Vegas.

Source: https://commons.wikimedia.org/wiki/File:Trump_hotel_Las_Vegas_2009.jpg—public domain, via Wikimedia Commons

from Washington, DC to Florida costs taxpayers $3 million and also generates a substantial carbon footprint.[38]

While many have focused on Trump's use of Twitter as the distinguishing aspect of his leadership, his seizing of vertical power is equally important. During his first months in office, he has intensified drone strikes and aerial assaults in multiple countries, paved the way for further deregulation and privatization of orbit and outer space, and prevented Muslims from several countries from entering the US at airports. Rather than interpret Trump's vertical maneuvers as unique to his administration, I understand his actions as part of a longer series of political and economic transformations that have taken shape since, and even before, 9/11.[39] As discussed throughout this book, similar strategic uses of US vertical power through the air, airport, orbit, and spectrum took shape during the terms of George W. Bush and Barack Obama, even if these Presidents differed on many issues. I present the details above to emphasize continuities in US struggles for vertical hegemony in the context of the war on terror and to highlight Trump's inflections of these historical processes, particularly his more boisterous and flamboyant approach.

Publics come to know about vertical power largely through media coverage. During the war on terror, media ranging from air-dropped leaflets to drone strike scene photos, from airport security X-rays to satellite images have drawn public attention to the vertical field and made it matter as a site of power, meaning, and contestation. Though I focus in this book on vertical strategies of domination, I have also mentioned ways in which such strategies have been challenged, complicated, and resisted, whether by feminists' critiques of US militarism on the airwaves, diffractive readings of geospatial images, condemnations of racial profiling at airport checkpoints, or hiding from infrared drone sensors.

In the process of analyzing relations between media and vertical power, I have set out to rethink and question the concept of "media" itself. Many assume they know what "the media" means and treat it as a given. Yet the materialities of "media" are always dynamically shifting at micro and macro scales. In the context of digitization, understandings of media have changed not only from an industrial and regulatory perspective but also in their theoretical conceptualization. The moment has provoked scholars to research an extensive array of mediated materialities from celluloid to soils, from clouds to oceans, from platforms to algorithms. As Larry Grossberg writes, "Media studies too often assumes that media is a stable concept. . . . [and should] stop thinking about media or about media worlds, and . . . interrogate worlds that are mediated in ways that we have yet to conceptualize."[40] By conceptualizing media as vertical phenomena, I have attempted to interrogate how state forces, technologies, and cultures have come together during the war on terror to articulate power relations through the air, orbit, and spectrum in ways that become perceivable to publics. I describe such formations as vertical mediations and suggest that coverage helps to materialize them—to communicate and render them intelligible in various sites and forms. The glaring rupture of the vertical field by the 9/11 attacks necessitated a reconceptualization of power relations in the world, but also of their mediation—that is, of the expanding capacities of various kinds of domains and materials to articulate, carry, and register power and meaning, and, in turn, affect everyday life. Vertical mediations are not just representative of, but constitutive of the power relations that define the war on terror.

It is vital for media and communication scholars to study widely recognized forms of media such as radio, film, television, social media, and games, as well as the relations between them. I argue that it is equally important to be able to think about how mediated modes of communication—such as reporting, mapping, and monitoring—materialize dynamically through extensive vertical domains. As I suggested at the outset of this book, media cannot be understood only through a formalist approach focused on screens and narratives. As media scholars have shown, content always exceeds the bounds of the frame and the story; its very production alters time/space, and its distribution has the potential to affect the bodies and imaginations of those who consume it.[41] More work on media ecologies and what I call cultural atmospherics is needed to understand the dynamic and extensive materialities and affects of mediation.

While new research on "ubiquitous media" and "cloud infrastructures" moves in this direction, it sometimes overlooks the military paradigms and forms of "infrastructural exclusivity" in which such systems participate.[42] When it comes to questions of ubiquitous access or universal service, claims of coverage are always overstated. Like earlier media, so-called ubiquitous systems are mobilized unevenly across territories and economies. The cultural atmospherics such systems generate differ across rich and poor communities and are interwoven with racial imaginaries as well.[43] The racialization of the vertical occurred long before 9/11 or the digital age. Toni Morrison and Simone Browne explain in different works how white imaginaries have allegorized formations such as a thunderous storm or the darkness of night as blackness, using abstract expanses like weather or luminosity to produce racial difference as a threat.[44] Though racism and racialization are embodied, they cannot directly be pinned down. They too are a kind of terror in the air. They demand a mode of analysis that accounts not only for their ideological dissemination, but also for their material relation to political structures of verticality, stratification, and hierarchization. Only by situating notions of ubiquitous or cloud-based media in relation to diverse experiences, is it possible to recognize how deeply entrenched a racialized verticality is within dominant political imaginaries.

The fact that vertical domination has persisted with different US leaders at the helm raises questions about how such power can continue to be meaningfully contested. How do we process the pendulum swing from Barack Obama, the first African American President, to Donald Trump, a businessman turned President who has refused to condemn white supremacism? At the current moment, terror in the air is shaped not only by Islamic extremism, but also by the conflagration of privilege, wealth, whiteness, patriarchy, and militarism in the White House. Trump's presidency has clarified how vertical power is used to organize and sustain gender, race, and class-based social hierarchies. Once again, the articulation of vertical forms of power has brought about massive public demonstrations. Rather than protesting US drone wars as discussed in Chapter 4, people have taken to the streets to protest Trump's methods of "making American great again" across the US, in Washington, DC, Portland, Charlottesville, Boston, Los Angeles, and New York.

The streets have become significant in other ways as well—the sites of an emergent form of terrorism. If 9/11 was a kind of singularity—a spectacular vertical event with expansive repercussions, as described throughout this book— then a spate of recent terrorist attacks reveals the tactics to be turning. Islamic terrorists and white nationalists alike (in London and Charlottesville) have used trucks, vans, and cars to kill and injure civilians on the streets of Barcelona, Berlin, Chapel Hill, Charlottesville, Columbus, Jerusalem, London, Nice, and Stockholm. Rather than hijacking commercial airplanes and ramming them into buildings on a single day, terrorists have begun to use automobiles and GPS-equipped mobile phones to perpetrate their violence more episodically. This tactic did not emerge out of nowhere. Such attacks by Islamic terrorists, I argue, can be understood as a retaliatory response to drone warfare. In many cases, Islamic communities and insurgent groups have been struck by drones un-expectedly and lacked the capacity to defend themselves or equivalently fight back. Moreover, drone strikes have been used to target vehicles suspected of transporting terrorists in many remote areas. A 2014 report indicates that 25% of US drone strikes in Pakistan hit vehicles (trucks, cars, and motorcycles).[45]

Thus, attacks by drones or unmanned aerial vehicles (UAVs) may have provoked attacks by manned terrestrial vehicles (MTVs). Since 2010 Al Qaeda in Yemen has urged its allies to use pickup trucks to "mow down the enemies of Allah."[46] In a 2014 speech following coalition air attacks on ISIS, Abu Mohammed Al-Adnani advised jihadis to kill Westerners in whatever way possible: "Smash his head with a rock, or slaughter him with a knife, or run him over with your car."[47] Experts speculate that vehicular attacks will increase and note that they are "less sophisticated and less predictable."[48] Just as drone wars have changed the meanings of the sky for those living in their range, this form of Islamic terrorism turns the most common elements of Western life— automobiles, streets, and smart phones—against civilians.

Whereas military personnel conduct drone attacks in designated mission areas as they watch on monitors, MTV or "vehicle-ramming" attacks are displaced from the drone war theater and delayed. They are committed opportunistically in Western cities where insurgents can strike civilians and other soft targets. As drone war casualties and injuries have increased, so has the frequency of MTV attacks. The TSA reported that between 2014 and 2017, 173 people have been killed and more than 700 wounded in 17 ramming attacks around the world.

Of the 17 attacks, 13 resulted in fatalities.[49] In 2017 the TSA issued a report called "Vehicle ramming attacks: Threat landscape, indicators and counter-measures," that warns no community "large or small, rural or urban, is immune to attacks of this kind. . . ." Recognizing that the threat orbit has expanded beyond the airport, the TSA also created the First Observer Plus training program for transportation industry workers to help them identify suspicious activity. This program effectively turns all US taxi, bus, and truck drivers and highway workers into TSA agents, instructing them to report "DLR"—things that "don't look right."[50]

Though MTV attacks weaponize transportation and telecommunication infrastructure on the ground, they arguably have been motivated by prior aerial assaults and as such are effects of vertical power relations. Even beyond this connection, MTV attacks rely on vertical domains. For instance, to carry out such attacks terrorists use the mobile spectrum and geospatial imagery to navigate through urban spaces, and, in the aftermath of the attacks, news media use those same domains to produce and circulate coverage of grisly scenes of violence. In this way, the MTV attack brings together and combines elements of vertical mediation with logistical or locative media—software and systems used to facilitate and track terrestrial movement—to produce *automobile terror*, a kind of terror that is predicated upon the use of vehicles and mobile phones by almost everyone in Western societies.[51] In this way, such attacks may be more sophisticated than experts have indicated. Like the 9/11 attacks, vehicle-ramming repurposes existing systems and turns them against their owners. MTV attacks kill civilians without trafficking or igniting explosives. They use the metal exterior of vehicles as armor, enabling perpetrators to sometimes escape after the attack. And they can be committed almost anywhere by groups or "lone wolf" attackers. As such these attacks are less costly and more efficient than drone strikes.

While terrorists orchestrated the 9/11 attacks by commandeering air, orbit, and spectrum, the automobile threat formation may be even more pervasive and terrorizing. After 9/11, Slavoj Zizek argued that the attacks on the World Trade Center and Pentagon represented a kind of wish-fulfillment since fictionalized strikes on the US, including on the White House, had played out again and again in Hollywood movies. As Zizek put it, "The unthinkable which happened was thus the object of fantasy: in a way, America got what it fantasized about, and this was the greatest surprise."[52] Nearly two decades later the war on terror has expanded far beyond America and the manned terrestrial vehicle attack has brought about new kind of surprise. Fantasies of freedom and mobility ascribed to transportation and telecommunication have been used paradoxically to stop people in their tracks. Rather than understand these incidents only as violent attacks on Western life, it is important to consider their enabling conditions. A combination of factors since 9/11, including drone wars, youth unemployment, discrimination, on- and offline extremism, and long-term military conflicts have played a role in motivating such actions. Increasingly, civilians are caught in the crossfire between militants and militarized states. The meanings of the streets and sky have changed. And peace and diplomacy have become almost unimaginable. We only have a chance of successfully resisting such conditions by adopting a more complex understanding of how the material relations of war reorganize power, technologies, and publics.

Written in September 2017.

Notes

1 Spencer Ackerman, "US Commando Dies in Yemen Raid as Trump Counter-Terror Plans Take Shape," *The Guardian*, January 29, 2017, www.theguardian.com/world/2017/jan/29/al-qaida-suspects-yemen-killed-raid-us-commandos

2 Thomas Gibbons-Neff and Missy Ryan, "In Deadly Yemen Raid, A Lesson for Trump's National Security Team," *Washington Post*, January 31, 2017, www.washingtonpost.com/news/checkpoint/wp/2017/01/31/how-trumps-first-counter-terror-operation-in-yemen-turned-into-chaos/?utm_term=.c50de208978b; Spencer Ackerman, Jason Burke, and Julian Borger, "Eight-year-old American Girl 'Killed in Yemen Raid Approved by Trump,'" *The Guardian*, February 1, 2017, www.theguardian.com/world/2017/feb/01/yemen-strike-eight-year-old-american-girl-killed-al-awlaki; also see Eric Schmitt and David E. Sanger, "Raid in Yemen: Risky From the Start and Costly in the End," *New York Times*, February 1, 2017, www.nytimes.com/2017/02/01/world/middleeast/donald-trump-yemen-commando-raid-questions.html

3 Robert Windrem, et al., "SEAL, American Girl Die in First Trump-Era U.S. Military Raid," *NBC News*, January 31, 2017, www.nbcnews.com/news/world/seal-american-girl-die-first-trump-era-u-s-military-n714346

4 Tom LoBianco, "Donald Trump on Terrorists: 'Take Out Their Families,'" *CNN.com*, December 3, 2015, www.cnn.com/2015/12/02/politics/donald-trump-terrorists-families/; Ackerman, Burke, and Borger, "Eight-year-old American Girl."

5 Michael Shank, "Doubling Down on Drone Mistakes," *U.S. News and World Report*, June 29, 2017, www.usnews.com/opinion/op-ed/articles/2017-06-29/president-trump-is-doubling-down-on-president-obamas-drone-mistakes

6 Micah Zenko, "The (Not-So) Peaceful Transition of Power: Trump's Drone Strikes Outpace Obama," blogpost, *Council on Foreign Relations*, March 2, 2017, www.cfr.org/blog/not-so-peaceful-transition-power-trumps-drone-strikes-outpace-obama; Joe Wolverton, "Drone Strikes Up 432 Percent Under Donald Trump," *The New American*, March 16, 2017, accessed August 27, 2017, www.thenewamerican.com/usnews/foreign-policy/item/25604-drone-strikes-up-432-percent-under-donald-trump

7 Eric Schmitt, "U.S. Carries Out Drone Strike Against Shabab Militants in Somalia," *New York Times*, July 3, 2017, www.nytimes.com/2017/07/03/world/africa/airstrike-shabab-somalia.html

8 Jamie McIntyre, "US Confirms Drone Strike Killed Key Terrorist Leader in Somalia," *The Washington Examiner*, August 4, 2017, www.washingtonexaminer.com/us-confirms-drone-strike-killed-key-terrorist-leader-in-somalia/article/2630647

9 One official indicated described the raid and the proposal as an outgrowth of earlier Obama-era operations that have pushed al-Qaeda militants from their sanctuaries and have provided more opportunities for U.S. strikes. Gibbons-Neff and Ryan, "In Deadly Yemen Raid."

10 "Khan Shaykhun chemical attack," *Wikipedia*, accessed August 27, 2017, https://en.wikipedia.org/wiki/Khan_Shaykhun_chemical_attack

11 Sune Engel Rasmussun, "US 'Mother of All Bombs' Killed 92 Isis Militants, Say Afghan Officials," *The Guardian*, April 15, 2017, www.theguardian.com/world/2017/apr/15/us-mother-of-all-bombs-moab-afghanistan-donald-trump-death-toll

12 Sune Engel Rasmussun, " 'It Felt Like the Heavens Were Falling': Afghans Reel From Moab Impact," *The Guardian*, April 14, 2017, www.theguardian.com/world/2017/apr/14/it-felt-like-the-heavens-were-falling-afghans-reel-from-moabs-impact

13 W.J. Hennigan, "Air Force Drops Non-Nuclear 'Mother of All Bombs' in Afghanistan," *Los Angeles Times*, April 13, 2017, www.latimes.com/politics/washington/la-na-essential-washington-updates-white-house-drops-mother-of-all-bombs-1492102824-htmlstory.html

14 Amber Jamieson, "Fox News Sets Afghanistan Bombing to Toby Keith Song As Other Outlets Voice Doubt," *The Guardian*, April 14, 2017, www.theguardian.com/media/2017/apr/14/fox-news-afghanistan-bombing-media-reaction

15 Ibid.

16 Paul P. Murphy, "Satellite Images Show Before, After US Strike on Syrian Base," *CNN.com*, April 8, 2017, www.cnn.com/2017/04/07/politics/new-satellite-imagery-of-bombed-syrian-base/index.html

17 Tyler Rogoway, "Mother of All Bombs Certainly Did Its Job Based on These New Satellite Images," *The Drive*, April 20, 2017, accessed August 27, 2017, www.thedrive.com/the-war-zone/9524/mother-of-all-bombs-certainly-did-its-job-based-on-these-new-satellite-images

18 Alcis, "After the Dust Settles—Imagery Analysis of the Afghan MOAB Strike Location," *Medium*, accessed August 27, 2017, https://stories.alcis.org/after-the-dust-settles-d167fa0e7599

19 Jesse Chase-Lubitz and Adam Griffiths, "Mosul, Before and After, in Satellite Images," *Foreign Policy*, July 14, 2017, http://foreignpolicy.com/2017/07/14/mosul-before-and-after-in-satellite-images/

20 "Statement from President Donald J. Trump on the Liberation of Mosul," press release, Office of the Press Secretary, July 10, 2017, www.whitehouse.gov/the-press-office/2017/07/10/statement-president-donald-j-trump-liberation-mosul

21 Keith Cowing, "Congress Pushes Back Against Trump Science Cuts," *NASA Watch*, May 1, 2017, accessed August 27, 2017, http://nasawatch.com/archives/2017/05/congress-pushes-2.html; Zoë Schlanger, "A NASA Engineer Explains Why Trump's Plan to Cut the Space Agency's Climate Science Program is Harder Than It Sounds," *Quartz*, February 28, 2017, https://qz.com/919982/a-nasa-engineer-explains-why-trumps-plan-to-cut-the-space-agencys-climate-science-program-is-a-lot-harder-than-it-sounds/

22 Steven Mufson, Jason Samenow, Brady Dennis, "White House Proposes Steep Budget Cut to Leading Climate Science Agency," *Washington Post*, March 3, 2017, www.washingtonpost.com/news/energy-environment/wp/2017/03/03/white-house-proposes-steep-budget-cut-to-leading-climate-science-agency/?utm_term=.4281d172e 119; Alexis Wolfe, "Trump Budget Cuts USGS by 15%, Restructures Climate Research," *American Institute of Physics*, June 8, 2017, www.aip.org/fyi/2017/trump-budget-cuts-usgs-15-restructures-climate-research

23 Maria Gallucci, "Enjoy NOAA's Eye-Opening Satellite Imagery While You Can," *Mashable*, March 5, 2017, http://mashable.com/2017/03/05/noaa-satellite-images-trump-budget-cuts/

24 Anusuya Datta, "Tech World Dismayed Over Trump Decision to Pull Out of Paris Accord," *Geospatial World*, June 2, 2017, www.geospatialworld.net/blogs/tech-world-dismayed-trump-decision-pull-paris-accord/

25 See the act here: National Aeronautics and Space Administration Transition Authorization Act of 2017, S. 442, 115th Cong. (2017–2018), www.congress.gov/bill/115th-congress/senate-bill/442

26 "American Space Commerce Free Enterprise Act of 2017 Clears Committee," *Aero News Network*, June 14, 2017, accessed August 27, 2017, www.aero-news.net/index. cfm?do=main.textpost&id=f527e224-6202-4a73-b3d0-d404a1e45dfa

27 Stephen Clark, "Trump Signs Order Reviving Long-Dormant National Space Council," *Spaceflight Now*, June 30, 2017, accessed August 27, 2017, https://spaceflight now.com/2017/06/30/trump-signs-order-re-creating-long-dormant-national-space-council/; Shannon Stirone, "Our Next World War Might Be Fought in Outer Space," *New Republic*, May 24, 2017, https://newrepublic.com/article/142365/next-world-war-might-fought-outer-space-trump-reagan

28 These privatization practices are visually symbolized in a satellite image found in Google Earth, featuring a plot of land in Idaho with the gigantic white word "TRUMP" upon it. See Kimberly Smith, "Man Researching Satellite Images Finds Trump Sign Where He Least Expects It," *Conservative Tribune*, September 16, 2016, http://conservativetribune.com/man-finds-trump-sign-least-expects/

29 See photos here: www.chron.com/news/politics/article/The-best-anti-Muslim-ban-protest-signs-from-10894719.php; www.nbcnews.com/slideshow/trump-out-refugees-ban-sparks-protests-airports-across-nation-n713746

30 Emanuella Grinberg and Madison Park, "2nd Day of Protests over Trump's Immigration Policies," *CNN.com*, January 30, 2017, www.cnn.com/2017/01/29/politics/us-immigration-protests/index.html

31 "Trump Travel Ban: Questions About the Revised Executive Order," *BBC News*, July 14, 2017, www.bbc.com/news/world-us-canada-39044403; Edward Helmore and Alan Yuhas, "Border Agents Defy Courts on Trump Travel Ban, Congressmen and Lawyers Say," *The Guardian*, January 30, 2017, www.theguardian.com/us-news/2017/jan/29/customs-border-protection-agents-trump-muslim-country-travel-ban

32 Reuben Fischer-Baum, et al., "Which of Your Family Members Could Visit Under the Travel Ban," *Washington Post*, July 19, 2017, www.washingtonpost.com/graphics/2017/world/travel-ban-who-is-close-family/?utm_term=.4673e95da6c8

33 Reena Flores, "Terror Group Uses Donald Trump Soundbite in Purported Propaganda Video," *CBS News*, January 2, 2016, www.cbsnews.com/news/al-shabab-terror-group-uses-donald-trump-soundbite-in-purported-propaganda-video/; Paula Mejia, "Donald Trump's Muslim Comments Featured in New Al-Shabaab Militant Recruitment Video," *Newsweek*, January 2, 2016, www.newsweek.com/donald-trumps-muslim-comments-featured-new-al-shabaab-militant-recruitment-410991

34 "Global View—Trump properties around the world," Google Maps, accessed August 28, 2017, www.google.com/maps/d/u/0/viewer?mid=1t_0cRcqX5P9ZtNRSjGOA8 De4khU&hl=en_US&ll=-3.81666561775622e-14%2C-18.43838113706056&z=1

35 Katie Zavadski, "Trump Has Properties All Over the World. They're Now Major Terrorism Targets," *Washington Post*, January 3, 2017, www.washingtonpost.com/posteverything/wp/2017/01/03/trump-has-properties-all-over-the-world-theyre-now-major-terrorist-targets/?utm_term=.f8f5059e0c13

36 Benjamin Zhang, "Check out Trump's $100 Million Personal Boeing Airliner," *Business Insider*, November 8, 2016, www.businessinsider.com/donald-trump-boeing-757-airliner-trump-force-one-private-jet-2016–11

37 "Mr. Trump's 757," YouTube video, 3:30, posted by "The Trump Organization," August 18, 2011, www.youtube.com/watch?v=UZq3iCn2y74

38 Philip Bump, "How Much Is Donald Trump's Travel and Protection Costing, Anyway?," *Washington Post*, March 17, 2017, www.washingtonpost.com/news/politics/wp/2017/03/17/how-much-is-donald-trumps-travel-and-protection-costing-anyway/?utm_term=.d07f84871d39

39 Naomi Klein, The Shock Doctrine: The Rise of Disaster Capitalism (New York: Picador, 2007); and Naomi Klein, No Is Not Enough: Resisting Trump's Shock Politics and Winning the World We Need (Chicago, IL: Haymarket Books, 2017).

40 Grossberg, Lawrence. *Cultural Studies in the Future Tense*. Durham, NC: Duke University Press, 2010. For Grossberg, media are "modalities of articulation creating environs or organizations that define the allowable logics of discourse and mediation" (217).

41 Anna McCarthy observes, "as a source of images from elsewhere, a technology that interacts with the ethereal, unlocatable physics of the electromagnetic spectrum, TV does not exist solely on the immediate social scale of the place where it is viewed." Anna McCarthy, *Ambient Television: Visual Culture and Public Space* (London and Durham, NC: Duke University Press, 2001), 14. Echoing this thinking, Geoffrey Batchen provocatively asks, "What happens if we conceive TV ... not as a signal between two points, but as an indiscriminate and all-encompassing atmosphere of electronic data, a field of impulses that continually surrounds and traverses us whether a monitor is present or not?" Geoffrey Batchen, "Da[r]ta." *Afterimage* 24, no. 6 (1997), 5.

42 Recent works include, Tung-Hui Hu, *A Prehistory of the Cloud* (Cambridge, MA: MIT Press, 2016); John Durham Peters, *The Marvelous Clouds: Toward a Philosophy of Elemental Media* (London and Chicago, IL: University of Chicago Press, 2015); Paul Dourish and Genevieve Bell, *Divining a Digital Future: Mess and Mythology in Ubiquitous Computing* (Cambridge, MA: MIT Press, 2011); Ulrik Ekman et al., Eds., *Ubiquitous Computing, Complexity and Culture* (New York: Routledge, 2016); Mimi Sheller, "Materializing US-Caribbean Borders: Airports as Technologies of Communication, Coordination and Control" in *Communication Matters: Materialist Approaches to Media, Mobility and Networks*, Ed. Jeremy Packer and Stephen B. Crofts Wiley (New York: Routledge, 2012), 233.

43 For work that addresses these issues, see Ramesh Srinivasan's, *Whose Global Village?: Rethinking How Technology Shapes Our World* (New York: New York University Press, 2017).

44 Toni Morrison, *Playing in the Dark: Whiteness and the Literary Imagination* (Cambridge, MA: Harvard University Press, 1992); Simone Browne, *Dark Matters: On the Surveillance of Blackness* (London and Durham, NC: Duke University Press, 2015).

45 Bureau of Investigative Journalism, "Most US Drone Strikes in Pakistan Attack Houses," *Bureau of Investigative Journalism*, May 23, 2014, www.thebureauinvestigates. com/stories/2014-05-23/most-us-drone-strikes-in-pakistan-attack-houses; "Number of Domestic Buildings and Vehicles Hit in Drone Strikes, According to Time of Day," graph, *Bureau of Investigative Journalism*, accessed August 28, 2017, http://s3.amazonaws. com/assets2.thebureauinvestigates.com/uploads/Domestics-and-vehicles-hit-time-of-day1.png?mtime=20170206132917

46 CNN Wire Staff, "New Issue of Magazine Offers Jihadists Terror Tips," *CNN.com*, October 12, 2010, www.cnn.com/2010/WORLD/meast/10/12/mideast.jihadi. magazine/; "Terrorist Attacks by Vehicle Fast Facts," *CNN.com*, August 17, 2017, www.cnn.com/2017/05/03/world/terrorist-attacks-by-vehicle-fast-facts/index.html

47 Robert Windrem and William M. Arken, "TSA Report Warns Against Truck Ramming Attacks by Terrorists," *NBC News*, May 4, 2017, www.nbcnews.com/news/ us-news/tsa-report-warns-against-truck-ramming-attacks-terrorists-n754576; Kurtis Lee, "Concerns Over Terrorism Lead TSA to Issue Warning to Trucking Companies," *Los Angeles Times*, May 5, 2017, www.latimes.com/nation/la-na-tsa-truck-warning-20170505-story.html

48 Justina Crabtree, "Low-Tech Terrorist Attacks Like Vehicle-Ramming Look Set to Rise: Analyst," *CNBC News*, March 23, 2017, www.cnbc.com/2017/03/23/low-tech-terror-attacks-like-vehicle-ramming-look-set-to-rise-analyst.html

49 Office of Security Policy and Industry, "(U) Vehicle Ramming Attacks: Threat Landscape, Indicators, and Countermeasures," Transportation Security Agency, May 2017, https://publicintelligence.net/tsa-vehicle-ramming/; Windrem and Arken, "TSA Report."

50 "First Observer Plus," Transportation Security Agency, accessed August 28, 2017, www.tsa.gov/for-industry/firstobserver

51 Ned Rossiter, "Locative Media as Logistical Media: Situating Infrastructure and the Governance of Labor in Supply-Chain Capitalism," *Organized Networks*, February 5, 2014, http://nedrossiter.org/?p=380Logistical Media; Jeremy Packer, *Mobility without Mayhem: Safety, Cars, and Citizenship* (London and Durham, NC: Duke University Press, 2008).

52 "Zizek/Reflections on WTC: Slavoj Zizek Answers Peter Murphy," October 7, 2001, *lacan.com*, www.lacan.com/reflections2.htm

INDEX

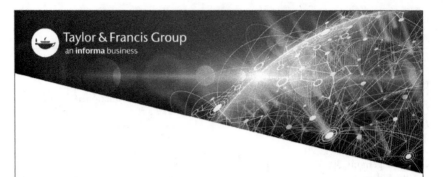

CPSIA information can be obtained
at www.ICGtesting.com
Printed in the USA
FSHW020956061219
64819FS